Graphic Design School
Fourth Edition

**A Foundation Course for Graphic Designers Working
in Print, Moving Image and Digital Media**

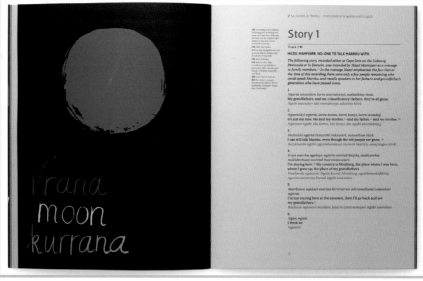

trana
moon
kurrana

Story 1

Track 1 ◄

HAZEL MAHIYARR, NO-ONE TO TALK MARRKU WITH.

The following story, recorded either at Cape Don on the Cobourg Peninsula or in Darwin, was intended by Hazel Mamiyarr as a message to family members.[1] In the message Hazel emphasizes the fact that at the time of this recording there were only a few people remaining who could speak Marrku, and recalls speakers in her father's and grandfather's generation who have passed away.

1.
Ngarla wuwulan, larra warrabanyi, waikitbay tbak!
My grandfathers, and my (classificatory) fathers, they're all gone.
Ngitit wuwulan lan wurrabanyi, alkwiny kbrk.

2.
Nguwalayt ngarla, larra kamu, larra bunyi, larra mundaj.
It's just me now. Me and my mother,[1] and my father,[1] and my brother.[1]
Nguwati ngabi, lda kamu, lda bunyi, lda ngabi atatatabong.

3.
Mukuski ngarla tbawalki Inkawart, nanatban tbak.
I can still talk Marrku, even though the old people are gone.[1]
Burukiwenbi ngabi ngalilabanbani inyman Marrku, isnangwart klrrk.

4.
Irtya marrku ngalayt, ngarla wuriad Majila, mutbarrka,
makitburbany wuriad tburrawuulan.
I'm staying here.[1] My country is Minjilang, the place where I was born,
where I grew up, the place of my grandfathers.
*Kutiburda nganini. Ngiti kuant Minjilang, ngeddalanbukking,
ngamwanyirmany kurak ngabi wuwulan*

5.
*Marrkuan ngalayt marran kirrirurun abranadbani wuwulan
ngarla.*
I'm just staying here at the nuunen, then I'll go back and see
my grandfathers.[1]
Bardawu nganini murdan, janira ayunwanyapu ngabi wuwulan

6.
Ngan, ngeni
I think so!
Nganini!

[1]

Graphic Design School
Fourth Edition

A Foundation Course for Graphic Designers Working in Print, Moving Image and Digital Media

David Dabner • Sheena Calvert • Anoki Casey

Thames & Hudson

First published in the United Kingdom in 2010 by
Thames & Hudson Ltd 181A High Holborn,
London WC1V 7QX

www.thamesandhudson.com

Copyright © 2010 Quarto Inc.

British Library Cataloguing-in-Publications Data
A catalogue record for this book is available from the British Library

ISBN: 978-0-500-28863-4

Printed and bound in China

12

Contents

Introduction

This book is written with a view to providing you with a thorough grounding in the principles that underlie all good graphic design, whether print-based, web or digital. The text has been constructed to mirror how the subject is taught in design colleges today, and the illustrations — a mixture of student and professional work — have been carefully chosen to illuminate specific teaching points. Many units contain step-by-step exercises and assignments, offer practical advice and point towards further resources.

The first half of the book — Principles — takes as a given that a thorough understanding of design principles should support the act of creating designs in response to specific briefs and problems, while allowing for visual freedom and self-authored experimentation. As you are gradually introduced to the basics of concepts such as research, typography, colour, photography, form and composition, you will learn how to become visually aware and design-literate.

In the second half of the book — Practice — you will be introduced to those invaluable practical skills that must be seen as equally important to the kinds of research, conceptual and compositional skills you will have developed in part 1, but which do not replace them. Remember: in order to be a well-rounded and successful designer, it is not only your ability to master a computer program or get something printed that makes you a good designer, but the whole range of conceptual

The 'Wire Tree' shows how text and image can work in creative harmony. This poster was silk-screened, and a full typeface was designed.

Rich, multi-layered imagery, painstakingly constructed in Photoshop, takes photomontage to a new level, in this illustration for the book *Wonderland*.

Deconstructed letterforms are reconstituted on separate sheets of glass, which can then be read when viewed from an angle where all the elements align.

and technical skills presented in this book. On the other hand, being a great visual designer is only half the story. Unless you learn the practical skills and technologies of design production, including how to work with images, set up files for printing or build and structure a website, you will be unable to get your work produced.

Finally, none of these visual skills can be viewed in isolation from the contexts in which design happens, and its larger role in society, and the world. Designers (working in any medium) are concerned with communication, and with creating messages that influence viewers or readers and/or convey information. However, with this comes responsibility, and it is crucial to be aware of the role of design in shaping the world we live in, and of changes to the profession which go beyond style trends or software. While any kind of comprehensive account of these topics stands outside the scope of this book, becoming visually literate and technically skilled should go hand in hand with an understanding of such issues as communication theories, the development of new and 'global' audiences, systems theory, ecology, sustainability issues in design and the changing role and potential of technology. These, and a general awareness of the world around you, alongside sound practical skills, will help you to become a well-rounded and versatile designer, whatever your career aspirations.

'The Wind is Free' is a campaign to sell the weather. Simple, cut-paper imagery forms the basis of an animation, while the DVD packaging contains instructions for users to create their own pinwheel.

Illustration, combined with hand-drawn lettering, produces an enigmatic effect, appropriate to the subject matter.

The installation entitled 'Crimson Hyperlink Hexagon', was part of the degree show exhibition at the London College of Communication in 2009. The titles of students' dissertations were displayed on the walls, in a 'cloud' configuration. These were then linked to other titles, via grey wires, creating new connections and associations. The work sits somewhere between typography, installation art, systems theory and information design.

Principles

The first half of this book is concerned with principles, or with learning the basic languages and methods of design. Every discipline or profession has its own set of rules, methods, languages and technical requirements. Each is rooted in the relationship between its history, theory and practice, but unlike learning law, or biology, the 'language' of design is predominantly a visual one. It involves developing a heightened awareness of not only visual principles, but the world, and what happens in it, such that a good designer can filter this information, and create relevant, engaging, visually eloquent design which responds to multiple problems, needs and contexts. In short, while a design student needs to develop the research, concept-development, compositional, layout and organizational skills associated with design, he or she also needs to become engaged with the world at large, and to be interested, aware and sensitive to the changing contexts in which design happens.

Unit 1 discusses different kinds of primary and secondary research, followed by an introduction to theories of the image, the importance of audiences and of organizing your work and time. In Unit 2, form will take centre stage: understanding form comes from the ability to see the intrinsic and subtle qualities of the various elements of a design, and from developing a sensitivity to the relationships between them. This takes practice, patience and an eye for detail. Form involves composition of the fundamental elements in a design (text/image/colour), and it requires an understanding of shape, proportion, balance

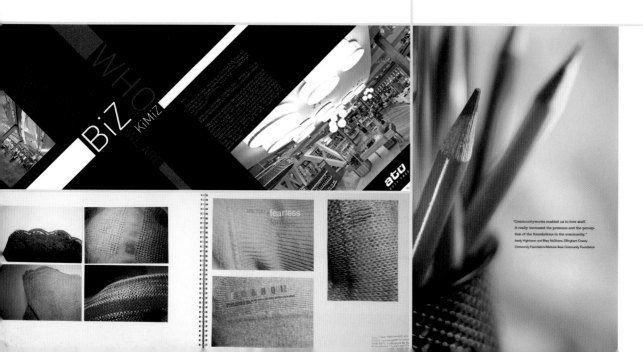

PART 1

and visual dynamics both within individual layouts, and as an integral part of coordinated design systems. Unit 3 introduces typography, which is a core skill for all designers, and cannot be underestimated in terms of its complexity, beauty and history. Developing a sound understanding of the science and art of typography is of crucial importance, and underpins most of the work represented in this book. Finally, in Unit 4, colour will be introduced as a primary factor in design, including a review of colour terminology, associations, legibility and the role of colour in conveying information.

Whatever design discipline you enter into, from editorial to web design, from information design to moving image, these basic principles will ground your work, and give you a solid foundation from which to proceed in your chosen field.

1 RESEARCH AND EARLY CONCEPTS

The first step toward becoming *interesting* is to be *interested*. The best artists of all kinds – painters, designers, writers, sculptors, musicians, playwrights – make the world their inspiration, and draw ideas and content from both experience and research. They make it a priority to stay aware of what is happening, not only within the world of design, but in the world in general, and this level of engagement enriches their work.

> ❝Design is everything. Everything!❞
> *Paul Rand*

PART 1	PRINCIPLES
UNIT 1	RESEARCH AND EARLY CONCEPTS
MODULE 1	**Basics of research**

You live in a media-saturated world, constantly bombarded with images and information. As a designer you need a heightened awareness of what is going on around you. Looking at the work of other designers and artists, cultural trends, technological developments and world events will influence you; you should make notes, keep sketchbooks – stay aware and alert. You never know when something you have seen will help you solve a design problem.

Whereas many people's interests are relatively narrow, you must always seek to broaden your horizons – increase your range of references – to successfully communicate with people of all ages, professions and lifestyles, and to contextualise your design work.
• Never read just one newspaper – change it every day, or read several, and compare stories, noting how information about the same events changes, how language tone is used to target various audiences and how imagery is used to support text.
• You can never read enough books, but don't limit yourself to the kind you usually read – be outward-looking. Limiting yourself to reading only about graphic design can be particularly dangerous:

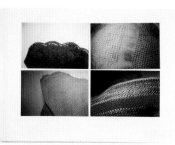
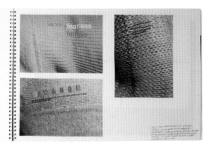
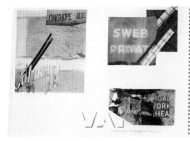

Worldwide focus

Ongoing research should inform the specific projects you are working on, but also engage you in a process of looking at, and understanding, the world around you. Keep notebooks/sketchbooks/ diaries as a way of seeking inspiration from the things you see/hear and as a way of documenting your ideas.

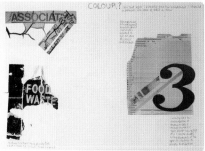

Extensive visual research

These pages show how the designer considers various options, including increasingly abstracting imagery and combining text and images, before working through the final design.

Simple combinations

Photographs and text explore the various connections between ideas and public and private space, as preliminary explorations on the topic. These early 'sketches' may or may not become part of the final work, but they move the work forward, and expand its potential.

although extremely useful for information and guidance, this may turn you into an armchair expert; you want to be an original practitioner. So add to your reading list: books on sculpture, architecture, art history, novels, plays, cooking, boxing, archaeology, travel, maths – it really doesn't matter, as long as they provide you with a broad spectrum of knowledge.

• Have as many varied experiences as possible: visit the kinds of shops, galleries and nightclubs you'd never normally go in, listen to music you've never heard before and eat food you've never tried before.

• Perhaps most importantly, talk to people. Share ideas, listen to what language they use, pay attention to what inspires them and learn from others, while sharing your insights. This is the stuff of life, the raw material common to every artist, and it's important to constantly observe and absorb it.

GLOSSARY

Contextualisation: The process of placing something within the inter-related systems of meaning that make up the world.

Primary research: Gathering material that does not pre-exist, such as photographing, drawing, making prototypes, interviewing people.

Secondary research: Gathering material that already exists, such as design work, colour samples, written texts, newspaper/magazine articles, archive images (eg, historical samples of advertising).

SEE ALSO: LINEAR REASONING/LATERAL THINKING P16
VISUALISING IDEAS P20

Initial photographic research

Abstraction of photographs and addition of text

Further exploration of text, looking at figure–ground relationships (see pages 38–39) and colour

Fragmentary numerals as an alternative

⌃ Experimentation

The design of a book cover develops through a series of initial experiments with imagery, and successive typographic experiments, to a final, dynamic text/image combination.

⌄ Research development

Part of a series of book cover designs, the development here shows a different approach to the previous design, while retaining a sense of unity.

Means of recording

Being human means forgetting things in the hustle and bustle of daily life. How often have you woken at night with an idea and forgotten it by morning? Or found yourself saying, 'I wish I had had a camera', or 'I'm sure I saw or read something about that recently'?

Every practising designer should always carry with them some form of recording device – a sketchbook, a camera, a voice recorder, a video camera – or several of these. Each should be updated on a daily basis; make time for research, take it seriously as an integral part of your work. Designers, artists, writers and illustrators all frequently keep scrapbooks/sketchbooks/collections of material that interests them. Often they will not know exactly why, or how, the material will come to be useful later on, but it forms an archive of ideas and inspiration from which to draw at a later date.

If something grabs your attention, draw it, note it down, photograph it or file it away immediately. Collect ideas and build upon initial thoughts by writing, drawing, sketching. Not only will your drawing and research skills improve by doing this consistently, but over time you will have built yourself a 'catalogue of inspiration' that can be drawn upon at any point in your career and especially when you are short of ideas. This kind of

Typographic experimentation

Integration of map as a background image

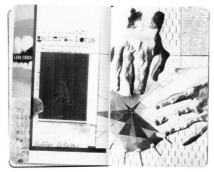

Extended photographic research, drawn from magazines

Further abstraction of imagery

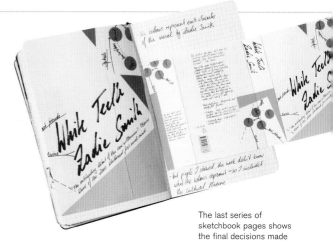

The last series of sketchbook pages shows the final decisions made

The final designs
show how
the research
impacted on the
decisions made

❝What you see and hear
depends a good deal on
where you are standing; it
also depends on what kind
of a person you are❞
C. S. Lewis

ongoing research also helps you to start to define your
own outlook, and to develop a personal 'signature',
since we are all different, and our individual perspectives
and experiences come to bear upon how we approach
a given problem.

⊙ ASSIGNMENT:
SPECIFIC RESEARCH/SKETCHBOOKS

In exploring ideas, you should aim to expand your
understanding of subject matter as far as possible. Research
done with an open mind will broaden your knowledge and
help you mature as a designer. It will also enable you to
achieve the most original solutions to a given project.

Gather items that suggest/promote/stimulate associations
with the project at hand. This might involve collecting possible
colours, letterforms, textures or formats; imagery from books,
magazines and newspapers; texts on related subjects, news
items, etc. Initial directions should be defined by the project
in question, but may branch out into many different areas.

Research may be quick, or it may take weeks to gather
materials, which can be done while working on other things.
Especially in college, you should take advantage of the luxury
of time, to explore and expand your research as fully as
possible, since in the professional studio, time is often at
a premium.

This process is as important as the final outcome, and you
should view it as a key factor of your work. A distinction is
made between primary and secondary research; both are
equally important aspects of the process.

sketchbook
ISTD
1002
LUCY BROWN

INTERNATIONAL SOCIETY OF TYPOGRAPHIC DESIGNERS PROJECT

This prize-winning project by Lucy Brown for the ISTD competition, 2007, involved looking closely at the architectural design and history of St Bride Library in London, to come up with a way of cataloguing its printing and typography collections. Detailed sketchbook pages show how the designer arrived at decisions about method, content and form.

Research reference on the simplest way to document books on a shelf

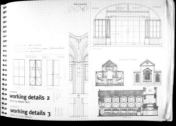

Research informing a detailed 'typographic' architectural elevation of the library

Early thoughts on type displayed on its side which informed the final layout

Expressing an interest in typographic hierarchy on a larger scale

Ideas on how a figure enables a sense of scale when showing a three-dimensional space

Sketches on how one represents a three-dimensional space on paper

Early visual reference of the perspective of a space and vertical typography

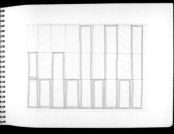

Getting a feel for the form of a vertical 'book-spine-like' structure on a page

Sketches informed by the visual spacing of typography in a public environment

Secondary research on grid systems and traditional letterpress frameworks

Research into the traditional and modern context of directional arrows and fists

Visual reference of secondary research material on Victorian library signage

Primary research on stock and print finishing

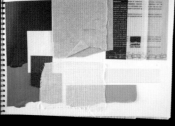

Further primary research on stock, materials and printing processes

Secondary research reference on the charm and form of brown paper envelopes

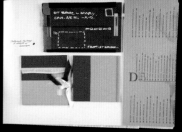

Examples of proposed finishing materials and print tests onto the chosen paper stock

The final designs reflect the intensive process of research, which has resulted in careful choices of materials and colour, and intelligent choices of references to the library's history and collections, through both the typography and binding.

Centred typography, in a traditional serif font, alongside condensed 19th-century typefaces, rules and pointing hands, shows the historical context of the library. The effect is highly sympathetic and well-considered, and sets the scene for what is inside.

The back of the catalogue includes an image of the chief librarian. The placement of the line of text next to the open hand is more modern in style, suggesting that the library houses not only historical, but contemporary collections.

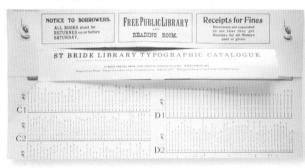

The catalogue features detailed typography set out in rows demonstrating the layout of the reading room. The spine of every book is set vertically as if viewing it in the building. The viewer is invited to consider the typography, the book spines and the building as a whole.

The paper sleeve in which the design is received continues the red/brown paper theme of the entire catalogue, suggesting a ribbon tied around the envelope.

RESEARCH TECHNIQUES

Primary sources/ factual research	Secondary sources/ factual research
• Previous knowledge/ opinion/memory • Observation • Conversation • Analysis • Role-play • Interviews: in person, by email, in a chatroom, by telephone • Questionnaires • Focus groups • Commissioned video/ written diaries (first hand) • Ethnographic research ('deep hanging out')	• Museums, archives, collections • Newspapers, magazines, journal articles • Published interviews • Films, TV broadcasts, theatre • Transcripts/recordings of film, TV, radio • Books • Music • internet: blogs, websites, forums, magazines • Surveys • Statistics • Organisations, agencies, gatekeepers • Lectures, public debates, conferences

Primary sources/ visual research	Secondary sources/ visual research
• Photography • Drawing/sketching • Media experimentation: 2D and 3D • Rubbings/casts • Typographic experimentation • Compositional experimentation • Image manipulation • Photocopying • Video/DV recording • Audio recording • Writing	• Exhibitions • Images/photographs from magazines, books, leaflets, internet, billboards • Work by other designers/ artists • Printed maps/diagrams • Ephemera (eg, tickets, receipts, packaging) • Found or bought photographs, postcards, drawings • Imagery taken from recordings of films, TV broadcasts, performances • Architecture

Other general work practices/approaches
• Put your own point of view into the subject
• Work in groups and respond to feedback from others
• Develop ideas by generating a number of visuals in response to one idea
• Explore the full capacity of your visual language

PART 1 | PRINCIPLES

UNIT 1 | RESEARCH AND EARLY CONCEPTS

MODULE 2 | # Linear reasoning/lateral thinking

In the initial stages of concept development, there are two main ways to approach a set brief: linear reasoning and lateral thinking. These are virtually opposites – the first focused and methodical, the second diffuse and expansive. However, both are equally useful as research and development tools.

Linear reasoning implies a strategic thought process, using step-by-step logic, and follows a specific trajectory (path). In other words, linear reasoning frequently involves a predetermined idea or concept that is then worked towards in stages. Generally, this will involve splitting the idea up into components such as colour or type, and working each through to finalise the form to fit the concept. Lateral thinking involves indirect exploration, generating ideas less readily available by linear reasoning (or hidden by the linear process, so that less obvious associations aren't readily seen or generated). The emphasis is on indirect, creative forms of research. The term was coined by Edward de Bono in 1967.

The process of brainstorming, or sketching in a non-linear diagrammatic way, approaches problems by exploring each component in as much depth and breadth as possible, finding connections and associations that then strengthen the concept. This process aims to push achievable boundaries. Another way to think of it is in terms of walking through a city. You may set out knowing exactly where you are going,

focused on the end goal: reaching your destination. Alternatively, you could take a stroll without any predetermined destination in mind. Each will provide very different experiences; in the non-predetermined form, you may notice things along the way that are not obvious if your sights are set only on the destination.

Sometimes, you might want to start out with a lateral thinking session, where you brainstorm as many ideas as possible, in order to generate your initial ideas, moving to a more linear process at a later stage. The two are not necessarily mutually exclusive, but often complementary ways of researching a design problem.

GLOSSARY

Lateral thinking: A form of research where the emphasis is on indirect, creative forms of enquiry and thinking.

Linear reasoning: A form of thinking that implies strategic thought process, one in which step-by-step logic is employed.

➕ **SEE ALSO:**
BASICS OF RESEARCH P10

▶️ ▶️ Brainstorming and storyboarding

Initial brainstorming, in the form of a spider diagram, allows for unexplored paths to open up in the early stages of the design process. Later development might take more linear forms, as in the storyboard, which outlines the sequence of a narrative and indicates preliminary character development and image choices.

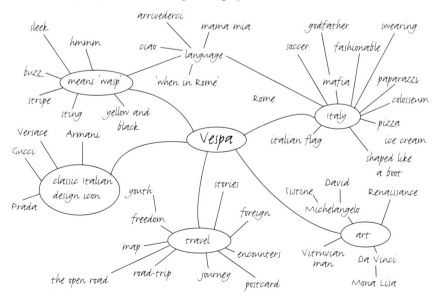

❯ Abstract interpretation

This piece is part of a body of work concerned with visual thought of the autistic mind and how this might be translated into the non-autistic world as creativity. Many autistic people record a piece of music note by note as an image in their mind in order to remember it. Bach's Prelude in C is represented here, determined by this possible autistic perception. It shows clearly how lateral thinking can be used to develop an idea.

❮ The thought process

The research notebook for the project at right shows how the designer applied a non-linear process to the development of the work.

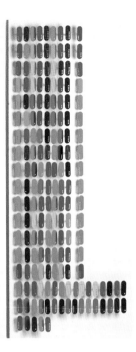

○ ASSIGNMENT: A CITY BLOCK

Produce a design (format to be decided by you, not limited to two-dimensional design) that explores a single city block, either historically, or as it exists in the present (or a combination of both), which conveys something about it to an audience of your choosing. This may sound very broad (and it is). Follow these steps to make the project manageable:

1 Choose a location.

2 Decide what kinds of recording devices might be used for a primary research investigation into the location (see Research Techniques on page 15).

3 Establish what secondary sources or research might be appropriate (see Research Techniques on page 15).

4 Decide on either linear reasoning or lateral thinking as the better research method. Or would a combination be productive?

Consider the following: Are there local library archives that could inform you about the history of this place? Would talking to passersby be useful research? What kinds of information would photography/video provide as opposed to drawing? Who is your audience? Local people, passersby, tourists, children? What do you want to tell them about this place and why? How might you express the passing of time, or the different meanings of a single place to a local community?

Compile a series of sketchbooks to show your research, and propose a final design solution, without necessarily producing a final design outcome. The emphasis of this assignment is on exploration/research, not on the finished product.

Try to expand your thought process and potential outcomes as far as possible by brainstorming, researching, analysing and evaluating your process as deeply as possible along the way.

PART 1 | PRINCIPLES

UNIT 1 | RESEARCH AND EARLY CONCEPTS

MODULE 3 | **Exploratory drawing**

The purpose of exploratory drawing is to explore ideas; it is a means of translating the outside world and of giving concrete form to abstract ideas. Sketching and drawing engage you in a constant process of looking, and aid in understanding the world around you. Whereas computer technology is another tool for the development of ideas, you should treat drawing as the basis of expression that underpins your design decisions.

Observational drawing, or drawing used to document, makes you see the subject as a shape or shapes, and colour as tones; it teaches you to understand and manipulate perspective, to understand how an object exists in space and to create the illusion of space and depth of field – it shows you how to convey texture and density. You should experiment beyond your comfort-zone, grasping as many forms of image-making as possible, both those that replicate what is seen (representational or observational drawing), and those where mark-making is freed from the need to represent what is seen (non-representational or non-observational drawing). The latter can generate valuable expressive drawn responses and gestures, and is widely used.

⌃ Another dimension The exploration of forms is achieved here through clear film and drawn line. Sketches do not have to take a two-dimensional form on paper, but can be produced in many different media.

⌃ Abstract drawing
Here lines are used in a non-figurative way, to suggest movement and create organic shapes. The effect invokes non-Western letterforms/calligraphy.

⟨ Figurative This representational drawing describes the scene. The drawn lines are expressive, but their primary purpose is descriptive.

You can always develop your drawing, regardless of how good you feel you already are. Continual practice is the key, and drawing should be a lifelong activity.

In observational drawing, train your eye to see diverse subject matter in detail. Whereas a still life helps you to observe static objects in detail, from a series of positions, going outside and visually researching the surrounding environment offers a stimulating variety of moving and static subject matter, which in turn changes how you draw. You can work directly in a sketchbook, or perhaps use a camera for more finished drawings at a later date. It is important to familiarise yourself with as many diverse aspects of form as possible.

Experiment with a variety of media, to determine and affect your created image. Whether charcoal or pencil, crayon or brush, each tool you use requires some understanding of its specific effects and mark-making qualities. For example, pencils allow tonal control, detailed modelling and a strong line, whereas ink and brush will generate an entirely different mark. Do not limit yourself to conventional media; other implements, such as a toothbrush, piece of string or even a sewing machine, can create interesting and valid marks. The aim is not merely to interpret the objects pictorially (representing them as they look), although of course this is useful for assessing various complexities of form. In short: both forms of drawing have their value and purpose, and should be treated as equally valid.

Understanding form

There are no lines around objects. They consist of their own solid form, and the light that falls upon them. It is tone that defines them. The normal procedure for understanding form is to create black-and-white drawings. Abstracting from real life, you are translating the language of colour into tone, substituting monochromatic tones for a wide range of colours in the existing object/objects.

Remember, too, that the media themselves are an abstraction, for while you may be drawing, say, a plastic bowl in charcoal, this medium has nothing to do with plastic. And if charcoal can be used to represent a plastic object, then why not try representing that same object in a non-conventional material, anything that enables you to express visually what you see? Experiment with a mix of media; explore both the linear and tonal nature of your subject matter.

Be as direct and spontaneous as possible. For immediacy, do several studies in a short space of time. Use materials to describe form and mass as areas of colour, replacing a monochromatic scheme, while using an outline only as a guide to subsequent layers. Concentrate not on an end product, but on the process of a rich description of forms.

❯ Extracting a theme
This experimental illustration examines the shapes and contours of maps, tracing their similarity to the forms of plants and flowers.

> ❝Matisse makes a drawing, then he makes a copy of it. He recopies it five times, ten times, always clarifying the line. He's convinced that the last, the most stripped down, is the best, the purest, the definitive one; and in fact, most of the time, it was the first. In drawing, nothing is better than the first attempt❞ *Pablo Picasso*

GLOSSARY

Abstraction: An aesthetic concept meaning something that is drawn from the real, but has been 'distilled' to its barest minimum form, colour or tone, often removed from its original context.

Documentation: The recording in written, visual or aural form of what is of interest.

Non-representation: The opposite of...

Representation: Something that looks like, resembles or stands in for something else. In drawing, this is also known as 'figurative', since it deliberately attempts to mimic the thing drawn.

⦿ ASSIGNMENT:
TAKING A LINE FOR A WALK

Linear drawing can be achieved in many ways; one is by 'taking a line for walk', first associated with the artist Paul Klee (1879–1940).

1 Choose a subject that offers variation in form.
2 Pick a visual point from which to start your drawing and continue without taking your pencil off the paper until your drawing is complete.
3 Experiment with the time you expend looking at the paper and your subject matter. Aim to observe the subject matter for a longer period of time than that of your developing drawing.
4 Finish a series of four studies, giving yourself a gradually increasing amount of time – between five and twenty minutes – to execute each one.

⦿ ASSIGNMENT:
THE LAST FLOWER

Choose a single live flower to document through drawing. Imagine that you have before you the last flower of its kind on Earth. There will never exist another one. Document it through drawing, both observational and experimental. What do you want/need to show? How could you 'draw' its scent?

Note
For research, the history of botanical illustration will give you numerous examples from which to find inspiration. See Maria Sibylla Merian (1647–1717).

⟩ ⓘ **Thumbnails** Sketches for business card layouts, book cover designs and packaging show a variety of options during the initial design stages. These can be shown to a client, before committing extra time to refining a design.

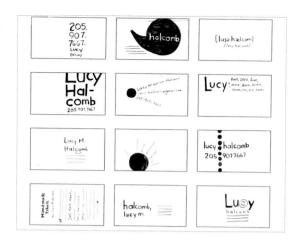

⌃ **Combining styles**
These logotype development sketches use quick visualisation techniques to explore possible layout and compositional solutions.

PART 1 | PRINCIPLES

UNIT 1 | RESEARCH AND EARLY CONCEPTS

MODULE 4 | **Visualising ideas**

As a student you need to develop the skill of putting ideas down on paper. This involves preparing rough visuals/design sketches – thumbnails, scamps or roughs. Students tend to bypass this process and set about producing ideas directly on-screen. This can inhibit the development of ideas because you may restrict yourself to what you are capable of achieving within the technology.

Initial ideas are generated much more quickly and prolifically if you first undertake a brainstorming session, in which your intial thoughts are scribbled down fast using various diagrammatic methods, or ways to structure information. In this process, coordination between brain, eye and hand is amazingly fast, and by working quickly you can generate many diverse (and sometimes unexpected) ideas, concepts and associations. Your mind starts flowing, loosening up and becomes open to diverse aspects of the project, swiftly moving the thought process forward. Literal and non-literal, lateral and non-lateral forms of thinking are used to maximum effect in these early sketches. Although roughs require a certain degree of drawing skills, these can be learned easily for this kind of work, where the generation of ideas is primary, not drawing as an end in itself. This is unlike observational drawing, or drawing as documentation, which needs to be precise.

Size and visualisation

There is no size to which roughs must be worked. 'Thumbnails' are, as the term suggests, small. You may feel more comfortable working to a third or a half of the actual size.

Remember that hand-drawn ideas can be vague and leave a lot to the imagination; this is a good thing: you don't read any detail into the sketch and so leave your options open. Designers use thumbnails to work out ideas. Usually these are generated on a sketchpad – thumbnails on a computer tend to look too fixed and

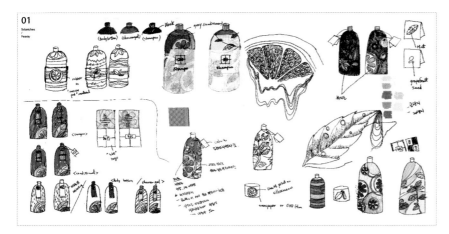

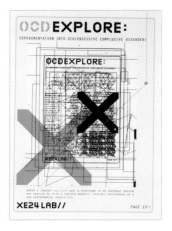

▲ **Cost-effective flexibility** Multiple versions of a single design can be swiftly generated on a computer, and colour can also be easily added and printed out.

◄ **Computer visualisation** The designer used a computer as a means of producing a vast number of visually dynamic designs. To some extent, the computer is replacing traditional visualisation techniques, but both are valuable skills.

polished: you are disinclined to change them or to be so critical. One way to capture the spirit of a thumbnail at full size is to enlarge it on a photocopier to the desired size.

Computers and visualisation

Once you have a number of ideas sketched out, you can step back and make judgments regarding their value, and potential for development, without having committed to any design in detail. This allows maximum flexibility and fluidity in the design process. However, once you have decided upon an idea or shortlist of ideas that you feel may have potential, computers come into their own, because they enable you to produce as many alternate versions of your ideas as you wish, changing colours, typefaces and images. Typefaces and grid measurements become fluid decisions when working digitally: you don't need to commit immediately, and in fact it may be better not to. It's fast and easy to change these on computers.

An important advantage of developing the ability to produce quick, effective roughs is that when presenting ideas to clients, alternatives can be quickly sketched out, keeping your approach fresh and relatively unrestricted. This in turn gives clients confidence in your willingness to be flexible and open-minded, while showing your design abilities.

⊕ **SEE ALSO:** EXPLORATORY DRAWING P18
LINEAR REASONING/LATERAL THINKING P19

SEE ALSO: EXPLORATORY DRAWING P18
LINEAR REASONING/LATERAL THINKING P19

Brainstorming: A visual aid to thinking laterally and exploring a problem, usually by stating the problem in the centre of a page and radiating spokes from the centre for components of the problem. Each component can then be considered separately with its own spokes, so that each point, thought or comment is recorded.

Thumbnail: Small, rough visual representation of the bigger picture or final outcome of a design.

PART 1 | PRINCIPLES

UNIT 1 | RESEARCH AND EARLY CONCEPTS

MODULE 5 | ## Theories of image and text

A design can communicate successfully, or be enhanced, through a number of visual strategies, depending on context. These range from highly pragmatic, where there needs to be as little ambiguity or opportunity for misunderstanding as possible – eg road signs, where clarity in message is potentially a matter of life and death – to work that allows for a much more 'poetic' approach – eg some editorial and arts projects, where subject matter invites interpretation, and where the designer has much more latitude in terms of imagery and message.

◗ Universally recognised
The 'stop' sign is part of the road signage system, but is understood in different contexts. Here, it indicates 'smoking prohibited' in a didactic, direct and unambiguous way.

◗ Strong association
Love is expressed through the symbol of the heart. Milton Glaser's famous 'I Love New York' campaign of the 1970s uses a rebus: I (image of heart = the spoken word love) New York. In rebuses, images substitute words, but in naming the image, we make the connection with the word.

⌃ Rhetoric These design campaigns use different forms of rhetoric (style of expression) to engage with different audiences. The message conveyed in the campaign (top) is subtle, graphically low-key and informational, whereas the campaign above is playful, childlike and fun.

Rhetoric

Originating in the Ancient Greek practice of public speaking, political argument or engagement in dialogue, rhetoric is a skill of persuasion, a style of speaking and a tone of voice. In both visual and linguistic terms it is important to carefully consider tone of voice – here, design can succeed or fail. For instance, in an advertising campaign to persuade children to eat more healthily, a visual rhetoric that is too 'adult' or serious may be off-putting; a playful, colourful, visual rhetoric may work better. However, in a series of books on politics or world affairs, such an approach is unlikely to work as well. With rhetoric, understanding your audience is all-important.

Semiotics

Ferdinand de Saussure developed this communication system into the theory that any sign can be broken down into a signifier and a signified.

Signs can consist of images, words, simple shapes, etc. For example, the sign for fire is made up of the word 'fire' (the signifier) and the concept or thing to which it refers: actual fire (the signified). The image (signifier) of an arrow indicates direction, and depending on which way it is pointing, people (the signified) know where to go.

Signs can also be denotative or connotative. Denotation is what a sign means – an image of a snake, for example, refers to a snake. Connotations are extended (extra) meanings associated with a sign (some of them emotional, personal, cultural). For example, a person described as a snake might be untrustworthy. An image of the Sun might suggest heat, light, joy or in the case of Japan, part of the national flag.

Signs and symbols

A sign stands in for something else. In this sense, it is close to a symbol, which also represents something other than itself (think of the shape of a red circle with a line diagonally running through it. This symbol is agreed to mean 'stop', or 'don't'). However, there may be rich layers of additional meaning in symbols, such as the symbol for a nation: a flag. While it's true that the flag is a sign for a country, and makes us think of that country when we see it, its symbolic associations go much deeper. There are natural signs, such as thunder, which usually points towards a storm; or footprints on the beach, which indicate that someone has walked there. These are called 'causal' signs. However, many signs are called 'conventional', in that they are agreed upon but bear no relationship to the meaning they stand for. All language consists of

▶ Open to interpretation
In the design at far right, while the imagery is simple, the possible interpretation is ambiguous (poetic).

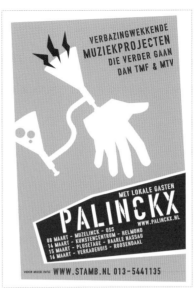

symbols. The word 'cat' makes us think of a cat, but the shapes of those letters have no particular relationship to a cat, in the same way that numerals stand symbolically for numbers, but don't resemble numbers, which are abstract.

Metaphor

Metaphors are words or images that set up associations or comparisons to other words or images. For example, a carrot is often used as a metaphor for an incentive (as in to 'dangle a carrot' in front of someone). A metaphor for learning is often an image of a book, or an apple with a bite taken out of it. Logos frequently employ metaphors to convey their meaning. They also utilise the extended meanings of a sign to suggest ideas (connotations – see above).

◉ ASSIGNMENT: ANALYSING SIGNS

Find three signs – logos, symbols, trademarks – whose denotations and connotations you can analyse and break down. Locate one design that operates didactically and another that uses poetic strategies. In your notebook, explain what kinds of rhetorical devices (including images, words, colours) are used, either unambiguously or ambiguously. It's important that you learn to analyse designs in this way, so that you can see how and why something does or doesn't work. Based on this information, can you suggest areas for improvement in any of the signs?

⊕ SEE ALSO: AUDIENCES, MARKETS, AND CONCEPTS P26

FURTHER READING

Roland Barthes, *Mythologies*

John Berger, *Ways of Seeing*

David Crow, *Visible Signs*

Ferdinand de Saussure, *Course in General Linguistics*

Semiotics for Beginners website: http://www.aber.ac.uk/media/Documents/S4B/semiotic.html

▶ The pointing finger The printer's index, or fist, is a symbol for drawing attention, which has been in use since the 12th century. The pointing finger is a universally understood symbol, since it shows part of the human body.

▶ Crossing the language barrier Several languages state the same thing: Caution. This design is rhetorically informational, and didactic, leaving no room for interpretation or misunderstanding.

Didactics

This method of pragmatically and unambiguously conveying a message gives clear, informative and instructive meaning. Road signs are a classic example: you do not want to spend time interpreting a sign as you drive down a busy road. Signage in airports and hospitals must also be unambiguous. Much information design relies on didactic forms.

Poetics

Poetic forms of work have much less immediately accessible or immediately given meaning. Sometimes, their meaning is referred to as opaque (less transparent). In this kind of work, the message being conveyed – the meaning of the work – is deliberately much less straightforward, and is open to numerous interpretations. Here, designers make a conscious decision to leave the work open. Many posters, advertising campaigns and book designs use poetic forms of work to engage audiences and to provoke thoughtful responses. They rely upon the viewers being willing to spend the time to interpret the work. In contrast, road signs, and other pragmatic forms of design, cannot rely upon this: function and immediacy are essential. Poetic work can often be seen as the other extreme to didactic/pragmatic work, being closer to fine art. However, all approaches exist on a wide spectrum, and so work can have elements of both, rather than be strictly categorised as one or the other. Designers are problem-solvers and communicators, but work that is rich in meaning and possible interpretations also has a place.

Abstract cover Silk-screen-printed abstract imagery is suggestive, but open to interpretation. The content of the book is implied, rather than described, and the use of subtle colour/texture and lines works to keep the meanings open.

Suggestive posters Poetic ambiguity inhabits these posters, whose imagery is beautifully sourced and sensitively judged, but open to multiple interpretations. There are references to mapping, targets and locations, but nothing concrete.

Brief:

Part 1: To create a sculpture influenced by the work and method of a designer featured in the Design Cities Exhibition, London (❯ top row)

The work of Owen Jones was the influence for this sculpture. Jones' work was heavily influenced by what he saw and learnt of the world when travelling at the beginning of his career. The work invites the viewer to see the world and be encouraged to travel. The box contains one whole atlas mixed up to evoke a fresh consideration of the many destinations to choose from.

Part 2: Design an alternative guide to London (❯ middle and bottom rows)

'The question then, is how to get lost. Never to get lost is not to live, not to know how to get lost brings you to destruction, and somewhere in the terra incognita in between lies a life full of discovery.' Rebecca Solnit

'I began by displaying posters to the public that stated "Get Lost in London Today" and later got three friends lost for the day in London. Observing both public and individual reactions to becoming lost, I realised that the key was to enable yourself to become lost *to* London not *in* London. The application of a verse from the Bible became my message: "Ask for London and it will be given to you. Seek London out and you will find it. Knock on London's door and it will be opened to you." Advertising boards, due to their common part to play in delivering messages within a city, became my format. The contextualisation of the boards within the city represents the individual Londoner's life as a daily existence of the boards' messages, acting as an invitation to others to engage with the city in the same way.' Lucy Brown, designer

❯ **'Get lost in London today'** Poetic and pragmatic dimensions of design co-exist in this body of work. The work references advertising boards and signage, which at first sight seem highly pragmatic and instructional. However, the work has a number of possible interpretations, depending on the attitude and experience of the viewer. This work exists somewhere in between didactic and poetic, and plays with elements of both.

PART 1	PRINCIPLES
UNIT 1	RESEARCH AND EARLY CONCEPTS
MODULE 6	**Audiences, markets and concepts**

Good graphic design is not simply the result of brilliant execution or technique. It is the strong expression of clever, well-formulated ideas, drawn from an ongoing engagement with research, and an interest in the world at large. In professional practice, as in school, extensive exploratory research is invariably the key to the most successful projects, and research into audiences is a primary tool of effective design.

It is vital to remember that everything you design is going to be seen by other people. You are not working in a vacuum. It is part of your job to discover what your audience wants/needs. Before designing, think about the people who will be looking at your designs. What is your target market? What do you know about them? What can you/should you find out about them? Your designs need to communicate with real people – not just work aesthetically. Design has to be functional and appropriate for the audience to which it is geared. Therefore, the more you can find out about your audience and their habits, the better informed your work will be, increasing its potential effectiveness.

Large companies have whole departments devoted to what is formally called market research. These people spend their time conducting surveys into their customers' needs and preferences. They do this by a variety of means, including questionnaires, telephone surveys and focus groups (where people carefully selected as representative of the target audience are brought together to discuss a product or campaign before it is launched into the public domain).

If you don't have time for this level of market research, then you should at least ask yourself the following questions every time you start a project: Who is the design aimed at? What messages are they supposed to get from looking at it? How will you grab and retain their attention?

Varied media The 'Man or Mouse' campaign challenged its audience to take up physical activity as a response to the increased use of computers in our daily lives. The campaign targeted both online and printed-newspaper readers. From top left, the various elements of the campaign are carried through promotional posters, printed newspapers, inserts to the newspaper, online newspapers and posters on bus shelters.

◄ Promoting ethical objectives The 'Address the Homeless' campaign aimed to establish the UK Royal Mail's social responsibility and corporate citizenship, educating its audience about homelessness and challenging preconceptions. Flyers and posters promoted the campaign as a community project, and aimed to generate corporate sponsorship. The designs, which place letterboxes in places where homeless people would be found, are stark in layout, informative in content and provocative in tone.

● ASSIGNMENT: **CONCEPT DEVELOPMENT**

Finding clever new ways of expressing your ideas visually is a bit of a daunting prospect. However, this is a skill that can be improved over time with practice. As already discussed, the starting point is often a piece of paper, a pencil and an open mind.

1 Take an example project: branding for a new dance music TV channel. What words and images immediately spring to mind? Noise, sound and rhythm: how can you convey these visually? What kind of type could express the broken, disconnected beats? Think about the people who listen to dance music. What do they look like? What about the musicians? What is the role of the DJ? What other things do fans like? What clothes do they wear? How about graffiti? Where do you normally hear this type of music (clubs, festivals, radio)?

2 Explore other formats (eg record, MiniDisc, CD, MP3): how are these differently presented in graphic terms?

This is just the beginning. Note down ideas, rather than relying on memory, because one idea will often obscure a previous thought. Each can spark off others and these can be connected together or followed up separately. Have as many ideas as possible down on paper, so you can move on to the next stage.

Audience: In its broadest sense, the consumers, voyeurs and occasionally participants of design work.

Customer profile/profiling: The process of creating a series of parameters or set of information that defines the desires, trends or interests of a demographic so that designs can be pitched or marketed to them.

Market research: The process of collecting and collating data from questionnaires, interviews and comments from the public regarding a concern, a problem or a possible solution.

❶ Dare to share
Talking about things often sparks off other trains of thought. Explaining ideas to others can help you really understand what you are trying to achieve. Be prepared to listen to opinions offered (remember: you do not have to act on them if you think they aren't relevant or helpful). Try not to take any criticism personally. Use it constructively to uncover which aspects of your ideas aren't working and what you can do to improve them. You will often have to listen to comments about your work, and they will not always be positive.

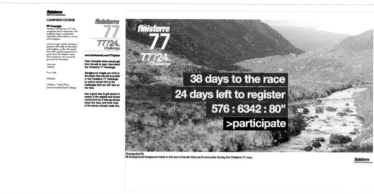

⊙ ⟨ ⌃ Multi-tiered campaign This Finisterre campaign promoted an ecologically and ethically manufactured surf brand. Billboards, online advertisements, sponsored race promotion, trade show exhibition designs, public relations and clothing designs are some of the elements of this extensive campaign. The clean, modern designs emphasise outdoor locations, physicality, lifestyle and a broad set of ethical concerns about the environment. The target audience had been carefully considered at all stages of the development of the design.

⊕ SEE ALSO: BASICS OF RESEARCH P12

LINEAR REASONING/ LATERAL THINKING P16

EXPLORATORY DRAWING P18

VISUALISING IDEAS P20

Conduct market research into driving schools, imagining that you are going to design a promotional campaign for your local one. Write up your findings into a report, as if you were presenting it to your local driving school, as evidence to back up your ideas.

- Go to the library to look at market analysis reports/statistics.
- Read newspaper/magazine articles.
- Look at company websites.
- Compile your own survey.
- Speak to customers/users.
- Try using the product/service yourself.
- Speak to people who work for the companies.

ELIMINATION PROCESS

Explore your ideas visually to see which have the most potential. Do not be too precious about detail; concentrate on expressing your ideas.

1 Make quick sketches to show you which ideas work well and have immediate impact. Use colour if it helps, but do not get bogged down in shades and tones.

2 Discard any sketches that are too complex or rely on tired visual clichés. Quickly getting rid of the bad ideas will help you focus on the good ones.

3 Select the strongest idea, then put together a presentation visual that demonstrates why your idea is so brilliant.

4 Now you can start working on the detail. The best ideas are often the simplest, but you need to show that careful thought and preparation have gone into your work. Consider how you will explain your idea to your client. You might need to 'sell' it to them, so think about what you would say to support your images.

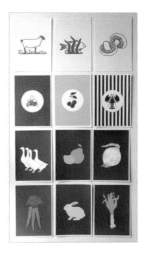

◀ ◆ ▶ **Extending the concept** Shopping bags, produced in a limited edition, were the core part of this campaign to educate consumers about the health benefits of food that is eaten during the correct season. There are also environmental benefits, since less transport is needed to bring food to the consumer, and local farming economies are supported. The campaign was developed beyond the initial shopping bags, into posters and product labelling, using hand-drawn illustrations and script typography.

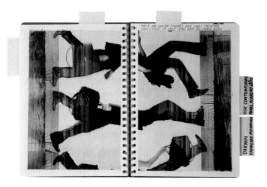

PART 1	PRINCIPLES
UNIT 1	RESEARCH AND EARLY CONCEPTS
MODULE 7	**Scheduling, organising and finalising**

The organisation of your thoughts into a coherent form is the end product of the design process, although the process of organisation starts right from the beginning, during your initial research. You should start all projects with a broad approach and gradually narrow your ideas down until you are ready to finalise decisions and resolve the minutiae.

⌃ Working through the detail

Sketchbooks are essential during the initial stages of developing a design, when you are researching, and exploring potential ideas (see pages 10–15). However, at some point, organising and finalising your design needs to move beyond the sketching and visualising stage. Macro (large-scale) issues and micro (small) details need to be worked out, and negotiated with your client.

Good design works both at a macro scale (the large, overview structure, as though viewed from 'above'), and at a micro scale (where the tiniest details are important, even down to letterspacing). Often you will have to give the information order and structure (hierarchy) as well as visual form. You will need to make micro decisions such as type size, individual page layouts and colour choices, and these will need to be balanced and related to the macro scale: the whole design needs to appear considered.

Design briefs always involve interpretation by the designer; some clients have little idea what they need – they look to the designer for clear analysis of, and a solution to, the problem. Other clients may have a clear idea of what they want, and these ideas need to be considered/respected, but also challenged if they are inappropriate. For example, green may be a favourite colour of one member of a group of clients, but it may be the wrong choice for the brief. Similarly, it's important to recognise that clients have valuable insight into the workings of their organisation and its needs, and although they may not have the design skills to implement their ideas, their input on these matters is crucial. Be open and flexible, but stand your ground when you know you are right.

There are as many different ways of solving the same problem as there are designers. Your job is to choose the solution that you think is the most appropriate. This decision-making isn't subjective; it comes from informed judgment.

(see pages 10–15)

GLOSSARY

Page plan/flat plan: A document with a series of numbered thumbnails set out in an ordered grid that represents each page in a book.

Storyboard: A document similar to a flat plan, but with a sequence of thumbnails that specifically lays out the narrative for a comic strip or film.

❶ Timescale

Research can be very time-consuming, so bear in mind that there has to be a cut-off point at which you have to start generating a visual concept. 'Design' is a verb as much as it is a noun: it's about doing things.

❶ Remember

• Write everything down. Don't rely on memory.
• Without a relevant concept your visualisation has no meaning.
• Create a flowchart/spider diagram with routes for different ideas.
• Look for professional criticism and use this constructively.
• Talk about your work as well as showing it. Learn to be verbally articulate, as well as visually.

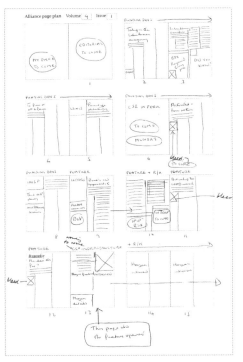

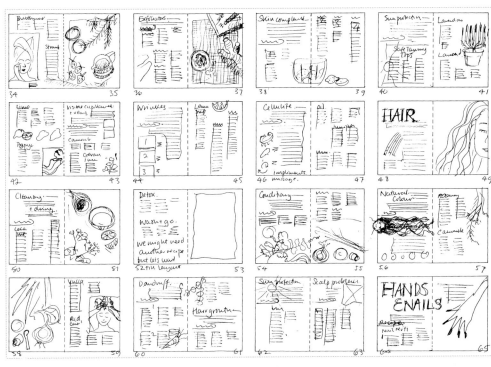

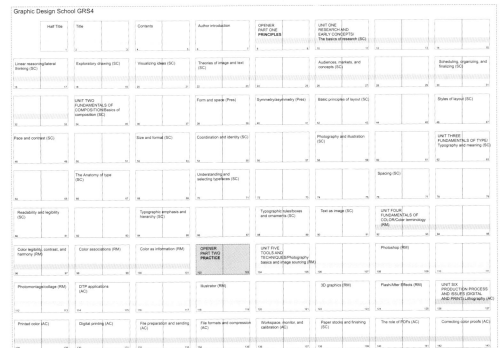

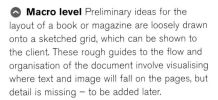

Macro level Preliminary ideas for the layout of a book or magazine are loosely drawn onto a sketched grid, which can be shown to the client. These rough guides to the flow and organisation of the document involve visualising where text and image will fall on the pages, but detail is missing – to be added later.

The bigger picture A more detailed set of sketches shows how a grid is used to organise material within a magazine. These sketches are valuable aids in developing the design on a computer, keeping the macro (overview) in mind as you design, not just the individual page or spread you are working on.

Organising content Flat plans or page plans represent a cohesive set of decisions about layout. Each spread is given a place, and organised in terms of content and/or visual rhythm. Clear chapter/section divisions can be seen, and the visual sequence of the entire book is available at a glance. This is the flat plan for the book you are reading.

WAYS TO ORGANISE THOUGHTS

Something as simple as making lists of tasks, of approaches or of time can clarify exactly what a particular problem is. Try organising your ideas by the following criteria:

- Alphabet – from A to Z
- Category – by type
- Chronological – by time
- Continuum – for example, from 'good' to 'bad'
- Magnitude – by size
- Location – by place

Scheduling and organisation

Time management and organisation are crucial aspects of design practice, and their significance cannot be over-stressed. Fix dates for yourself: organise your time, and plot out the progress of a project, from start to end, allocating time to different aspects of the process. To help you do this, make a schematic diagram to identify how long certain things may take. If you are working on a project for which there are numerous applications and different elements, you particularly have to bear this in mind.

Over longer jobs there may be only one deadline per week (eg interim presentations to the client); on shorter jobs this may be two deadlines per day (eg multiple proof stages). One way to organise ideas into sequence is to write everything down on self-adhesive reminder notes and only then put things in a logical order; you may surprise yourself with the final order. Computer programs such as Excel can be invaluable in plotting job progress, and in maintaining an overview. Organise your digital files logically, making sure everyone working on the project knows the system, and back up your files regularly. Many good designers miss the importance of time management and organisation, and their work and client relationships suffer as a result. Get into the habit of good time management – now!

Storyboards

Storyboards give the client or production person enough information so that each can take them and begin to design their assigned spreads or pages of the final product.

Website plans show how pages link up in a logical order. The organisation of a website reflects the actual body for which the site is designed. It is important to get the structure right before designing the look of the pages.

Storyboards are used to design individual pages or sequences before engaging a web designer. As well as in multimedia design, storyboards are commonly employed in films, comic strips, animation and TV commercials. The storyboard contains a sketch of the visual aspect of the screen, information that will be present, descriptions of animations, interactions (eg dialogue boxes), sounds and any other media. Although storyboards were originally linear (for film), non-linear elements are incorporated.

Page plans/flat plans

There has to be a logical visual (and conceptual) sequence in any design project. A magazine or a book illustrates this point well. Magazines and books are normally laid out in miniature on a 'page plan' several times before full-size layouts are started. The page plan may consist of no more than the article title but can be much more specific, including a list of all the page elements or a thumbnail drawing of the layout with text blocks and artwork sketched in. The page plan is intended to clarify logical sequence, distribution of colour, change of pace and so on.

➕ **SEE ALSO:** BASICS OF RESEARCH P10

VISUALISING IDEAS P20

COORDINATION AND IDENTITY P55

❱ ❱❭ **Stages of animation**
Design for an animation starts out as rough sketches, and develops into more detailed storyboards, before the final production phase.

CRS4 graphic design.xls

(Screenshot of a spreadsheet titled "Graphic design school 4th edition" with columns for Batch 1 to Batch 4, scheduling rows such as Text/pic list in, Edited, Props in, Other photos, Pic list in, Selection, Pic costing, Pencil roughs, Author check, Finished artes, Rough layouts, to authors, Final layouts, Proofread, Disk out, Synopsis revised, Dummy revised, Planning meeting, Author contract, Publisher stages, Budget status, Sample?, presentation due from author, and styling/set-up notes.)

Schedules A schedule may be a handwritten list with dates, in the case of a simple production task. However, if you are working with a client, it's always a good idea to send a typewritten schedule, to avoid any confusion. More complex projects, with many disparate elements to pull together, may require a more formal schedule. A spreadsheet is ideal for this.

ASSIGNMENT: BUILD A SCHEDULE

In a flowchart program such as Excel, create a scheduling/organisational document for design projects that you are currently working on, or plan to work on in the future. Establish beforehand the categories you will need to build in, such as the different development phases of a project, from initial design ideas through to print or uploading (in the case of websites or other digital work). You will need to incorporate ways of tracking expenses, overall budget to and accounting for the various elements of a project. This document may change to address the different needs of individual projects, but will be a sound basic template that you can modify over time.

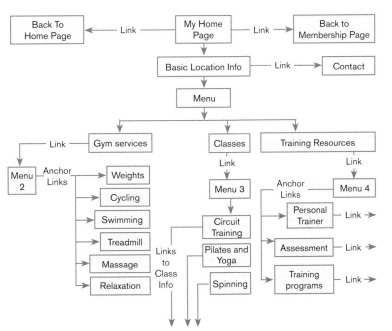

Web flowcharts You can map out the structure and organisation of a site, with its various sections and subdivisions, using a flowchart. In the planning and conceptualisation stage of a website, it's important to create a chart, outlining the site's overall structure and showing how the viewer will navigate through the site. Any potential problems can be identified and resolved, before designing/coding.

2 FUNDAMENTALS OF COMPOSITION

Successful graphic designers are masters of the visual fundamentals that underlie all aspects of design. The way that you present design elements on a page should be led by concern for spacing, visual organisation, style and the size and format of the finished work.

Any project should be designed to maintain interest while cohesively bringing together a variety of text and images.

◀ **Contrasting colour**
The varied sizes and placement of these circles activates space in different ways, causing the circles to recede or advance.

❝Visual literacy also is an ability to view any image as an abstraction, to understand what is happening in purely visual terms as well as knowing and understanding visual terminology. It involves training the eyes to see minute detail and being sensitive to colour, shape, form and line. It has little or nothing to do with content or style❞ *Rob Roy Kelly*

PART 1 | PRINCIPLES

UNIT 2 | FUNDAMENTALS OF COMPOSITION

MODULE 1 | **Basics of composition**

Composition refers to the visual structure and organisation of elements within a design; it concerns the process of combining distinct parts or elements to form a whole. Composition involves seeing the whole as greater than its parts, and is just as important as the individual elements that make up a design (text, images, etc.).

Designers primarily organise images and text – consisting of shapes, sizes, colours and textures – in many different forms of media. These are produced in a wide range of formats, from two- and three-dimensional, black-and-white design, through full-colour work, to three-dimensional, web-based and time-based (moving) imagery.

A practical understanding and exploration of composition is crucial for effective visual communication: it teaches control, so that the desired effect is achieved, and the intended message is communicated. Developing good compositional skills is of the greatest importance in creating effective designs, whatever medium you are working in. This takes time, patience and practice, but the confidence it gives and the rewards it brings are immense.

Throughout the history of the visual arts different theories of composition have been advanced. Vitruvius, the Roman architect and engineer, devised a mathematical formula for the division of space within a picture. His solution, known as the Golden Section or the Golden Mean, was based on a set ratio between the longer and shorter sides of a rectangle. The French painter Henri Matisse (1869–1954) put greater emphasis on inspiration, maintaining that composition is the art of arranging elements to express feelings.

Positive and negative space

Positive space is a form or object that, to the eye, appears to exist. This might be a solid shape (large or small), a line or a texture. Negative space is everything

Shape and space You need to be familiar with the various visual effects that figure/ground, compositional and symmetrical/asymmetrical relationships create. The best way to do this is to experiment with simple forms in a given space (the space used here is a square), which allow you to see the effect of sometimes very small decisions on a design. The relationship between negative and positive forms, and the dominance of vertical/ horizontal shapes, or shapes that draw the viewers' attention towards a particular part of the composition, are crucial parts of a designer's visual vocabulary. Practise, practise, practise – preferably before moving to a computer.

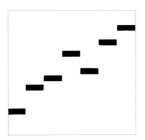

Repetition of unequally spaced lines creates movement and rhythm. Putting these elements at the page edge implies that the pattern continues beyond.

The illusion of gradation is created by an intervention into the space by finely tapering lines. The right edge of the square dissolves; the left edge is reinforced.

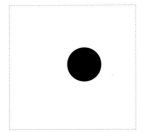

An off-centre circle within a square implies movement to the right. Designers use this imbalance to shift the visual focus.

Dynamic forms and negative/ positive spaces create the illusion of directional arrows. The eye closes the breaks in the lines.

As with the image above, lines create movement and continuation beyond the page edges. The directional movement here is diagonal, however, and the intervals between the lines are even.

The centre of the square is reinforced by four triangles, pointing towards it. It's unclear which is the figure and which is the ground, confusing the eye.

Unevenly spaced vertical lines create tension between the left and right edges of the square, breaking up the surface in rhythmic ways. Vertical lines tend to imply power, strength and stability.

Despite the small square being dominated by the larger, the eye moves towards the small square because it is the figure, reinforced by the surrounding space.

Typography In this series, the compositions refer to typographic elements, which may be combined with images and/or rules. Be aware of how the same compositional issues seen in the two series above also apply to typography. Text must also be treated carefully when it comes to composition, since the meaning of the words and the connection between titles and body text (hierarchy) needs to be respected.

Centred lines of text are a classic form of title page design for books. The space is symmetrical, stable and restful to the eye.

The relationship between the blocks of text and the thicker line conveys separate yet related elements.

The bar and small text block that runs at a right-angle to it are connected, while being visually contrasted.

Text and title are related in sequence by the bar that is of the same width as the left-hand column of text.

◉ Visual rhythm A series of objects related to one another by similarity of form (curved lamp bases) shows how the visual rhythm between elements is of great importance. Here, the rhythm created is harmonious to the eye.

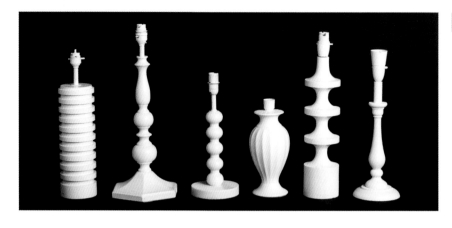

⊕ SEE ALSO: FORM AND SPACE P39

COLOUR LEGIBILITY, CONTRAST AND HARMONY P96

else around or within an object: this is the 'empty' space left over. It is important to learn to effectively control the relationship between positive and negative space, and to explore this in basic compositional studies, before moving on to more complex designs. Carefully consider the effective use of positive and negative space, and recognise that, in general, negative space works to support the positive 'image' in any given area (also called the 'picture plane'). Don't leave the relationship between positive and negative elements to chance; be in control of them, to create a more considered and effective composition.

White space creates tension and contrast; you can easily see the effects of 'unused' space on the overall feel of a composition by altering the ratio of positive to negative space. If you place a single dot in the centre of a relatively large square of white paper, far from disappearing, the dot becomes emphasised. This is because the expanse of white space highlights and focuses attention on the dot itself. Sometimes you can actively encourage ambiguity between picture elements and background. For example, a particular group of forms can come together to support each other and compete in such a way that the (normally negative) space is given form by the positive elements, as in 'figure–ground' relationships (see page 38).

Point and line

A point exists in its own right as a point in space (a dot), but is also the start of a line, since it has the potential to extend into a line whether it does so or not.

Many points together start to set up a rhythm, or pattern, which (depending on uniformity, repetitiveness or change in size or quantity) can suggest regularity or variation.

A line is a pathway between any two points. It can be straight, curved, thick, thin, horizontal, diagonal, jagged, solid or broken. Soft, sensuous lines imply tranquility and harmony, whereas sharp, zigzagged lines invoke jarring and discordance. Two converging lines imply a point disappearing in the distance, and the illusion of three dimensions in a two-dimensional space. Horizontal lines suggest horizons; vertical lines suggest power and strength. Lines usually imply motion, momentum, rhythm and upwards or downwards movement, and are usually orientational and directional, but broadly suggestive of different effects.

Look at the artist Franz Kline's use of strong, emphatic painted line, or Cy Twombly's wandering, fragile drawn and painted lines for their expressive qualities. In design, see Wolfgang Weingart's use of line in typography, as a way to structure information, or Russian Constructivist Alexander Rodchenko's powerful use of red and black line. El Lizzitsky and Piet Zwart also used lines emphatically and expressively in their work.

> ❝Line: a thin, continuous mark, as that made by a pen, pencil or brush applied to a surface. Lines are a human convention. They are intellectual constructs to impose order such as a line of thought, or a line of flight. In the visual world, lines are generally a shorthand for edges. We perceive objects because of the dozens of ways they differ from their surroundings. We abbreviate these differences by drawing a contour line❞ *Tim McCreight*

◉ ASSIGNMENT: **COMPOSITION FROM LINES**

1 Drawing

Using tracing paper and a pencil, rule two horizontal lines 230mm (9in) apart. Beginning at the left, draw four different lines, ranging from 1 (nearly straight) to 4 (extremely active). These must flow without points or breaks, running from top to bottom; they must enter and exit the composition vertically.

Produce a total of ten sets of lines in which variety, symmetry/asymmetry and relative tension are considered. They should not be broken, and you should be aware of the quality of the line itself; for instance, poorly drawn or broken lines are not acceptable. Make sure they are interesting visually, and relate to one another (see example).

2 Positive and negative

Choose the four most interesting sets of lines. On tracing paper, working at the 230mm (9in) square size, use a combination of marker pen and black paint to fill in the shapes made by the lines. Explore positive and negative possibilities. They can have a combination of black/white shapes and black/white lines. Be aware of figure–ground qualities, and of ambiguity in spatial readings, which are most interesting. Tensions between lines and shapes create variety and richness in final compositions.

• Play one line against another. Consider the dynamics of opposition: lines working against lines, pointed curves against flat curves or straight lines, activity against static, etc.

• Avoid parallels such as a flat curve against another flat curve or straight line creating nearly parallel shapes; modify the curve to a sharp pointed curve so that the shape is continually increasing or decreasing.

• Examine each line in relation to others in terms of shape, not just the shape created between two lines, but also those made between one line and all others, ie pay attention to the whole design, not just individual lines.

• Finalise the compositions and choose the three most successful, in which you think the figure–ground relationships have been resolved in interesting ways (and that address the considerations above). Rank these from 1 to 3 in terms of success (1 = the best). Work at your highest level of skill, and be aware of every detail.

3 Colour

Now add different quantities of colour as an element in four of your designs. Consider carefully how this can enhance a line, or create strong positive or negative spaces. Does the use of colour contribute to establishing 'opposites', for example, by using green across a similar-sized field of red? How does an orange shape surrounded by a larger area of grey affect the design? Experiment, play, explore.

4 Texture

Now add texture (surface qualities of marks on paper) and/or pattern as an element in two of your designs. This can be created by rubbing, drawing or photographic means. Textures and patterns can be light or dark, large or small, regular or irregular.

◉ **Experiment** Texture, line and solid shape can produce rich results within compositions.

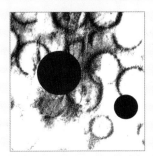
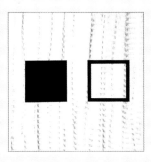

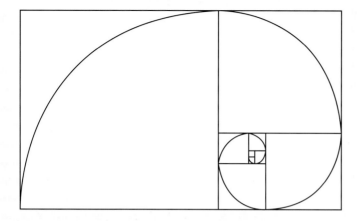

🔺 **Fibonacci spiral** Each time a square is taken from the section, a smaller rectangle remains with the same proportions as the original. The spiral (also known as the Golden Ratio) can be used to create a proportional and harmonious composition.

🔻 **Tricks on the eye** Figure–ground relationships produce different effects that confuse the eye. For example, the Rubin vase (top left) relies upon a visual confusion between figure and ground, so that the eye sees either faces or a vase.

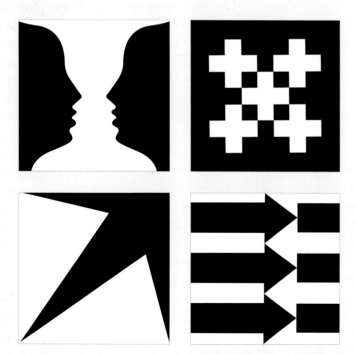

MODULE 2 │ # Form and space

In order to develop good compositional skills, it is important to understand the role of visual perception (the way our eyes and brains make sense of what we see), and its role in communication.

Whether consciously or not, our eyes are constantly supplying information to our brain, which processes and makes sense of that visual input. Being able to control that process and understand how it works is crucial. Good design thinking also requires an understanding of the relationship between things. The relationship between visual elements strongly affects the way we perceive them. In this section of the book, we will look at some of these relationships, and learn how to control and exploit them.

Figure and ground

A form is always experienced in relation to the space it occupies and to other forms that may be present in the format. We call this the figure–ground relationship (where 'figure' refers to any object in a given space, and 'ground' refers to the background, or space in which that object is seen). Another way to talk about this relationship is in terms of negative and positive space. Visual elements are therefore always seen in relation to a visual field, background or frame. In other words, every form is seen in context and cannot be totally isolated. Generally speaking, a form is considered to be positive and the space around it negative. The space within a format (the ground) is an extremely important element of any design and not just something left over once a form is placed on it: it matters within the overall design, since the ground affects the figure and vice versa. Usually, we tend to notice the figure before we see the ground, or what is in a space, before we see the space itself. However, a well-known example of where this relationship becomes confused is drawn from Gestalt psychology, specifically

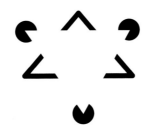

the well-known example, the Rubin vase, where the effect depends on whether we see the figure as the white element, with the ground as the black, or whether we see the black shapes as the figure. As we can see in the example opposite, the lines that define the black and white areas can be seen as pointing either inwards or outwards, so that the eye swiftly reverses the figure–ground relationship, flipping back and forth between the two.

The law of closure

Another phenomena drawn from Gestalt psychology is the law of closure, which argues that we tend to 'close' or complete lines or objects that are not, in fact, closed. This can be a useful device in design, and is related to figure and ground, since it relies on our ability to collapse the space between foreground and background.

⌃ The law of closure
The shape of the star is completed mentally, even though the form is incomplete.

GLOSSARY

Composition: The arrangement of elements or parts of a design (text, images) on the page.

Gestalt psychology: A theory that suggests that the mind perceives and organises holistically and finds patterns in that which appears to be unconnected.

Ground: The page, surface or area in which the design will be placed.

Law of closure: The mind creates a solid object on the page from suggestions of contours and shapes.

⊙ Filling in the gaps The smaller circles, although separated by white space, suggest a closed circle due to the law of closure, which dominates our perception even though visual information is missing.

⌃ Emergence The image of the dog sniffing on the ground becomes visible in a single moment, during which disparate pieces of visual information suddenly cohere.

⊙ ASSIGNMENT: FIGURE VERSUS GROUND

Rearrange shapes cut out of paper to try and find the point at which the figure disappears into the ground.

1 Cut out a series of shapes from black paper – squares, rectangles, circles and random shapes – in a variety of sizes, from small to large.

2 Working with a square piece of white paper, place shapes of different sizes into the white space, one at a time, moving them around.

3 Try to find the point at which it becomes unclear which is the figure, and which is the ground. Does it depend on which shape dominates the space: black or white? Or is it about the position of the shape within the space? Think about how important figure–ground relationships are in composition and design.

⊙ Question

How many examples of design can you find that use the principles of figure–ground, law of closure or emergence?

⌃ Subtle symmetry
This poster design
by Almar Mavignier
uses symmetrical
design principles in
a subtle form.

❯ Zang Tumb Tumb,
by F. T. Marinetti in
1919, uses creative
asymmetrical typography
to express the sounds
of battle. In typography,
'Onomatopoeia' refers to
the use of type to express
sounds in a literal way.

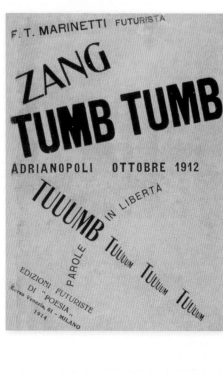

PART 1	PRINCIPLES
UNIT 2	FUNDAMENTALS OF COMPOSITION
MODULE 3	**Symmetry/asymmetry**

Symmetry in design refers to a spatial relationship between elements, and specifically to a situation where the elements in a layout are centred, having equal space to the left and right, or above and below them.

Frequently, title pages of books, before the 20th century, use centred text in their design, where each line of type is centred in relation to the others. In symmetry, if you were to fold a sheet of paper with text or image(s) on it, in half, you would see that the left-hand side of the design 'mirrors' the right. However, the second meaning of symmetry is more general, and refers to a sense of harmony, or balance, which in turn is seen to reflect beauty. Symmetry carries associations of tradition, order and rationality.

Designing without symmetry

In asymmetrical design (which means without symmetry), elements are not centred, but utilise the whole format, creating dynamic compositions that play with scale, contrast, space and tension between elements. Negative space is less passive in asymmetrical design, and becomes fully 'activated', or evident as a part of the design. Asymmetry is generally associated with fewer rules and limits, and more expressive possibilities. However, each kind of composition has its place, and the important thing is to learn how to identify when it is appropriate to use one over the other. While asymmetrical design may seem less rigid, it is crucial to spend time learning how asymmetry activates elements in a given space, and to carefully control the effects you want to achieve, rather than randomly placing elements in a design.

Choosing symmetry or asymmetry

Similar questions arise in any design you undertake. How should the picture surface be divided up? In what way should the subject matter occupy the surface space? The elements chosen do not simply have to sit in a central position on the paper but can appear to protrude out of or enter in from the edges. As explained above, a symmetrical composition makes for a calmer, more peaceful work, while something more dynamic can be achieved if the elements are arranged asymmetrically. Symmetry tends towards balance and lack of movement, while asymmetry injects movement and spatial tension into a design.

In the examples shown, which use simple black squares, the relationship between the black square and the space conveys different meanings, even though all that changes is the placement of the same element.

> [The] liveliness of asymmetry is an expression of our own movement and that of modern life *Jan Tschichold*

❯ Yin/yang The yin/yang symbol is a perfectly balanced, symmetrical design.

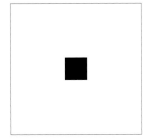

❂ Questions

• When would a symmetrical design be appropriate, as opposed to an asymmetrical one?

• What kinds of design work do you see that use these different compositional modes, and can you identify why?

❂ ASSIGNMENT: (A)SYMMETRY EXPERIMENT

1 With a sharp pencil, draw a large square frame in the centre of a piece of paper. (Repeat to make about 20 sheets.)

2 Cut out double the number of black squares (these need to be accurately cut so that they are perfect squares) in varying sizes to experiment with.

3 Place one or two squares within the frame, to achieve the following visual effects (some of the results are shown below):

• Entering left
• Movement to the right
• Movement to the left
• Movement downwards
• Movement upwards
• Balance
• Tension
• Symmetry/asymmetry

4 Produce at least two different versions of each effect, recording your results each time. Explain in one or two sentences what you wanted to achieve (as shown below).

GLOSSARY

Asymmetry: A composition where elements are juxtaposed and do not mirror the other forms on the page.

Symmetry: A composition where elements are balanced or mirrored on a page.

Testing the theory

In these examples, various effects are achieved by simple variation of the position of the square within a stable frame.

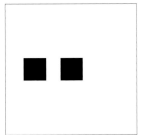

1 Balance
The centred square is stable or static, as the space around the square is equal on all sides.

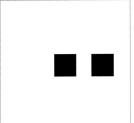

2 Movement to the left
When a second square is introduced, visual forces develop. There is a sense that the squares are moving left.

3 Movement to the right
Changing the position of the two squares suggests movement to the right.

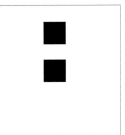

4 Upward movement
The position of the two squares hints at movement upward.

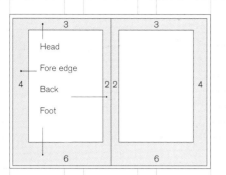

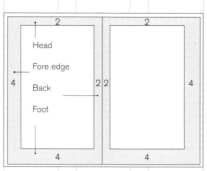

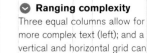

Type area In the diagram to the far left, the head and back margins are half the amount; left, a deeper text area results in a smaller foot but is still proportionately bigger than the head.

Ranging complexity Three equal columns allow for more complex text (left); and a vertical and horizontal grid can be broken into 16 units (right).

PART 1	PRINCIPLES
UNIT 2	FUNDAMENTALS OF COMPOSITION
MODULE 4	**Basic principles of layout**

The term 'layout' refers to the organisation of disparate material that makes up the content of a design. Your aim is both to present information in a logical, coherent way, and to make the important elements stand out. Use of a grid and consistently styled elements also helps the reader to absorb information in a visually pleasing way, which enhances the communication of the content.

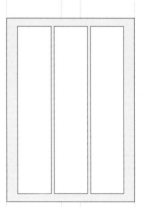

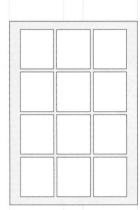

There are three basic stages in producing layouts. First, the designer receives a brief from the client, establishing what material should be included. This usually involves a combination of text (eg main text, display copy [headings], boxes or sidebars, captions) and images (eg photographs, illustrations, maps, diagrams). The brief should also indicate the desired look or 'feel' of the work, which in turn will depend on the target audience. Should the layout look authoritative? Should it be densely packed with information? Or does the client prefer a lean and structured design, with lots of white space?

Practical factors

You will need to consider the format and budget. If there are many pictures and extensive copy for a small space, this will affect the look of the layout. Agreement should be reached on hierarchies (emphasis) within the copy; an editor may already have labelled their headings 'A', 'B', 'C', and so on, to indicate their relative importance. Such elements can be indicated typographically for emphasis, through differences in type size, weight, form and choice of colour.

Underlying grid This design is strongly linked to the structure of the grid, but uses heavily cropped images and changes of scale to emphasise certain elements.

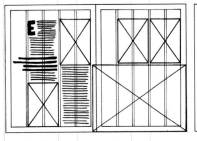 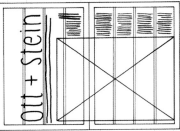 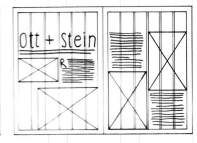

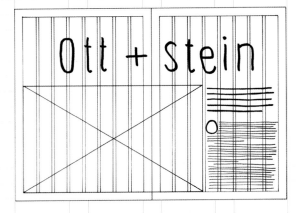

Grids

The third stage involves organisation. In print-based work, this means developing a grid, in which various elements can be placed within a ready-made structure that underpins the entire design. The grid enables the layout of columns, margins and area for text and images; it is a tool for structure and order in documents. A well-designed grid allows for a degree of flexibility of layout on individual pages, while providing an underlying system that gives visual coherence across a series of pages. This is obviously crucial in any kind of editorial work, including books and magazines, but also applies to website 'pages', where some elements stay the same and others change.

Margins, grids and structure

For books and other publications, you should first construct a double-page spread that can then be

Flexibility Many variations of the layout can be explored as thumbnail sketches, before committing. Here, you can see the kind of flexibility a simple grid provides, giving indications of structure without limiting creativity.

The top of the x-height of text blocks. No text (except for running heads/page numbers) would normally appear above this line

Master grid Margins, columns and non-changing typographic elements such as page numbers and running heads can all be placed on the master grid, which provides the design template. The grids have been printed over this module to show how they structure the design.

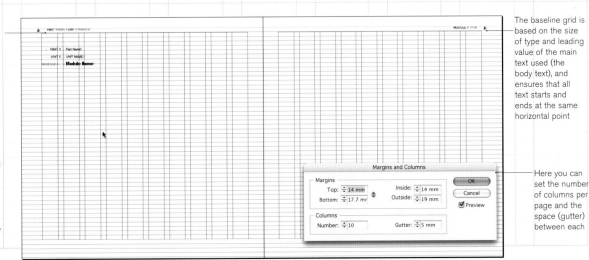

The baseline grid is based on the size of type and leading value of the main text used (the body text), and ensures that all text starts and ends at the same horizontal point

Here you can set the number of columns per page and the space (gutter) between each

applied to the entire publication. This is important, since you need to see how the verso (left-hand page) relates to the recto (right-hand page) and judge how well they balance. Established practice suggests that the back (inner margin) should be half the fore edge (outside margin), and the foot (bottom margin) greater than the head (top margin). These rules should ensure a balance, with the type area sitting comfortably in the format. Remember that the eye will need to move from one page to another, so the gap, or gutter (the two back edges combined), should not be too large.

When establishing page margins, bear the type of material in mind. For example, paperbacks tend to have tight margins to keep page numbers (and therefore costs) down, whereas illustrated books have more generous margins. Economic considerations play a part: sales brochures and promotional items tend to have bigger budgets, so more white space is possible.

The grid shows the layout of columns, margins and areas for main text, captions and images; it also shows the position of repeating heads (running heads) and page numbers. These elements normally stay the same over a series of pages.

After drawing out your double-page spread you can prepare some layout 'roughs': these may be small thumbnails or half-sized visuals in which first ideas are sketched out. This preliminary thinking time is important in the overall layout process: it's where you make important decisions about the composition of pages and organisation of material. Preliminary sketches can then be transferred to the computer and several variants quickly produced, based on the main grid. The time it takes to sketch ideas is infinitely faster than trying to create designs directly on-screen. The computer is simply a tool; it cannot think for you. With initial sketches the imaginative designer can fully explore ideas and options, before moving to the production phase.

Using a grid

The grid divides the available type area into proportioned units, providing an overall visual structure, and helping to unite all elements. The most basic grid structure – used primarily for text-based material, such as reports or novels – is that of a single measure. The measure should relate to legibility. With complex layouts, in which text, images, diagrams and captions must be integrated, a more sophisticated horizontal and vertical grid is needed; those comprising between three and six columns enable you to use all kinds of elements. The more units used, the more flexibility you have to accommodate both smaller pieces of copy, such as captions; longer measures, such as section openers; and displayed material. Do not simply follow your computer's default settings for columns, but decide your own, which ought to be in whole numbers for every unit.

Ideally, a grid should have vertical controls, both for structure down the page and for order to layout. Give headings, subheadings, captions and page numbers set positions for continuity. Finally, be flexible. After two or three spreads the grid may seem too rigid, so adjust it. Grids should not be restrictive, but provide structure, while giving rich compositional variations to spreads.

❯ **Creating subtle differences** Structure, authority, tradition and contemporary style are some of the variations that can be achieved when using a flexible grid in a thoughtful way. The three examples shown here use various means such as serif and sans-serif type, ranged left and justified text, large and small images and background tints to achieve different tones of voice.

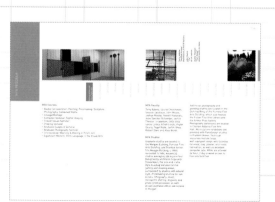

❮ **Think it through** This design shows a strong grid, which has been well utilised. It has contrast, rhythm and consistency, and the body text is set on the same baseline grid, while smaller elements of vertically set text provide an interesting counterpoint to other pieces of text.

Urban life
the fumes, **the future, the facts**

Left: Duis autem vel eum iriure dolor in hendrerit in vulputate velit esse molestie consequat, vel illum dolore

Korem ipsum dolor sit amet, consectetuer adipiscing elit, sed diam nonummy nibh euismod tincidunt ut laoreet dolore magna aliquam erat volutpat. Ut wisi enim ad minim veniam, quis nostrud exerci tation ullamcorper suscipit lobortis nisl ut aliquip ex ea commodo consequat.

Duis autem vel eum iriure dolor in hendrerit in vulputate velit esse molestie consequat, vel illum dolore eu feugiat nulla facilisis at vero eros et accumsan et iusto odio dignissim qui blandit praesent luptatum zzril delenit augue duis dolore te feugait nulla facilisi. Lorem ipsum dolor sit amet, consectetuer adipiscing elit, sed diam nonummy nibh euismod tincidunt ut laoreet dolore magna aliquam erat volutpat.

Ut wisi enim ad minim veniam, quis nostrud exercitation ullamcorper suscipit lobortis nisl ut aliquip ex ea commodo consequat. Duis autem vel eum iriure dolor in hendrerit in vulputate velit esse molestie consequat, vel illum dolore eu feugiat nulla facilisi at vero

erat annum et iusto odio dignissim qui blandit praesent luptatum zzril delenit augue duis dolore te feugait nulla facilisi.

Nam liber tempore cum soluta nobis eleifend option congue nihil imperdiet doming id quod mazim placerat facer possim assum. Lorem ipsum dolor sit amet, consectetuer adipiscing elit, sed diam nonummy nibh euismod tincidunt ut laoreet dolore magna aliquam erat volutpat. Ut wisi enim ad minim veniam, quis nostrud exerci tation ullamcorper suscipit lobortis nisl ut aliquip ex ea commodo consequat.

Duis autem vel eum iriure dolor in hendrerit in vulputate velit esse molestie consequat, vel illum dolore eu feugiat nulla facilisis.

urban life
the fumes, the future, the facts

Korem ipsum dolor sit amet, consectetuer adipiscing elit, sed diam nonummy nibh euismod tincidunt ut laoreet dolore magna aliquam erat volutpat. Ut wisi enim ad minim veniam, quis nostrud exerci tation ullamcorper suscipit lobortis nisl ut aliquip ex ea commodo consequat.

Right: Duis autem vel eum iriure dolor in hendrerit in vulputate velit esse molestie consequat, vel illum dolore

Duis autem vel eum iriure dolor in hendrerit in vulputate velit esse molestie consequat, vel illum dolore eu feugiat nulla facilisis at vero eros et accumsan et iusto odio dignissim qui blandit praesent luptatum zzril delenit augue duis dolore te feugait nulla facilisi. Lorem ipsum dolor sit amet, consectetuer adipiscing elit, sed diam nonummy nibh euismod tincidunt ut laoreet dolore magna aliquam erat volutpat.

Ut wisi enim ad minim veniam, quis nostrud exerci tation ullamcorper suscipit lobortis nisl ut aliquip ex ea commodo consequat. Duis autem vel eum iriure dolor in hendrerit in vulputate velit esse molestie consequat, vel illum dolore eu feugiat nulla facilisis at vero eros et accumsan et iusto odio dignissim qui blandit praesent luptatum zzril delenit augue duis dolore te feugait nulla

aliquip ex ea commodo consequat. Duis autem vel eum iriure dolor in hendrerit in vulputate velit esse molestie consequat, vel illum dolore eu feugiat nulla facilisis. Nam liber tempor cum soluta nobis eleifend option congue nihil imperdiet doming id quod mazim placerat facer possim assum. Lorem ipsum dolor sit amet, consectetuer adipiscing elit, sed diam nonummy nibh euismod tincidunt ut laoreet dolore magna aliquam erat volutpat. Ut wisi enim ad minim veniam, quis nostrud exerci tation ullamcorper suscipit lobortis nisl ut aliquip ex ea commodo consequat.

facilisi.

Nam liber tempor cum soluta nobis eleifend option congue nihil imperdiet doming id quod mazim placerat facer possim assum. Lorem ipsum dolor sit amet, consectetuer adipiscing elit, sed diam nonummy nibh euismod tincidunt ut laoreet dolore magna aliquam erat volutpat. Ut wisi enim ad minim veniam, quis nostrud exerci tation ullamcorper suscipit lobortis nisl ut

Above: Duis autem vel eum iriure dolor in hendrerit in vulputate velit esse molestie consequat, vel illum dolore

Urban life the fumes, **the future, the facts**

Kremipsumdolorsitamet, consectetuer adipiscingelit, seddiamnonummybibh euismod tincidunt at laoreet dolore magna aliquamerat volutpat. Ut wisienimadminim veniam, quis nostrud exerci tation ullamcorpersuscipitlobortisnislutaliquipex ea commodo consequat.

Duis autem vel eum iriure dolor in hendrerit in vulputate velit esse molestie consequat, vel illum dolore eu feugiat nulla facilisisat vero eros et accumsan et iusto odio dignissimquiblanditpraesentluptatumzzril delenit augue duis dolore te feugait nulla facilisi. Lorem ipsum dolor sit amet, consectetuer adipiscing elit, sed diam nonummynibh euismod tincidunt ut laoreet dolore magna aliquam erat volutpat.

Ut wisi enim ad minim veniam, quis nostrud exerci tation ullamcorper suscipit lobortis nisl ut aliquip.

Duis autem vel eum iriure dolor in hendrerit in vulputate velit esse molestie consequat, vel illum dolore eu feugiat nulla facilisis.

Duis autem vel eum iriure dolor in hendrerit in vulputate velit esse molestie consequat, vel illum dolore eu feugiat nulla facilisis at vero eros et accumsan et iusto odio dignissim qui blandit praesent luptatum zzril delenit augue duis dolore te feugait nulla facilisi.

Nam liber tempor cum soluta nobis eleifend option congue nihil imperdiet doming id quod ipsum dolor sit amet, consectetuer adipiscing elit, sed diam nonummy nibh euismod tincidunt ut laoreet dolore magna aliquam erat volutpat.

Duis autem vel eum iriure dolor in hendrerit in vulputate velit esse molestie consequat, vel illum dolore eu feugiat nulla facilisis.

Duisautemveleumiriuredolorinhendrerit in vulputate velit esse molestie consequat, vel illum dolore eu feugiat nulla facilisis at vero eros et accumsan et iusto odio dignissimquiblanditpraesentluptatumzzril delenit augue duis dolore te feugait nulla facilisi. Lorem ipsum dolor sit amet, consectetuer adipiscing elit, sed diam nonummynibh euismod tincidunt ut laoreet doloremagnaaliquamerateratvolutpat.

Ut wsi enim ad minim veniam, quis nostrud exerci tation ullamcorper suscipit lobortis nisl ut aliquip.

Ipsum dolor sit amet, consectetuer adipiscing elit, sed diam nonummy nibh euismodtincidunt utlaoreetdolore magna aliquameratvolutpat.Utwisienimadminim veniam, quis nostrud exerci tation ullamcorper suscipit lobortis nisl blandit praesentluptatumzzrildelenitaugueduis.

Ipsum dolor sit amet, consectetuer adipiscing elit, sed diam nonummy nibh euismodtincidunt utlaoreetdolore magna aliquameratvolutpat.Utwisienimadminim veniam, quis nostrud exerci tation ullamcorper suscipit lobortis nisl ut aliquip.

Ut wisi enim ad minim veniam, quis nostrud exerci tation ullamcorper suscipit lobortis nisl ut aliquip.

CHECKLIST FOR BEGINNING A LAYOUT

- Who is the target audience for the design?
- What different kinds of text will be included?
- Will there be photographs, illustrations, diagrams or a combination of all three?
- How many colours can be used (the budget will affect this in print-based work)?
- What is the format and final size of the job (also related to budget)?
- What parts of the text need emphasising?
- Is the client looking for a particular style?

⊙ ASSIGNMENT:
UNDERSTANDING GRIDS

Take a magazine, newspaper or book that includes images and text. Lay tracing paper over the top of three spreads (both left-hand and right-hand pages). Using a pencil, and measuring carefully, trace the grid underlying the page layouts, removing specific text elements or images; just draw the grid lines. Note column widths, and margin sizes at the top, bottom and to the left and right of the main body of text. Is your document based on a two-column, three-column or other type of grid? Which elements stay the same on each page, and which others change?

FURTHER READING

Jost Hochuli and Robin Kinross, *Designing Books: Practice and Theory*

Allen Hurlburt, *The Grid*

Josef Müller-Brockmann, *Grid Systems in Graphic Design*

⊕ **SEE ALSO:** AUDIENCES, MARKETS AND CONCEPTS P26

STYLES OF LAYOUT P46

PACE AND CONTRAST P48

SIZE AND FORMAT P52

TYPOGRAPHIC EMPHASIS AND HIERARCHY P84

I'm rather fond of... I'm not so fond of...

Asymmetrical Serif and sans-serif text are incorporated sympathetically into this design, which is asymmetrical in its layout.

Symmetrical This typography is organised around the axis of a central vertical gutter, which runs between the left and right parts of the text.

Influences Strong diagonals, highly contrasted colours and use of rules are direct descendents of Russian and German experimental design from the early part of the 20th century.

MODULE 5 | **Styles of layout**

Layouts can be divided into two basic styles: symmetrical and asymmetrical. In broad terms, symmetrical style has a traditional approach in which design is structured around a central axis. This type of layout has its origins in early printed books, which, in turn, borrowed their layout from handwritten manuscripts of the medieval era. Asymmetrical style is non-centred, dynamic and associated with 20th-century modernism and contemporary design.

Symmetrical layouts are most commonly seen on title pages of books, where each line of type is centred on the others. Part of the tradition is the use of serif typefaces, often set in letter-spaced capitals, with, perhaps, the addition of an ornament or printer's flower. It is considered traditional because, until the 1920s, most publications were designed this way. Achieving a balanced-looking composition within symmetrical design is not easy. Type size must be carefully judged, and spacing between each line considered, since certain information belongs in the same typographic 'unit', and should be grouped accordingly; fine-tuning horizontal line-spaces is crucial. These judgments must be made while maintaining balance and compositional quality. For superb examples of symmetrical typography, see the work of Aldus Manutius, the Dolphin Press and the Venetian printers from the late 15th century.

The asymmetrical revolution

Asymmetrical layouts can be traced back to the 1920s and 1930s, and in particular to the German school, the Bauhaus. Artists such as Kurt Schwitters and Theo van Doesburg experimented with layouts based on an off-centred axis, which they saw as creating more tension and dynamism. In this style, type is primarily ranged left; ranged-right setting is kept to a few lines, as reading from left to right is ingrained in the West, so ranged right can be tiring to read. Other predominant designers are Armin Hofmann, Wim Crouwel and Josef Müller-Brockmann.

The modern movement also rejected ornament, and sans-serif typefaces dominated because of their clean lines and modernity. The work of the Bauhaus and their stylistic descendents, such as the Swiss typographers of the 1950s and 1960s, is usually set in sans-serif faces, and often completely lowercase. Rules, in a number of weights, are another distinctive feature, often in two colours, such as red and black.

Another interesting typographer, whose work over a long career shows both styles well, is Jan Tschichold. Early on he was heavily influenced by the modernist philosophy of the Bauhaus, and is considered a pioneer of the asymmetric revolution. However, he later changed direction, rejecting the hard-line approach advocated in his book *Asymmetric Typography*. Tschichold later returned to the frequent use of centred, serif typography, but continued working in both styles.

Integrating styles

Today's designers often integrate the two styles; the division is somewhat arbitrary, and contemporary typographers such as April Greiman and Philippe Apeloig use both in their search for visual solutions. You need to understand both styles and their historical precedents and contexts so that your judgments are based on sound knowledge rather than guesswork. The best advice is to follow the philosophy of Jan Tschichold and use both styles, but understand that mixing them needs to be undertaken with caution. Apart from anything else, learning as much as you can about the different ways of designing, and keeping your options open, will give you more flexibility in reaching appropriate solutions.

⊕ SEE ALSO: BASIC PRINCIPLES OF LAYOUT P42 SIZE AND FORMAT P52 SYMMETRY/ASYMMETRY P40

❯ Classically centred
The *Hypnerotomachia Poliphili*, printed by Aldus Manutius's Dolphin Press, Venice, in 1499, is an example of the highest art of Renaissance printing. Its symmetrical typography harmonises with the wood-engraved illustrations.

⊙ ASSIGNMENT: BOOK DESIGN

Choose a book that you have read.
1 Set the text for the title, author, publisher, etc, and design a title page in both symmetrical and asymmetrical formats. Use serif type for the symmetrical versions and sans-serif for the asymmetrical designs. Do at least six versions of each, working through them in detail, and paying attention to the type style, type size, where type lines should be broken and so on.
2 Carefully work with the spacing in each style, to establish correct grouping for the information. For example, should the author's name be closer to the title of the book than to the publisher? Make notes of what you find the most successful outcomes in each style.
3 Finally, mix both symmetry and asymmetry in one design.

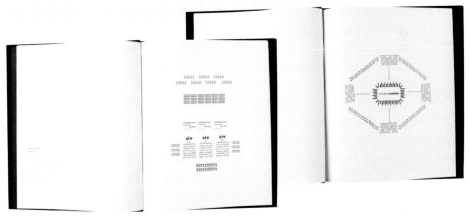

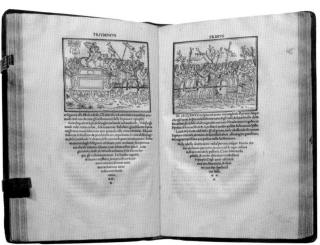

⌃ Combining symmetry and asymmetry In this unusual design, there are elements of both centred and ranged left text in use, and the result is striking and original.

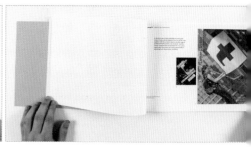

⌄ Linking through movement Images, text and fields of colour are used to create a strong sense of horizontal movement throughout a series of spreads.

PART 1	PRINCIPLES
UNIT 2	FUNDAMENTALS OF COMPOSITION
MODULE 6	**Pace and contrast**

Pace and contrast are vital qualities for maintaining a reader's interest in a design: they provide variety. This is true particularly in magazines and image-heavy books, where it is critical to be able to direct the eye to different pieces of information. Think in terms of choreographing a stage show, where the audience should be given different experiences. In a middle-distance athletics race, runners alternate between fast and slow, and end with a sprint finish. This is a useful metaphor for pace in design.

⌄ ⌐ Contrasting layouts
Different rhythms and pace are shown here: the design to the right is quiet and typographically centred; the one below references visually active forms of design such as Dada and 'zines'.

In continuous text, the reader takes more time to cover information, whereas in a highly integrated design – with panels, pictures, captions, quotes and so on – there is much more variety: an article may be skim-read; some pages will be scanned for pictures; in another section, the reader might be seeking a specific piece of information. The pace will be dictated by the content and space available. Contrast is closely linked to pace: when you want to inject pace into a design you can create visual emphasis in the form of large type and imagery, or unusual cropping. Alternatively, you can create a quiet interval by having text-only spreads or employing white space liberally.

Thumbnails

In order to achieve a good pace, with contrast and visual rhythm over a succession of pages, an overall plan is needed. Too much visual complexity can be counterproductive, but a succession of similar-looking spreads will become boring, and risk losing the reader's attention.

An invaluable technique is to construct a flat plan, showing the total number of pages in the publication (see page 30). The flat plan can be drawn small (thumbnail size) in double-page spreads. It should contain page numbers, titles and content. A quick survey of this plan gives you a broad overview of how your material will unfold.

First, you should meet the editor/client, with a list of questions on all-important content. The editor/client will know what information they are trying to impart, and what needs emphasis; your role as designer is to interpret that information, and make decisions on how to lay out the text and imagery in a dynamic and interesting way. Text with a complicated argument may need a slower pace with clean, clear typography, allowing the reader to focus on the content. In contrast, strategic messages may require a bold, lively image for the point to get across effectively.

Creating momentum and rhythm

The beginning of an article or section can create momentum and rhythm in the form of large headings, bold type, colour changes, etc. Many variations are possible in laying out images and text. You can use pictures as a frieze – a narrow sequence of images running along the top of spreads. You can have one large picture and five smaller ones. You can break out of the grid at strategic points. Depending on picture content, you can create vertical movement with narrow vertical images. Conversely, with landscape pictures, you can create a strong sense of horizontal movement. Contrast can be achieved with vertical and horizontal movement on the same spread or on consecutive spreads.

You can create pace by juxtaposing black-and-white images with colour, or black-and-white with duotones. Variation between narrow and wide text measures will certainly add pace to your pages; however, you need to decide this at grid-design stage. Using strong background colours, or reversed-out type at specific points, can also create a sense of movement, change of speed and vary the rhythm. Indeed, any kind of formal variation will result in a change of pace.

Magazines versus books

In magazine design, pace and contrast is fundamental. There is probably more variety in magazines than in any other category of design. They range from highbrow, political, economic or philosophical journals, to sporting, arts, satirical and leisure titles. They require different kinds of pace depending on content and readership. Magazine readers differ from book readers because the way they view the product is unpredictable. Some will be led by the cover straplines to the contents page, where they will select their

◀ Contrasting layouts

Pace and contrast are well developed in this catalogue of photographs by Fin Costello through the use of large-scale images next to smaller ones; and intelligent use of space, along with strong black-and-white contrast in the images. Design elements such as fine red keylines around the smaller images and ranged-left typography give consistency, while the combination of different scales of images and text allows for variation and visual interest to emerge.

⊕ **SEE ALSO:** BASIC PRINCIPLES OF LAYOUT P42

COLOUR LEGIBILITY, CONTRAST AND HARMONY P96

FURTHER READING

Herbert Matter, *Alberto Giacometti*. For a beautiful example of pace and contrast.

Marshall McLuhan, *The Medium is the Message*. Quentin Fiore has made design decisions with the content firmly in mind.

❯ **Online rules** When designing for websites, the same principles of pace and contrast that affect print apply. However, the issues of time, screen navigation and the limits and possibilities of digital typography and moving imagery also need to be addressed. For example, readers' attention spans are shorter in a digital environment, so the designer needs to be aware of this, and design accordingly.

❯❯ **Literary choreography** Book design requires the coordination of various elements of text and image across a series of pages, engaging the reader. This book uses liberal white space, coloured paper, unusual materials and strong typography to keep the readers' attention, and create a sense of drama and anticipation.

articles in an ordered way; others will dip in and out of any part of the magazine; while others will always read certain sections in a peculiarly personal order. This is why some kind of visual interest has to be created on almost every page.

In illustrated books, change of pace is also required. Generally, readers behave in a relatively logical way, moving through the publication from start to finish. They too will dive in but not to the same extent as magazine readers. Economic factors will also play a part. If plenty of pages are available, then you can introduce section openers, and use lots of white space to create drama with headings and so on. As a general guide, try to create a style that has a strong visual identity. If the spreads are too diverse, this can have a hazardous effect on the book, creating confusion. Try not to place all the text in one place together: readers often find this off-putting after viewing lots of images. If the text has to be positioned in one area, then at least introduce subheads and, perhaps, quotations to give the reader visual relief.

A master of magazine layout is American designer Alexey Brodovich, who worked primarily in the 1940s and 1950s. Bradbury Thompson also understood the importance of pace and contrast (see Westvaco Inspirations).

The digital revolution

Electronic magazines require different strategies; type and images interact much more immediately on-screen. Imagery is much easier to manipulate and adapt to a variety of purposes. Some of the principles in print-based work may not apply directly to screen-based designs: one obvious difference is that, instead of turning pages, viewers scroll up and down a screen, which poses a separate set of challenges. Again, instead of using weight, style or position for emphasis, type can move or a headline can be flashed on-screen. Sound and graphics will increasingly integrate more effectively.

In short, a whole new aesthetic is developing hand in hand with digital technology. Ultimately, though, basic issues of pace and contrast for print still apply, in part, for screen. How do you navigate the viewer through the maze of available information? Learning the basics of layout from the model of print design is a stepping-stone to the development of new ways of working in digital environments.

○ ASSIGNMENT: COMPARING DIGITAL AND PRINT MEDIA

Compare the design of an online magazine, blog or website, in terms of pace and contrast, with a printed magazine, book or journal. What differences can you see between the kinds of design strategies used in the two formats? Bonus points for comparing a publication that has both online and printed versions.

◉ **Controlling pace and contrast** The use of a mixture of black-and-white, colour and sepia photographs is an effective strategy to inject pace and variety. The subdued typography has been carefully positioned in relation to the imagery, and white space has been used as a means of emphasising the broken pencil on the last page. This design is effective and dynamic.

PART 1	PRINCIPLES
UNIT 2	FUNDAMENTALS OF COMPOSITION
MODULE 7	**Size and format**

Size and format are important considerations in any printed design. They are affected by budget, practical restraints such as postage costs and by the needs of the job. Part of how a design 'works' is in the experience of holding it in your hands; it involves not only physical size, but also weight and texture of the paper, choice of binding, etc.

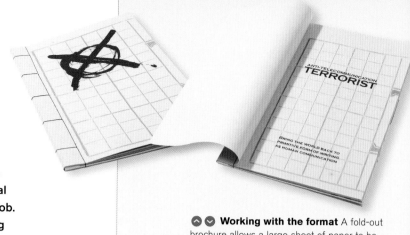

Working with the format A fold-out brochure allows a large sheet of paper to be used cost-effectively. This design uses only two colours, but works imaginatively within the available format, moving from landscape (when closed) to portrait (when open).

In terms of format, the designer is often limited by external factors. Items such as reports, stationery and official forms must be a standard size; other factors, however, may also have to be considered. Cost issues loom large: can the size selected for printing be cut economically from a bigger sheet of paper, or will there be unnecessary (expensive) waste? Carefully evaluate the sheet size with the number of copies required. Will the finished work have to be posted out? If so, a larger format will prove more expensive to send by post. Can your job be folded economically in relation to the grain of paper?

Unusual formats This non-traditional artist's book uses folded sheets to create a scroll-like form.

Content determines format

In book publishing, format should be determined by purpose or nature. Text-only books pose fewer problems than illustrated books. For continuous reading, a good type measure with adequate margins normally determines format (portrait or landscape), and in paperbacks, which need to be both cheap and portable, size is typically small. In illustrated books, images need

Tactility Alternative binding can enhance the experience of reading a book, and reinforce the content in subtle ways.

to be of a reasonable size, so a larger format is required, but the danger is that the book may become unwieldy. Illustrations do not necessarily lose information value if they are smaller than first anticipated, and there are benefits in making a product easier for the reader to handle. The biggest sizes are generally reserved for fine-art books and museum catalogues, in which good-quality illustrations are central to the book's success.

Where possible, content should determine format. Illustrated books on trains, rivers and panoramic views would, because of the shape of their subjects, lend themselves to a landscape (sideways) format; whereas those on skyscrapers, totem poles and giraffes would be better suited to a portrait shape. Multilingual publications pose their own set of problems. It is probably best to try to accommodate two or three languages side by side to achieve a consistent flow of text and, if illustrated, to ensure that text references are on the same page as pictures. A landscape format is probably the best answer.

Although international standardisation in paper sizes helps keep prices down, the same old formats can become a bit boring. There are several solutions. By folding sheets differently, you can effect simple changes: fold on the short side for an elegant long format. Or trim standard sizes for unfamiliar shapes at no extra cost.

Folds and binding

With leaflets and brochures, folds can play a big part in enticing the reader into the subject matter. The aesthetically pleasing square format is simply achieved by folding the sheet in a different way. Organising copy to follow folds – whether rolling folds or concertina folds – creates a sense of fun, and is an excellent way to entice the reader into the publication.

Simple binding ideas also enhance the appeal, such as trimming each spread a little shorter than the preceding one, giving an area at the end of the page to use as an information tag. An untrimmed fore edge makes for an attractively handcrafted feel, as does coloured thread for the stitching. Such ideas are easy to implement; they don't necessarily cost a lot, and can make your designs different and memorable. (See top left for an example of a stitched binding.)

◀ Inherent challenges Vertical formats present their own problems, especially where text needs to be read from a distance, as in these street banners.

◀ Making the most of it This concertina-fold brochure maximises the impact of colour, imagery and text, across a series of eight panels.

● ASSIGNMENT: CREATIVITY WITH PAPER

Take a single sheet of paper of any size, and see how many different folds, formats and shapes you can make out of it. Remember that the trick is not to waste paper, but to use the paper as creatively and economically as you can.

GLOSSARY

Concertina folds: Folds in alternate directions.

French folds: Sheets of paper are folded in half, so that they are double thickness. The two folds are at right angles to each other, and then bound on the edge.

Gatefold: A way of folding paper so that the outer quarters of a page are folded to meet in the centre. The result works like symmetrical doors that open onto an inner page.

Paper grain: The direction of wood fibres that make up a piece of paper.

Perfect bind: Method similar to paperback binding, where loose sheets are encased in a heavier paper cover, then glued to the book spine. Edges are trimmed to be flush with each other.

Rollover folds: A way of folding a page so that successive folds turn in on themselves and the page is folded into a roll.

Saddle stitching: Binding method where sheets of paper are folded in the centre, stitched together along the fold, then glued into the cover spine.

● SEE ALSO: BASIC PRINCIPLES OF LAYOUT P42

STYLES OF LAYOUT P46

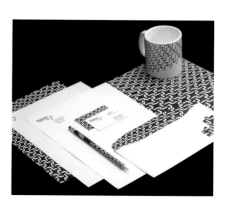

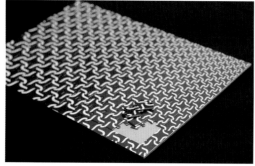

 **Secret of success** From the logo design, to stationery, cups and website, this identity scheme has been carefully implemented. The essence of a good design scheme is flexibility, along with visual consistency across different elements, over time and in different contexts.

PART 1	PRINCIPLES
UNIT 2	FUNDAMENTALS OF COMPOSITION
MODULE 8	**Coordination and identity**

In the commercial world, few things are designed to work as stand-alone pieces. Look at a successful corporate identity: the logo, advertising campaigns, direct mail pieces and annual report all have common design elements, binding them together and identifying them as part of the same set. Or look at any newspaper: the information changes every day, yet the paper looks consistent, day after day; at a glance we can easily and immediately identify which paper is which on the shelf.

So how is this identity achieved? The answer is a coordinated design and effective design strategy that allows for changes, but is consistent throughout. With newspapers, this is achieved by strict rules and principles. For example, major headlines will be set in one font and ranged left; secondary headlines in another font and centred; body text in yet another font with fixed point size, leading and justification; feature articles in a bolder font with looser leading and alternate justification. These rules are never broken, but they should be comprehensive enough to allow for any situation while maintaining a consistent 'look'.

Most authors write more than one book, and publishers almost always use coordinated designs for their book

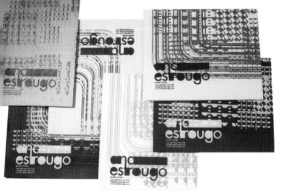

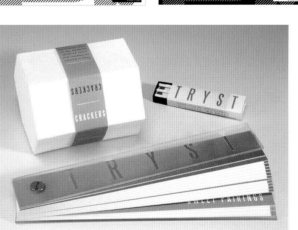

Unity Detailed, large-scale black-and-white photography is the unifying aspect of this series of posters. Typography is consistently applied to establish a unified look.

Central themes Colour, abstract imagery, paper stock and typographic treatment are the key elements of this identity scheme.

Schematic Consistent typography, treatment of images, colour and layout have been applied throughout this design scheme.

Minimalist The dominant unifying aspect of this identity scheme is the typography and minimal use of colour.

covers. If a publisher is repackaging the back catalogue of a bestselling author, they use a coordinated strategy for the covers that allows for changes of colour, image and title, but also enables book buyers to identify the titles as part of a set. Perhaps the unchanging element is the type, set in the same face, at the same size, and in the same position throughout. Or it could be the style of the photographs used (black and white, full colour, abstract) or the illustration (pen and ink, scraperboard, collage). A good designer ties together all elements, creating a template that not only makes each jacket striking in its own right, but also ensures easy identification with its counterparts.

❯ Unity through diversity
The use of photomontage techniques, along with varying styles of typography and strong colours, unifies this series of posters.

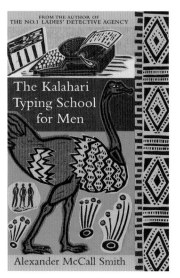

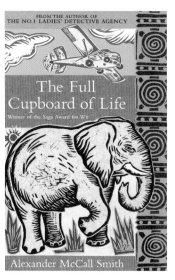

❮ Out of Africa These book covers use vibrant colours and Africa-inspired illustrations to create a consistent look for the series, but also to portray the themes of the books.

Creating identifying characteristics

A book jacket is, in effect, a piece of packaging that advertises both product and publisher; it should be approached in the same way as an advertising campaign. Each jacket must compete with all the others on display, leaping out from the shelf before informing potential buyers as to what the book might be about, and why they should buy it. However, in many bookshops limited space dictates that only the spines will be visible, so how these appear as a 'patch' will be crucial. For example, a series of covers with spines in bold black text on acid colours will create an impressive patch when a dozen or so are stacked along a shelf.

The creation of these identifying characteristics motivates all manufacturers and organisations competing for attention in the marketplace, whether the product is books, chocolate, an art gallery or an online music service. Next time you go out shopping, or attend a cultural event, open your eyes to this principle and you will notice that many of the products that have the most eye-catching and coordinated identity schemes are those of the most successful manufacturers and organisations. This is no coincidence, and the designer that can successfully coordinate a brand or company will always find their services in demand.

Know the content

A concept for a book jacket design will be influenced by a number of factors: whether the book is fiction or non-fiction; if it is the author's first book or

Adding value Products need to be placed in the public consciousness through strong use of coordinated design. The use of colour, typography and minimal imagery is carried through on all elements, from packaging to the design on the side of delivery vehicles.

Keeping a sense of unity
These newspaper spreads demonstrate how coordinated design helps to forge a unique identity. A good exercise for any designer is to recreate exactly any page from a newspaper. It's harder than you think!

○ ASSIGNMENT:
NEWSPAPER PAGE

Choose any organisation, company, series of books or other situation where a design scheme has been used. Take some time to research the various ways in which their visual identity has been implemented/coordinated. In your sketchbook, make a detailed study of the various ways in which this identity scheme has been established, through photography, colour, format, typography, etc.

they already have a band of loyal followers; the genre the book belongs to; the subject matter — is it fun, grave, romantic or scary; and, most importantly, who the book is being aimed at. When designing book jackets, good designers make it their business to ask the publisher lots of questions — and to read the book! After all, your jacket must inspire people to buy the book, so what does it contain that makes it a 'must read'? Penguin books are an excellent example of coordinated design strategy over an extended period of time, and one that has changed to address design and technologies of the time.

PART 1	PRINCIPLES
UNIT 2	FUNDAMENTALS OF COMPOSITION
MODULE 9	**Photography and illustration**

Whether to use photographs, illustrations or even type as image (or all three together) are important design considerations. A well-coordinated look is a hallmark of good design, and the way you plan, edit and incorporate images significantly affects the outcome.

Boundaries between photography and illustration are becoming increasingly blurred by digital art techniques; a straightforward choice between a realistic photograph and an illustrator's interpretation is still possible, and computer-montage techniques allow for a merging of the two. Within the three categories are relatively direct or obscure approaches, so you need to think how you want your message to be understood and interpreted.

Much will depend on the industry in which you are working. In advertising, for example, it is often crucial to show the brand your client is endeavouring to sell. Food packaging or car advertisements tend to feature beautifully photographed and highly realistic pictures showing the product in as flattering a light as possible. If you are working in corporate design, the company's ethos, enshrined in its 'mission statement', is as important as its products or services. Here a more abstract or 'suggestive' set of images could also work. In magazines and books, the look of the images will have been considered at the initial styling stage, when all the questions about the target audience will have been discussed. Here a mix of diverse styles – illustrations and photographs – can be used to differentiate between the various editorial sections.

Creative constraints

Clients might send you the pictures they want you to use along with the initial brief, so sometimes the decision has already been made for you. Photography might not always be possible for logistical reasons – distance, budget or difficulty in gaining permission – and then commissioning an illustration is the only route.

Technical manuals, company reports, educational books or anything that aims to explain how things work, benefit from visualisation. This tends to be a specialised area of illustration, in which designer, illustrator and author/originator must liaise closely.

Budget and schedule

Commissioning an intricate illustration, say a big design of a busy street scene, might not be appropriate unless you have a large budget; it's better to get a photograph. Conversely, asking a photographer to set up a shoot involving several models, a make-up artist and a hair stylist, as well as complicated sets and props, would also be expensive. Here, it's cost-effective to commission an illustration.

Occasionally you may have to produce something for which there is no budget. Don't be thrown by this – there are always possibilities. Sometimes, for instance, evocative type can function as an illustration, and copyright-free pictures can always be found if you know where to look.

Where to start

You may be working on a self-initiated project or to a brief; either way, the illustrative approach may be immediately clear, or you may have to work harder to decide on the right style of image. First, ask yourself what would be suitable for the market and the message you are trying to put across; then research a source that does the job within the constraints of budget and schedule.

Start by researching sources. You may have to create them yourself, or commission a freelance illustrator or photographer. There are many ways of looking at people's work beyond flipping through a portfolio – on the internet, at exhibitions and agencies and in other graphic works such as magazines.

Picture libraries represent photographers and illustrators, or buy in their work to sell on to the media. If you type 'picture library' or 'illustration agency' into a search engine, you will get many names. Generally, such companies allow you to use a low-resolution version for rough concepts, either for free or for a small fee. Then when you have finalised your idea you can buy the rights to use that picture. Always check what

◀ Dramatic background The highly detailed, simple and subtle photography in these posters is effective in the context of a series of musical performances. Their placement on black dramatises the images and achieves striking effects that illustration would not be able to replicate.

◀ Abstraction The top illustration is highly abstract and simplified, using computer-generated imagery. The design below combines a silhouetted image that has been abstracted from a photograph, alongside a collection of computer-drawn illustrations. Both use abstraction, but the style of each image is carefully chosen to reflect the content and intended audience.

❯ Carefully composed
These photographs employ a visual language as seen frequently in advertising: full-colour unmodified photographs, with a high degree of focus on the content of the image, and less emphasis on typography. Illustrations would have been less visually arresting and also less literal.

❮ Integration Black-and-white photomontage is used in an interestingly abstract way, to reinforce a sense of ambiguity about the content of the book. Typography has been integrated into the image, rather than treated as a separate element.

❯ Reinforcement The message in this poster design is reinforced by the imagery, which employs a knowing reference to advertising photography for travel brochures.

the final fee will be before committing yourself. These sources now produce downloads, scans, or CDs of royalty-free images – you can use them without paying further fees. If you intend to cover a certain subject or style repeatedly, it might make sense to buy one of these.

Another source is (copyright-free) clip art, which can be useful as backgrounds to text. Although mainly old black-and-white engravings, they can be used in both modern and traditional ways.

Finally, keep an image bank of your own. Most designers keep notebooks or files of photographers' and illustrators' work, mainly torn from magazines. Sometimes you'll receive promotional work that has been sent in speculatively. If you like it, or think it might prove useful in the future, file it away carefully for potential future use.

➕ **SEE ALSO:** EXPLORATORY DRAWING P18
THEORIES OF IMAGE AND TEXT P22
PHOTOGRAPHY BASICS AND IMAGE
SOURCING P104

◉ ASSIGNMENT:
ZODIAC SYMBOLS

Create a series of 12 images for the horoscope page of a teenage-market magazine. Begin by researching your audience: look for existing examples, and research the history of each symbol. The illustration can be created in any medium, but should take all factors into consideration (see right). You should be able to reproduce the images in four colour, and they will be used in 65mm (2.6in) width. Remember, you can use photographs, illustrations, computer-generated imagery or a combination of all three.

⬆ **Playful imagery** Hand-drawn illustration is the most appropriate solution to suggesting children's drawings (top). Cut paper and simple shapes are effective in the middle design. Rich, colorful, painted illustrations give a warm, tactile quality to the lower design.

CHECKLIST FOR SELECTING IMAGES

• **Age/gender/social class of the target audience** The visuals for the horoscope page of a teenage magazine, for example, could be more 'quirky' and abstract than the imagery for a company report and accounts.

• **Shelf life** The images in a weekly magazine can be transient, whereas those in an expensive book with a selling potential of ten years or more need to have more lasting resonance.

• **Clarity of information** The images for a CD cover could be obscure, whereas those for a technical manual have to be clear and didactic.

• **Perceived value** This is tricky to pinpoint, since quite often something that is cheap is marketed as more expensive through its image, and something that is expensive can seek to appeal to a mass market.

• **Design criteria** Do you want a dynamic cut-out shape or a square image bled off the page? Do you want it in black and white or colour?

• **Theme** Often it is important to create a set of images that all work around one theme or style.

• **Be contrary** Just for a moment or two, consider the opposite of what is expected – this will either give you a new angle or help to consolidate your original thoughts.

• **Budget and schedule**: Check that your solution is affordable and feasible in the time available.

3 FUNDAMENTALS OF TYPOGRAPHY

Typography is the process of arranging letters, words and text for almost any context you can imagine: it is everywhere.

As a designer, you must learn to use typography with imagination and a sense of exploration, while maintaining respect for its rules and traditions.

Typography is the visual manifestation of language – utilising all its expressive and practical qualities. Typography occupies a place somewhere between art and science. You need only look at work presented by concrete poets, or to various art movements such as Futurism and Dada, to see typography's significance as an aesthetic medium. It also involves the functional setting of type for both legibility and communication of information, and in these instances, aesthetic experimentation takes a backseat to pragmatic concerns.

Some assignments in this unit require you to carry out tasks by hand. Drawing letterforms, experimenting with layouts and 'feeling your way', before working onscreen, are essential stages in learning about the subtleties of typography.

PART 1	PRINCIPLES
UNIT 3	FUNDAMENTALS OF TYPOGRAPHY
MODULE 1	**Typography and meaning**

By definition, a typographic message, aside from an intrinsic beauty, must convey a meaning. Meaning, and its expression, is at the core of typographic activity – at the level of both individual words and entire passages of text. This is called 'linguistic meaning', since it resides in language.

Letters and words have an abstract beauty, seen and appreciated through experiments in type anatomy, which isolate the forms and separate elements of individual letters, and frequently reveals them as shapes, rather than meaningful linguistic objects. However, the instant words materialise on page or on-screen, they also express ideas, and possess this elusive quality we call 'meaning'. Linguistic meaning, an essential element of typography, can be expressed, controlled and amplified through such typographic variables as size, weight, typeface, placement on the page and letterspacing.

Sometimes – as in the pages of a book – the visual aspects of typography must take a backseat to the process of understanding (see print historian Beatrice Wardes' essay 'The Crystal Goblet'). However, designers use such visual techniques all the time, to communicate messages effectively; building confidence in working with text in this way is important, so that linking typographic form to linguistic meaning becomes second nature.

But what is 'meaning'? An alternative term is 'semantics', an important subtopic within all aspects of design, which is worth exploring in more detail. Semantics is the study of meaning, and applies to both images and language. 'Syntax' (or grammar) refers to the rules that govern the organisation of elements of a sentence or paragraph, so that meaning is conveyed. If the syntax is wrong, then language becomes nonsense, or meaningless. In a general sense, to say that something has a meaning (a semantic value) relies upon its ability to present its idea in a form that can be communicated and shared. In linguistic meaning (the

a b c

language-based meaning that typography participates in), this communicability is based on sets of symbols in the given language, which includes letters and words, but also space between words, and punctuation.

Typographers such as Wolfgang Weingart, Willem Sandberg and H. N. Werkmann pushed the expression of meaning in typography to its limit, and in so doing, expanded its visual vocabulary and expressive potential by working at the boundary between language and meaning. Dada and Futurist artists such as Kurt Schwitters and Tristan Tzara, Marinetti and Wyndham Lewis experimented with the relationship between language and meaning, around the time of World War I. Such historical practitioners are worth studying closely, for their inspirational typographic experiments, including the work of the concrete poets e. e. cummings and Apollinaire, and designers such as Robert Massin and Johanna Drucker.

Meaning is communicated not only through words, but also through various media, including images, sounds, performance – for example sign language for the non-hearing community; body language, such as the 'thumbs-up' sign; facial expressions for sadness, joy or anger; also Braille, musical notation, Morse code and semaphore.

Vibrancy This book spread shows how typography can express the meaning of words: various typefaces and sizes express the vibrancy of dancing.

All a blur The typography here is manipulated in such a way that it conveys ideas of light dissolving and lack of focus.

❝Type well used is invisible as type, just as the perfect talking voice is the unnoticed vehicle of the transmission of words and ideas❞
Beatrice Warde, 'The Crystal Goblet', or 'Printing Should Be Invisible'

Mixed elements This book cover is consciously composed of elements that are both readable and abstract. The mixture of fragmented images, symbols and letterforms at the centre of the design does not try to convey meaning as much as suggest an atmosphere.

ABCDE
FGHIJK
LMNOP
QRSTU
VWXYZ

Cut and paste This typeface design applies a digital cut-and-paste technique to printed letters in a highly effective evocation of the themes of Mary Shelley's *Frankenstein*.

Wheel of motion Visually rotating text creates an intense illusion of motion. By varying the degree of blurring, different 'speeds' can be portrayed.

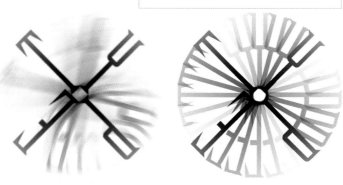

Using light The qualities of light are suggested by transparency, shadow and distortion.

❝A love letter is the beginning of typographical wisdom. That is, the love of letters as literature and the love of letters as physical entities, having abstract beauty of their own, apart from the ideas they may express❞
John R. Biggs

The word 'typography' comes from Greek: *typos* = form and *graphein* = to write

FURTHER READING

http://www.papress.com/thinkingwithtype/index.htm
Based on the book by Ellen Lupton (2004), *Thinking with Type: A Critical Guide For Designers, Writers, Editors, & Students*. Subjects include anatomy, big families, classification, families, kerning, line-spacing, size, tracking, x-heights.

http://www.typeculture.com/academic_resource
A digital type foundry and a resource for essays and short videos on typography and typeface design.

http://www.typotheque.com/site/index.php
A digital type foundry, which also has a large number of texts and articles on graphic design and typography.

During this assignment, concentrate on, and carefully consider, the word in terms of what its meaning is, and how typography can help to convey it.

1 Choose two words from the list below:
- Compression
- Transition
- Contraction
- Addition
- Subtraction
- Disruption
- Repetition
- Elimination
- Migration
- Expansion

Also, create a 'new' word, which has no dictionary definition, and a meaning that only you know; for example, the word 'roleean', which doesn't appear in the dictionary, to mean round, and leaning to the left (you decide its meaning). Your typographic treatment of this 'word' might involve emphasising/dramatically enlarging one of the 'o's within the word, and using italics to have that letter leaning to the side.

2 Create three different compositions, one word per composition. In each, arrange each word to express its meaning, using either colour or black and white. Consider all and any means at your disposal: dramatic scale contrasts, cutting, repetition, letterspacing, etc.

Each composition should utilise a US tabloid or (A3) format. Vary the size, spacing, placement and orientation of letters. Be aware of how the word (or words) interacts with the entire format. Consider the entire format as an important design element: use all available space; don't simply centre the word – think of this as an opportunity to direct attention

throughout the entire 'poster'. Experiment. Play. Push to the edges of the page; repeat elements if it helps to get the meaning across. Be very simple, if that's most appropriate.

Use only one typeface for each composition, noting the appropriateness of the choice of typeface to the word explored; you can mix variants of one (light, bold, condensed, capitals, lowercase). You may repeat, omit, slice, block or overlap words or letters. However, do not use drop shadows or horizontal/vertical scaling (distortion). Consider the entire space of the format as part of the design.

Suggested materials

You can initially execute your project and explore ideas by tracing letters, cutting and pasting computer-generated words, photocopying, photographing or by any combination of these methods. Be inventive. Later, once your ideas are developed, you can use a program such as InDesign, Quark or Illustrator to rework and refine the design. Take time to consider the various options; don't just do the first thing that enters your mind. Explore all possibilities for enhancing ideas.

● **Question**

If you look long enough at a word, at what point and why does it become a set of meaningless shapes?

◉ **Different languages** The subtleties of communication in Italian and English are explored through letterpress typography, and a carefully applied second colour.

PART 1	PRINCIPLES
UNIT 3	FUNDAMENTALS OF TYPOGRAPHY
MODULE 2	**The anatomy of type**

Familiarity with the basic structure of letterforms – type anatomy – is essential to understanding how typefaces differ, what characteristics they share, and allows the designer to make decisions about selecting and using the multitude of typefaces now available. The most basic element of typography is the letter, and each typeface has unique characteristics, while sharing a basic language that describes its parts.

Typeface Classical letterpress typographic processes form the basis of this design by Strichpunkt Design for the packaging of a Typometer (typographic ruler) for desktop publishing use (DTP).

Roman capitals The inscription carved in stone on the base of the Trajan Column in Rome (AD 106–133), similar to the one shown, is acknowledged to be one of the most beautiful examples of classic Roman capital letterforms. These letters formed the basis of many subsequent typeface designs, which emulate their symmetry, balance and rhythm.

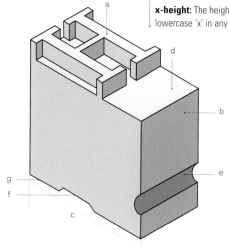

Common terminology of typefaces includes the size of the x-height, counterform, serif style and stress of the letter (ie vertical/oblique). The ability to compare these terms between typefaces establishes essential knowledge about suitability. By providing valuable information, or 'earmarks', about how typefaces relate to classification systems, such as old-style, transitional, modern, serif/sans-serif, knowledge of type anatomy helps the designer to identify and select appropriate typefaces for different purposes.

Technological advances in ways that typefaces are designed and produced has led to difficulties in deciding which typeface to use. Because of the relatively easy method of producing type through digital means, there are now countless new fonts on the market. Some of these are of limited use – they do not have much to offer; arguments can, of course, be made that they appear different or experimental, so could be used in certain circumstances, for example in an experimental style magazine. For general use, however, it is better to select the well-known or classical fonts. Criteria for selection should normally be made on a more rational basis than simply that it looks different or is unusual.

Typeface A block of letterpress type, showing the face of the letter, whose surface is inked and printed, giving us the term 'typeface'. **a** face, **b** body or shank, **c** point size, **d** shoulder, **e** nick, **f** groove, **g** foot.

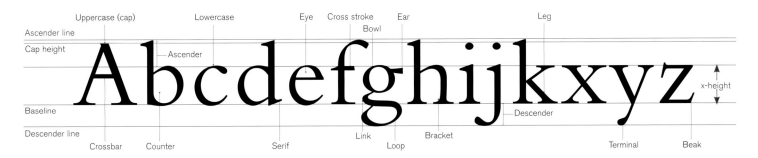

Uppercase (cap) — Lowercase — Eye — Cross stroke — Ear — Leg
Ascender line
Cap height — Ascender — Bowl
x-height
Baseline — Descender
Descender line — Crossbar — Counter — Serif — Link — Loop — Bracket — Terminal — Beak

---

Oblique, angled stress, associated with old-style

Semi-oblique stress, associated with transitional typefaces

Vertical stress, associated with modern and sans-serif typefaces

⌃ Language of letterforms

Each distinct part of a letter has its own name, forming a 'language of letterforms'.

❯ Counterforms

Eliminating the counterforms within letters does not necessarily detract from readability, and in this case, creates an interesting logotype.

⌃ Identifying characteristics

The different stresses of typefaces are essential information in identifying their place within the classification systems, and to locating them within an historical timeline.

❯ Linking the parts

This poster shows a good knowledge of type anatomy in its design, which is sensitive to the relationship between the different parts of the old-style Roman letters.

FURTHER READING

An excellent additional resource for information on type anatomy can be found at: http://typomil.com/anatomy/index.html

Key terms

There are over 25 anatomy terms applicable to letterforms. For general typography it's not necessary to know all of them, but some are essential to making visual judgments that aid typeface selection for different situations, and you should be able to describe those differences in a technically correct way. For example, you may want to argue for the use of the 18th-century typeface Bodoni in a particular design, in which case, being able to state that its characteristics include a vertical stress and a high degree of contrast between thick and thin strokes is important language and information to have at your disposal.

Information such as the difference between x-heights of typefaces is very helpful, since this allows the designer to choose typefaces that are more or less readable at smaller sizes. The x-height is the size of a lowercase 'x' in a given typeface, and the ratio between x-height and the ascenders and descenders of the lowercase letters, such as 'g' and 'h', defines the overall appearance of a font, including the fact that type that has a large x-height may need more space between

Times New Roman   Bodoni Book   Times New Roman   Bodoni Book

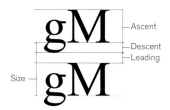

Ascent
Descent
Leading
Size

Measuring The point size of type is measured from the baseline of one line of type to the baseline of another. Leading is the vertical space between lines of type, and affects the readability of text.

Impact of x-height The x-height is the height of a lowercase x and determines the visual size of type. The x-height size varies from typeface to typeface: some, like Bodoni, have a small x-height, whereas Times New Roman has a large x-height. However, each type has the same body size. Type with large x-heights tend to have small ascenders and descenders, whereas type with small x-heights have large ones.

Large x-heights

In typefaces with large x-heights, such as Bookman or Helvetica, the lack of white space above and below the lowercase letters, and the larger white spaces within the letters, requires more space between lines. Increase the leading so that text is easier to read, and the overall 'colour' (another term for density or texture of the type) on the page is less heavy.

Small x-heights

In typefaces with small x-heights, such as Caslon and Futura, there is more white space above and below the lowercase letters. Such type is easier to read because the eye can travel back and forth along lines without difficulty. Use less leading in these typefaces, or even set them without any additional leading ('solid'), and set them in a larger point size.

the lines (leading), so that it doesn't appear as visually heavy on the page.

Typefaces of the same size can appear larger or smaller. Futura has a small x-height, and long ascenders/descenders, whereas most sans-serif typefaces, such as Helvetica, typically have large x-heights. Although a general understanding of the terminology of typefaces is adequate for most designers, if you are interested in designing typefaces, you will need to develop an intimate knowledge of type anatomy, in all its nuances, and have an excellent understanding of typeface history and development.

1234567890

1234567890

Numerals Aligning (above, set in Palatino) and non-aligning (or old-style) numbers (below, set in Bembo Expert).

STAGES OF WORK

Here are some key steps to follow when you are given a piece of typography work.
1 Analyse the information and make sure that you fully understand all the terms. Select those terms you wish to convey in your design.
2 Fully explore your design scheme using thumbnails or half-size visuals. At this stage you need to make your design as dramatic as possible, while still maintaining comprehension.
3 Work up your designs to full size, as working drawings. Use layout paper or cartridge paper.
4 Think about colour. Do you want each element to be different or the same? Or perhaps you'd prefer to work with a limited palette of colours?
5 Before going to the computer you need to develop hand-rendered artwork. Work produced on the computer should be an extension of your hand-rendered layouts.

Helvetica   Futura   Bembo

Typefaces of | the same size | look different sizes | because they | have varying | x-heights |

Bodoni   Bernhard Modern   Times New Roman

Minimalist The barest information can be used to construct a font, since once the system is established, even a straight line can be understood (in context) to be a letter.

Know your letters The logo used on this envelope employs subtly overlapping letterforms as part of its identity scheme. Knowing the heights of letters, and how they will interact, is essential in this kind of design work.

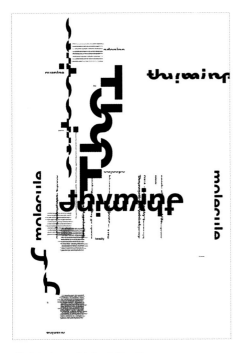

Playing with legibility This experimental design relies upon the knowledge that the upper part of the letterform is more readable than the lower part, so that by cutting lines of text in half the words are still legible.

Attractive interaction The circularity of the chosen letterforms here enables the designer to combine them in an appropriate and visually sensitive way.

Grasp of anatomy These designs rely upon an understanding of type anatomy, explaining terms while experimenting with ways to convey them.

ASSIGNMENT: GETTING TO GRIPS WITH LARGE-SCALE LETTERFORMS

Print out a series of letters, both capitals and lowercase, in several different typefaces. Test your knowledge of type anatomy by naming as many parts of the letters as possible, using arrows. Then, check your answers against the diagram on page 67, to see if you are correct.

ASSIGNMENT: TYPE ANATOMY INFORMATION SHEETS

You are asked to design a series of information sheets explaining the anatomy of type to someone new to the subject. The main object of the sheets is to convey the terms and corresponding parts of the letters as clearly as possible, in a visually interesting way.

1 Working with a single typeface, or comparing up to three typefaces, enlarge or reduce, cut out sections or overlap parts – anything that helps explain the terms to the viewer. Use a maximum of three colours to full effect by using the second and third colours sparingly, and solely to add emphasis. For instance, explanatory text could be in one colour, and the parts of the letterforms in the others. Show at least three terms on each of the sheets, for example x-height, cap height, body size, counter, serif, ascender, descender, bowl, baseline, stress/axis, stroke weight, bracketed serif.

2 The explanatory copy can be taken from the information in these pages. The format should be 210mm (8¼in) square. There are three stages to the design and a production stage, when you will produce your designs on the computer. The point of having different design stages is so that you will fully explore ideas before going to the computer to produce them.

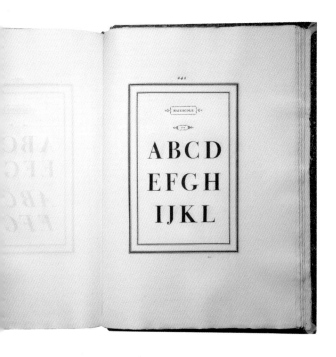

❯ **Choose your font** Digital type finders group together typefaces in related families and in many different sizes and weights.

PART 1	PRINCIPLES
UNIT 3	FUNDAMENTALS OF TYPOGRAPHY
MODULE 3	**Understanding and selecting typefaces**

Since the introduction of digital typefaces, the number of fonts available has increased exponentially; it is virtually impossible to know them all, or be able to reference all of their attributes. However, it is advantageous to know a typeface's historical background, since this can help in relating its characteristics to the content of the text. Selecting and understanding typefaces is a complicated business, one that becomes easier only with practice.

⬥ **Beauty of Bodoni**
The *Manuale Tipografico* by Giambattista Bodoni, printed in 1788 and again in 1818, is an exemplary specimen showing all the variations of this beautiful typeface. It is an extraordinary document, and Bodoni is still one of the most popular modern typefaces.

❝*By all means break the rules, and break them beautifully, deliberately and well. That is one of the ends for which they exist*❞
Robert Bringhurst

To give a simple example of important issues in typeface selection: a sans-serif typeface such as Univers references modernity in a way that a serif font such as Garamond does not. Bodoni, designed in the late 1700s, has certain formal characteristics that, in their own era, were considered 'modern', including its use of perfectly vertical stress, and sharp contrast between thick and thin lines, departing from 'old-style' typefaces based on pen-drawn forms. However, in a modern setting, this font is associated with classicism and history. Although it can be used in a contemporary way, it's important to understand Bodoni's history, and associations, and to take these into account when considering its use. Understanding a typeface's historical origins and references, and its associated formal (visual) characteristics, is crucial information in matters of selection. Broadly, contemporary typefaces such as Univers tend to work in modern contexts, whereas traditional type such as Garamond would be more apt for a literary classic – as book text. Of course, all these conventions are there to be played with and broken, but only in full understanding of their significance.

Before examining the various factors involved in selecting type, it is worthwhile considering the broad categories into which they can be placed: type classification systems. Categorising type is never an exact process, due to its many idiosyncrasies. Nevertheless, a rough guide can help in recognising typefaces and learning the different functions appropriate for the various type families. A clear initial division is between text and display type, each of which has its own criteria for selection.

Text type: old style, transitional and modern

Primarily, text types are meant to be read in continuous form or at least with few interruptions.
• Old-style serif typefaces, such as Bembo, Garamond and Caslon, are ideal for this purpose. They are now regarded as 'classic' fonts because they have stood the test of time and still command respect. These Roman fonts have been in use since the origins of printing in the 15th century. During the 1930s a number of new 'Romans' were introduced to coincide with the new Monotype hot-metal system; many of the classics were also recut for the same purpose. Times New Roman and Imprint are good examples of this group, known as 20th-century Romans. Later the German type designers

Hermann Zapf and Jan Tschichold added, respectively, Palatino and Sabon to this group. Contemporary Romans, such as Minion and Swift, have now been designed using digital means.

• Transitional Roman fonts have a vertical stress, sharp and bracketed serifs and in most cases a medium to high contrast between thick and thin letterstrokes. Baskerville and Century Schoolbook are prime examples. The term captures a movement away from the old-style group, influenced by pen-drawn forms, towards modern faces, which are rooted in geometry rather than the pen.

• Modern faces also have a vertical stress, but an abrupt contrast between the thick and thin letterstrokes, fine horizontal serifs and a narrow set width (in most cases). Bodoni is one of the earliest and best-known examples; Walbaum is a slightly more contemporary version of a 'modern' typeface.

There are many fonts in these three groups, which cover pretty much all kinds of book work. They can also be found in brochures and magazines, but other groups are more often used for this kind of publication.

Display type

Major social changes in the 19th century brought about the need for display type. In Britain, the Industrial Revolution brought the masses into the cities, increasing production and consumption of goods and services, which led to the need to communicate to a wider audience. Existing fonts were used primarily for books, which were limited to an elite sector. Printers found the available typefaces inadequate for the new billboards, posters and pamphlets produced, especially since there were many more messages being displayed in public spaces, vying for attention. Bolder, stronger faces were needed to suit this new context, and to meet demand.

The sans-serif typeface was bolder and more 'industrial' in its look, along with slab serifs, and thickened modern letters known as 'fat faces'. Mostly, these rather crude faces died out after 1850, but Ultra Bodoni is an example still in use today. The Victorians were innovative; their typefaces are full of vigour and still fascinate today. John Lewis' book *Printed Ephemera* has excellent examples of Victorian display fonts used on posters and flyers advertising plays.

Juxtaposition Many styles are evident in this street poster, which makes use of sans, slab serif and outline letterforms.

Contrasts Large wooden type and a smaller font, both printed letterpress, are used in a truly contemporary way, since the small text consists of a long list of Facebook updates, collected over a period of time, meticulously printed.

Wooden type Originally used for producing posters by letterpress printing, wooden type is a good source of alternative letterforms.

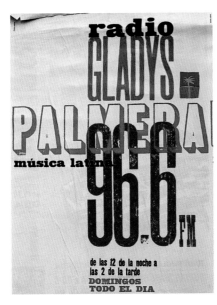

SERIF

oAad   oAad   oAad   **oAad**

Humanist Old-Style

Typefaces of the 15th and 16th centuries are based on hand-drawn calligraphic letterforms. They are characterised by having slanted (oblique or diagonal) stress, bracketed serifs and low contrast between thick and thin strokes. Sabon, designed by Jan Tschichold in 1966, is a contemporary example, based on the 16th-century typeface Garamond.

Transitional

A more vertical axis is visible in these 18th-century typefaces. The sharp contrast between thick and thin strokes was considered controversial at the time. Serifs are still bracketed, but they are moving away from the calligraphic influence. Baskerville is an example of a transitional typeface.

Modern

In the late 18th and early 19th centuries, typefaces became significantly more abstract. Bodoni shows a highly exaggerated contrast between thick and thin strokes, a perfectly vertical stress, and serifs that are no longer bracketed, but straight lines.

Egyptian and Slab Serif

In the early 19th century, in response to the industrial revolution, many new typefaces were designed for use in advertising. Their bold, robust, decorative forms grew from this context. Egyptian typefaces are typical of this period, with their heavy, slab serifs, and 'industrial' quality.

SANS SERIF

oAad   oAad   oAad

Humanist Sans Serif

Sans-serif typefaces originated in the early 19th century but became dominant in the 20th century. Gill Sans, designed in 1928, combined the characteristics of both old-style serif, and sans-serif fonts, with its calligraphic qualities but lack of serifs.

Anonymous Sans Serif

Sans-serif fonts were first produced by Caslon in 1816 (in capitals only), and William Thorowgood in 1832 (with lowercase), and they were known as Grotesques, since they were thought to be ugly. Helvetica was designed in 1957 by Max Miedinger, and is one of the best known sans serifs.

Geometric Sans Serif

Typefaces such as Futura (designed by Paul Renner in 1927) are extensions of earlier sans serifs, but have a more geometric design, based on monolines (lines of one thickness, with no variation of thick and thin as in old-styles), perfect circles, and triangular shapes. Such typefaces are associated with Modernism in the early part of the 20th century, but continue to be popular.

Sans-serif and script typefaces

The 20th century saw the extensive development of the sans serif, notably by the Bauhaus school in the 1920s and 1930s. Their philosophy was to sweep away the traditional forms characterised by excessive ornament, employing the principle of 'form equals function'. Simple typographic structures called for clean, functional typefaces, hence the interest in the sans serif with its monoline and functional forms. Futura was introduced in 1927, and two years later Gill Sans was unveiled. In the decades that followed, well-known fonts such as Helvetica and Optima in Europe, and Franklin Gothic and Avant Garde in the USA, kept the sans serif among the most popular of type styles.

A significant advantage of the sans serif is the large number of potential variants within one typeface. In 1957 Adrian Frutiger introduced a complete family of different weights and forms when he conceived the design of Univers, which comprises 21 variants ranging from light condensed to bold expanded.

Selecting fonts

The content of the material and the purpose of the design are the main factors in deciding your choice of font. Design clarity is essential in information, and it is telling that sans-serif types, with

Classifying differences Type classification charts are useful guides to the various characteristics (sometimes known as 'earmarks') of different typefaces. They allow you to place typefaces within their historical contexts, and to see how their basic visual attributes are shared across different, but related, fonts. For example, Romans always have serifs, while sans-serif humanist typefaces such as Gill Sans share properties associated with both old-style Roman and sans-serif typefaces.

Newspaper fonts Sans-serif fonts were first seen in 1786. Shown above is an early use of a sans serif working with serif fonts in a French newspaper, from 1898. Until this time, all newspaper text and headings were set in serif fonts, and to this day, text setting is usually in serif.

Correct fonts

Italic **Bold** SMALL CAPS

Pseudo fonts

Italic **Bold** SMALL CAPS

Unless you choose a real italic from the font menu, a computer will only slant Roman letterforms

Pseudo bold is simply thickened digitally rather than being the true, carefully crafted font

Small caps are used within lowercase text when smaller, non-dominant capital letters are required. They are used for emphasis within traditional typesetting

their simple monoline structures, are used for road signage. Sans serif is also ideal when type size has to be small, as in some diagrams and maps.

• Font choice can be influenced by subject matter, and a knowledge of the font origins can help in the final decision; for example, Caslon and Baskerville are classical English, Garamond is French, Goudy American, Bodoni Italian and so on. You do not have to rely on classical fonts; contemporary serifs such as Minion, Swift and Meta are ideal for modern material.

• Magazine designs can be more adventurous because readers tend to dip in and out of the text, rather than reading from cover to cover. Serifs designed for text, such as Century, Serifa and Glypha, are vigorous and appealing. With small segments of copy, unusual fonts can bring a freshness to the overall feeling of the design. However, it's wise not to mix too many fonts together in one design.

• Display types offer much more variety than text types because their purpose is expression rather than readability, so you can engage in playful experimentation.

• Sans-serif and slab-serif faces are seen as more authoritative and bolder than typefaces that are designed for reading over long periods. If you are reversing out type or printing onto tints in small sizes, sans serifs are a good bet. For elegance, serifs have the advantage.

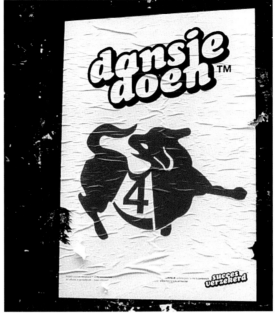

◀ **Matching text with image** The choice of an outlined, lowercase typeface is unusual, but in the context of this poster it works with the image, since it has a similar rhythm and movement. The text has a strong visual presence in its own right.

▼ **Themed book covers** The different content of these books requires varied typographic treatment. Serif, sans-serif, bold, condensed, hand-painted and lowercase type are used to suggest the themes of the text.

Condensed Expanded
Condensed Expanded

Artificially condensed or expanded letterforms should be avoided, since the computer distorts them by applying a percentage reduction or expansion. Always use a 'true' condensed or expanded typeface

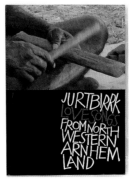

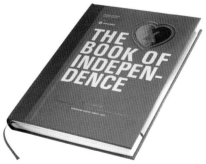

Stone Sans Semibold
Stone Sans Medium

This intro type is set in Stone Serif Semibold.

This body type is set in Stone Serif Medium. Designed in 1987, the Stone family consists of three types of font – a serif, a sans-serif and an informal style – all designed to work together. The styles are legible, modern and dynamic, combining the old with the new. The range of Stone fonts integrate perfectly with each other, giving the typeface a wide range of design applications.

Officina Sans Bold
Officina Sans Book

This intro type is set in Officina Serif Bold.

This body type is set in Officina Serif Book. Designed in the 1980s, the aim was to create a versatile family of fonts, suitable for office and business use. Officina fulfilled the brief, proving to be an extremely legible and popular typeface, with five weights available in both serif and sans-serif versions. The font is also robust enough to meet the demands of low-resolution printing.

Sans serif: Without serif. Typefaces such as Univers, Helvetica, Aksidenz Grotesque and Futura, characterised by their lack of serifs. Predominantly associated with the 19th/20th centuries.

Serif: Structural details at the ends of some strokes in old-style capital and lowercase letters.

⌃ **Perfect harmony** Type designers have recently produced serif and sans-serif versions of the same typeface, for example Officina and Stone. The advantage is that you can use a serif for the text setting and a sans for the display, and they will harmonise perfectly because they have been specifically designed to work together.

⌄ **Cultural interpretations** This adaptation of the book *The Strange Case of Dr. Jekyll and Mr. Hyde* makes historical references through choice of typefaces (below), which are then applied to clothing and an umbrella, in the style of 19th-century newspapers (below left). The film *Blade Runner*, and the book *Frankenstein* have been treated within an unconventional 'accordion-fold' format (below right).

⊕ **SEE ALSO:** THE ANATOMY OF TYPE P66

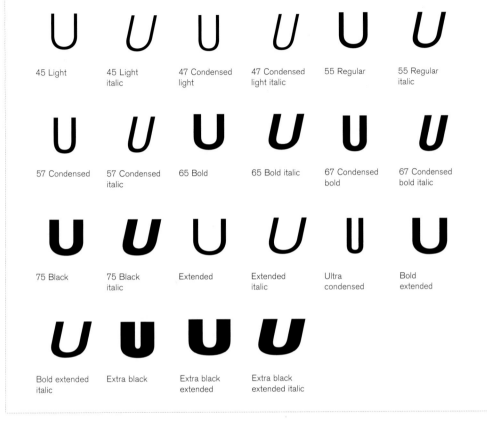

45 Light	45 Light italic	47 Condensed light	47 Condensed light italic	55 Regular	55 Regular italic
57 Condensed	57 Condensed italic	65 Bold	65 Bold italic	67 Condensed bold	67 Condensed bold italic
75 Black	75 Black italic	Extended	Extended italic	Ultra condensed	Bold extended
Bold extended italic	Extra black	Extra black extended	Extra black extended italic		

◉ ASSIGNMENT:
COLLECTION OF TYPE

1 Find four typefaces that fit the classification old-style Roman, four that fit transitional and four that fit modern.
2 Find three Victorian display typefaces, or ones based on older types but digitally redrawn.
3 Locate two sans-serif typefaces based on geometrical elements, and two that are non-geometric.

   Bonus points for finding one font that has the attributes of both old-style, pen-drawn letterforms, and the simplicity of a sans serif, combined in one typeface. Pay close attention to anatomical differences between typefaces, which tell you what classification group they belong to. Keep all this information in your sketchbook, along with details of who designed the typeface, when and in what context the typeface is usually seen, ie as a display or text face.

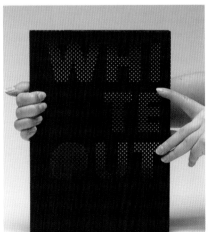

◀ Legibility The heavy forms, and larger surface area of the bold version of a sans-serif typeface such as Helvetica or Univers can 'hold' information better than an equivalent size of serif font. Here, the text is readable, even though only very minimal information (in the form of dots) is used in the last few letters of the title.

⌃ Univers Designed by Adrian Frutiger in 1954, Univers is a modular system, with 44 numbered typefaces in various weights, widths and oblique versions. This flexibility makes the font ideal for incorporating many differing levels of information within a design. It's interesting to compare the slight but important differences with other sans-serif typefaces such as Helvetica. You should learn to observe the fine distinctions when choosing between one sans serif and another.

◉ Question

In a piece of either historical or contemporary design of your choice, do you think the typeface used is appropriate to its purpose?

PART 1	PRINCIPLES
UNIT 3	FUNDAMENTALS OF TYPOGRAPHY
MODULE 4	**Spacing**

Understanding how to deal with space in typography is essential. Proper spacing affects legibility, and space is also an integral and powerful part of any composition, whether symmetrical or asymmetrical. The most important thing is to develop an eye for detail, and to consider the role of space in both legibility and meaning, as you progress at every stage of the design.

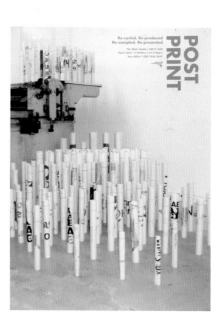

GLOSSARY

Alignment: The setting of text relative to a column or page.

Centred: Text that is aligned neither to the left nor to the right: symmetrical, with an even gap at the end of each line.

Hyphenation: The point at which a word is broken at the end of a line in continuous text, and a hyphen is inserted.

Justification: Text that is aligned on both the left and right margins of a column (lines are equal in length).

Kerning: Adjustments to the spaces between two letters (used extensively for capitals).

Leading: The horizontal space between lines of type. Related to the historical use of strips of lead in letterpress.

Letterspacing (tracking): The space between letters, which can be adjusted.

Optical adjustment: Making adjustments to letterspacing by eye, not mechanically.

Ranged left/ranged right: Text that is aligned to a column, either left or right.

IEFKHN OQ AVID

Space needed

These upright letters appear much tighter visually than the rounded letters below

Rounded shapes give the illusion of more space between each letterform

The V has been moved closer to the A but there is still an unevenness of visual spacing in the word, so adjustments need to be made

Limit it Small amounts of ranged-right type can work well on a poster, but are ill-advised for larger quantities of type.

Kern your caps Kerning is the process of optically adjusting the space between (mostly capital) letters, so that they appear evenly spaced.

The lowercase i is a good guide

Word spacing is traditionally based upon a space equivalent to the body width of a lowercase "i."

t o o m u c h l e t t e r s p a c e

Too much spacing between letters looks awkward and can inhibit readability

Grouping information Centered or symmetrical type needs to be adjusted carefully both horizontally and vertically. The various sizes of type are used to "group" information.

In most cases the designs you produce will consist of a mixture of pictures, illustrations, captions and copy, in the form of either headings (display type) or main copy (text). Display type ranges in size from 14pt and upwards, whereas the main text (also referred to as body copy or body text) generally falls between 6 and 14pt. As you design, important choices will need to be made regarding typefaces, sizes and measure (width of line). You will also need to decide about spacing (letter, word and line) and, later, adjustments will need to be made by eye, which is where developing that keen eye for detail becomes essential.

Letterspacing

When you key text, a computer sets the type at default space settings, both for between individual letters and for between lines of type (leading); it doesn't make the fine-tuning decisions that a designer must. If your type is too close together, with the letters almost touching, the letterspacing needs to be adjusted (called kerning). If they are too far apart, individual word shapes break down and legibility is affected. When starting out, one of the most common mistakes that designers make is to letterspace their text either too closely or too widely, or to accept the computer's spacing decisions. Designers need to learn as much as possible about the ways in which leading affects readability and impacts on the overall texture, sometimes called 'colour', of the text on the page.

Extra or negative letterspacing can be inserted into lowercase type or capitals to reinforce a particular conceptual idea, but these are the exceptions. With regard to text sizes, in general letterspacing should not need to be altered from the default computer setting. Type designers for software programs are careful to produce settings for good visual spacing between letters at different sizes. However, never take this for granted. For instance, condensed typefaces should always be treated cautiously, as should those set in justified measures: in these cases, small additions or subtractions can improve the evenness of spacing or allow a word to be taken into a line to avoid widows or orphans (single words from the end of a paragraph left at the end or beginning of a column of text).

Objectives

The main aim in display and text type is to try to achieve visual evenness throughout a series of characters. Consistency is important because readers interpret shapes of words rather than individual letters. If there is unevenness in letterspacing, the eye can be distracted by space rather than seeing words.

You can test the importance of even letterspacing by setting text with different spacing, including altering it within the same line. As type size increases the unevenness can worsen, requiring the designer to make optical adjustments. This problem is prevalent with capital letters, because the way they fit together is complicated by their inherent forms. Characters with straight stems such as 'I', 'J', 'E' and 'F', when placed together, require more space between individual letters than those with rounded shapes, like 'O' and 'Q', or those with diagonal strokes, such as 'A', 'V', 'Y' and 'W'. This is because the letters occupy different amounts of space, having varied widths.

'Kerning' allows for individual reductions or incremental increases to letterspacing; 'tracking' increases or reduces space between words. Always trust your eyes. Other letters in a word may, for instance, need adjusted spacing to compensate for the reduced space between characters, such as 'A' and 'V'.

ℹ Left versus right
Ranged-right text is harder to read than ranged left, because the eye travels to the end of the line and seeks a consistent location for the beginning of the next line. If the lines (on the left) are uneven, it's more difficult to do this.

❝Anyone who would letterspace lowercase would steal sheep❞

After Frederick Goudy

⊕ SEE ALSO: THE ANATOMY OF TYPE P66

READABILITY AND LEGIBILITY P80

◀ ▶ Breaking the rules Negative leading and overprinting can produce dramatic experimental effects, but are not always conducive to the reading experience.

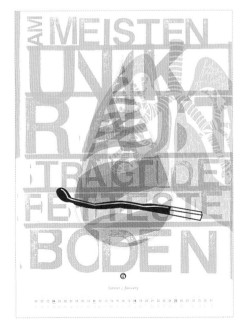

Word spacing

In display type, a gauge for the amount of space to leave between words is the width of a lowercase 'i'. Anything more will exacerbate difficulties in reading. It is therefore best not to try to force display lines out to preconceived measures.

Word spacing in text type also needs careful scrutiny; typesetting style plays an important part. There are two basic setting styles for continuous reading: justified and ranged left. With justified setting, word spacing will vary because words are pushed out to fulfill the requirements of the measure. Space between words can become excessive, particularly if the chosen measure is too small or the typeface too large. Hyphenation (word breaks) can be adjusted to even out word spacing as far as possible, but justified setting is always tricky unless type size in relation to set measure is considered. Setting justified text on a short measure with many long words is especially

❯ H and Js Hyphenation and justification can be fine-tuned manually giving an excellent level of control; here the dialogue boxes from InDesign are shown.

Changes space between words

Changes space between letters

Applies horizontal scaling to characters

Controls a single word occupying a line

Enter values to control how words are hyphenated

Amount of white space at the end of a non-justified line

How many consecutive lines can be hyphenated

With justified setting, that is, alignment on both the right and left of the measure, the word spacing will vary because words are pushed out to fulfil the requirements of the measure. Herein lies the problem. The space can become excessive, particularly if the chosen measure is too small or the typeface too large. The result is often bad word spacing, which can cause 'rivers' of space to run down the page.

Hyphenation can be adjusted to even out the word spacing as far as possible, and avoid ugly spacing. Hyphenation specifications are sets of automatic hyphenation rules that you can create and apply to paragraphs. You can specifiy the smallest number of characters that must precede an automatic hyphen (the default is 3), and the minimum number of characters that must follow an automatic hyphen (the default is 2). These controls do not affect manual hyphenation.

With ranged-left setting you have the decided advantage of being able to space words consistently – the inherent difficulties of justified text can be avoided. For this reason, many designers prefer this style, though problems of legibility can still arise. As mentioned earlier, style of type also plays an important part in the amount of word spacing to have. Percentage adjustments can be made within hyphenation and justification (H and J).

◖ No H and J This justified setting has no word breaks. You can easily see the problem of excessive word spacing, which causes rivers of space to form.

◖ Hyphenation Using hyphens can help to reduce the problem of excessive word spacing, but don't hyphenate too often in a block of text.

◖ Unjustified Excessive word spacing can be made to disappear with the ranged-left style of setting. With no word breaks you can shorten lines, giving a ragged look.

‹ **Style reflects message** Carefully adjusted leading that brings lines of type close but not touching produces a tight yet typographically subtle setting.

difficult, since few words end up on a line. You can often see this problem in newspapers.

With ranged-left setting you have the advantage of being able to space words consistently. For this reason, many designers prefer this style, although problems of legibility can still arise and 'ragging' text becomes a major issue. Type style also plays an important part in word spacing. Percentage adjustments can be made within the hyphenation and justification (H and J) settings of page layout programs, to accommodate closer or wider word spacing depending on the width of character of the typeface. In general, ranged-left setting should not be hyphenated, except sometimes for shorter column widths; otherwise you can end up with lines of uneven length.

Leading

This term derives from 'hot metal' typesetting (where strips of lead were placed between lines of type) and refers to the amount of horizontal spacing between lines of type. In display type the designer will invariably have to adjust individual lines and not just rely on a constant setting. Each line of type is spaced differently, according to need. The role of leading becomes particularly important when setting large areas of text, for instance in books. There are no clear rules regarding adjustments of line-spacing for display matter; it is a matter of skill in developing an even look and letting your eye be your guide: every time you use display type, analyse each case individually. For example, designers often use negative leading (in which the leading has a lower numerical value than the type size). This can be effective in giving a dynamic visual appearance, but should be used with care.

All type settings are enhanced by the careful consideration of leading. Factors such as x-height, measure and weight of typeface will all influence the amount of leading that you should employ.

X-HEIGHTS AND READABILITY

Helvetica Medium, designed in 1957 by Max Miedinger, a Swiss type designer, is a sans-serif typeface that has a relatively large x-height in relation to its ascenders and descenders. This means that when setting text in this font, you will need to add extra leading (space between the lines) to ensure maximum readability. The text you see set here is in 8pt, with 4 points of leading, or 8/12pt.

The same size of type in Futura Medium, designed in the mid-1920s by Paul Renner and based on simple geometric forms, has a relatively small x-height for a sans-serif typeface. However, its long ascenders and descenders (see the 'l' and the 'y') mean that when setting text in this font you may need to add extra leading (space between the lines) to ensure maximum readability. This text is set in 8pt, with 4 points of leading, or 8/12pt.

This text is set in the same size of type, in the transitional serif typeface Times New Roman, designed specifically for the Times newspaper in 1931, by Stanley Morison. It has a smaller x-height in relation to its ascenders and descenders, and therefore an overall smaller appearance on the page, needing less leading. The text you see here is set in 8pt, with 3 points of leading, or 8/11pt.

The same size of type in the old-style typeface Bembo, originally cut by Francesco Griffo in 1496, has an even smaller x-height, although it is in the same size as before. This means that when setting text in this font, you may want to reduce the space between the lines (leading) to ensure maximum readability. This typeface also looks less visually dense when set as text on the page, because the weight of its strokes is less heavy. This text is set in 8pt, with 2 points of leading, or 8/10pt.

○ ASSIGNMENT: ADJUSTING SPACING

1 Typeset and arrange in a US letter or A4 format the heading RAILROADS IN CRISIS in a 60pt sans-serif face. Do not adjust any letterspace.
2 Print out the setting and mark on the proofs any adjustment you feel is necessary to achieve visually even spacing.
3 Return to the computer and apply kerning (see page 76).
4 Print out the new version and compare the two proofs.
5 Continue adjusting the kerning until it is perfect.

RAGGING TEXT

Creating ragging text, which is ranged left, takes time, practice and patience. The key is to create a 'soft' right-hand edge to the type, by bringing words down onto the following lines, and avoiding making harsh, obvious shapes, such as diagonals, at the right edge of the text, which would distract the eye. A rule of thumb is to alternate longer and shorter lines. Avoid putting in hyphenation to solve ragging problems – work with the natural flow of the words in the copy, and only break if absolutely necessary.

Adding emphasis These three book spreads illustrate the use of a variety of type sizes, styles of type and settings for emphasis.

Mix it up This spread mixes sans-serif and serif fonts, in capitals and lowercase, and introduces letterspacing. The text is legible, yet playfully handled.

Stylish combinations The justified setting for the main columns of text is offset by the captions, which are on a shorter measure and ranged left. This creates typographic variety, while respecting legibility.

Short and sweet Curved lines of type are acceptable in this poster design, since only a small amount of copy is involved.

PART 1	PRINCIPLES
UNIT 3	FUNDAMENTALS OF TYPOGRAPHY
MODULE 5	**Readability and legibility**

Intense debate continues between traditionalists and modernists as to whether sans-serif typefaces are more or less legible than serif faces. Traditionalists argue that serifs aid legibility by helping to differentiate letterforms – all factors that keep the eye moving along the horizontal line. However, modernists argue that sans serifs do not really decrease legibility; it is just a question of readers becoming culturally acclimatised to the sans-serif face, which is historically a much more recent phenomenon.

Rules have evolved about setting type and using letterforms. One is that long passages composed entirely of either capital letters or bold text are difficult to read. The reason capitals are difficult to read is that the words have similar visual shapes or outlines, all of the same height; ascenders and descenders in capital and lowercase settings aid the differentiation between words.

> Since an uneven line ending creates a pattern of broken eye movement, you might expect that justified type would be easier to read. Again, reading experiments do not confirm this. It may be that the additional white space provided by unjustified type compensates for the less eye movement pattern
>
> *Betty Binns*

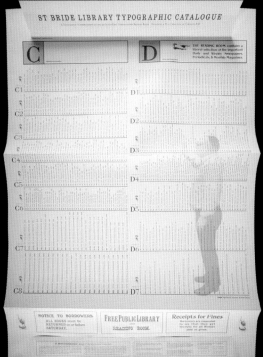

Combining ranges The use of both ranged-left and ranged-right type, which meets at the centre of this menu, can be effective. However, ranged-right type needs to be carefully handled.

Refining the detail The refinement of typographic detail in terms of leading, line length and typeface choice makes the large amount of complex information readable and accessible.

Justified versus ranged left

Another perennially hot topic is the relative virtues of justified and ranged-left settings; justified text may be no easier to follow than lines ranged left. Ranged-right settings force the reader to search for the beginning of each line, which in over-long passages can get very annoying and should be avoided. Generally, if you are reversing type out of black or a colour, then a sans-serif typeface is a safer option than the alternative, with its finer lines and serifs. Much will depend, of course, on the size of type and quality of paper.

Between 60 and 72 characters per line (on any given measure) is the best number for optimum readability. However, these parameters change according to type size. When lines are too long the eye loses its place; too short, and you become distracted by the constant returning to the start of a new line. The text throughout these paragraphs is set in Berthold Akzidenz Grotesk at 9 points, with a leading measure of 11 points.

Question

Which size of type do you consider to be the most legible based on the information given here? Can you say exactly why?

KEY FEATURES: READABILITY

Measure (line length), type size and leading (spacing between lines) work together, which affects readability.

• The optimum number of characters per line is between 60 and 72. Any more and the eye has problems picking up the next line. Conversely, fewer characters per line can interrupt reading flow, since the eye has to constantly move back and forth from one line to the next. Of course, the needs of different design types will influence these decisions; in fact, context is everything. In magazines measures tend to be shorter because readers dip into articles rather than reading from cover to cover. Novels, which have to satisfy a criterion of continuous reading, look very different from advertisements, in which impact is a primary concern. Indeed, it is a useful exercise to ask why certain publications – telephone directories, timetables, cookbooks, etc – differ in their standards of readability depending on the function they fulfil.

• Choice of type size and measure also depends on the amount of copy. Readers can cope with small amounts if the setting is smaller or on a narrower measure than the recommended optimum.

• Typefaces with large x-heights have reduced ascenders and descenders, resulting in less differentiation in word shapes. Therefore, these typefaces need to have more leading.

• Leading is a major element in readability, since if there is insufficient space between lines the eye will be hampered from moving to the next line. Increased leading is also required if the typeface is condensed, or a serif typeface with a heavy or bold characteristic is being used.

Excellent legibility This is an important aspect to a design identity. As seen in this example of a corporate design manual (a guide for both the company and the designer, showing how a design scheme should be implemented), the logo must be legible at all sizes, and the typography consistently applied throughout, whether in the context of advertisements, printed literature or even on the side of vehicles.

Room to breathe Text set in uppercase needs to be given more leading, to avoid the lines visually crowding in on one another, decreasing legibility.

Keep it short Ranged-left, sans-serif type is highly legible in short amounts. However, there is debate about its legibility across large quantities of texts, such as books. Here, it is effective, readable, and visually attractive.

⊙ ASSIGNMENT: (A)SYMMETRY EXPERIMENT

Using InDesign, set a piece of text of approximately 300 words in length.

1 Apply a number of different line lengths, leading values, fonts, typestyles (including capitals, lowercase, bold, condensed, serif/sans-serif, etc) and sizes.

2 Switch between ranged left, ranged right and justified settings.

As you proceed, carefully keep all your printouts, and mark them with an indication of the variations. This will build a collection of examples quite quickly. In each instance, ask yourself which are the most legible examples of text-setting. Make notes on the printouts and keep them in a file for reference.

Another useful exercise is to start a collection of text-setting from books/magazines, etc. that you think are good and/or bad. Make a note of typefaces, sizes used, measures, etc so that you can start to see what does or doesn't work.

◄ Suitable settings

This book cover design uses a good length of line (measure), ranged left, on a well-chosen leading, in a sympathetic typeface (sans-serif).

▶ Space your capitals

Capitals used sparing in titles are legible if properly letterspaced (or kerned, see p76). Here the designer has used justified text, instead of ranged left. The text is quite closely line-spaced (or leading, see p76), and may have benefited from extra space between the lines. However, it makes a striking companion design to the one above.

◯ Well judged The typography in this design is beautifully judged in terms of line length, size of type, measure and leading, making it easily legible.

PART 1	PRINCIPLES
UNIT 3	FUNDAMENTALS OF TYPOGRAPHY
MODULE 6	**Typographic emphasis and hierarchy**

Learning how to solve problems of emphasis using type is a crucial skill. This involves considering the relationship between size and weight of type, position on the page, and between elements, along with developing an understanding of how these decisions call forth some contents while suppressing others. These kinds of typographic decisions relate to what are called 'hierarchies' of information, since in any design, some things will need to be read first, whereas other information is secondary.

Key data The use of large-scale serif typography and fields of colour/reversed-out type call attention to the date, creating a hierarchy of information that emphasises the important content.

Page structure The bold slab-serif typeface and varied sizes of type clearly differentiate titles from text, establishing a strong structure.

Before starting any design, it is crucial to understand where the main points of emphasis fall in terms of headings, subheadings, intro copy, captions, quotes and so on. These levels of importance are called hierarchies. Once established, hierarchies can be indicated in various ways, mainly by space, weight and form.

• Adding vertical space in the form of a one-line space or half-line space, above or below a heading (separating it from surrounding elements) creates emphasis. You may not need to employ extra spacing around headings if you use bold type.

• The density of black ink creates its own visual emphasis. Sans-serif typefaces, such as Univers, are good for this because they typically have various weight combinations you can use: light with bold, medium with extra bold and so on. Bear in mind that a smaller size of bold type is visually 'heavier' than a larger size of regular-weight type.

• Changing the typestyle is a third method – switching from roman to italics, for example. Italics add informality and movement to a design and are also effective for highlighting key phrases within text. Because of their more delicate form, you will probably need to increase the size proportionally for italic headings.

• Changing some lowercase to capitals can add formality to a design. Capitals need more letterspacing, and so consume more space, though you don't have the problem of ascenders clashing with descenders. Small capitals provide an even more subtle shift of emphasis.

The power of contrast

Other techniques involving the use of contrast can be applied to add emphasis effectively.

• Contrasting condensed with extended type can be effective, but you have to be careful not to overdo the visual shift of emphasis. Remember, too, that condensed type requires more leading, and expanded type pushes out the length of the copy. A simple yet effective form of emphasis is to use indents at the start of paragraphs or sections.

• Colour is another technique you can employ. Make sure that you have sufficient contrast between the colour and the stock on which you are printing. When adding colour to type, consider using a typeface with more weight, which provides a larger area of colour. Reversing out type or adding rules are other ways of drawing attention to parts of the text.

• Changing type size or weight is a popular option. Again, be careful when using shifts of size for emphasis to ensure that there is a substantial difference between the main text and the heading. If the sizes are too close, then the point is not made. The difference in size has to be great enough to make the point.

Less is more

Try not to have too many means of emphasis going on at once. Too many techniques in one place means the eye becomes quickly confused. 'Less is more' is often a good principle when trying to work through problems of emphasis and hierarchy. For instance, don't overstate your points by setting type in a large size, bold, italics, underlined and at an angle. This would be overkill. With computers, it is easy to change things and you need to be disciplined to avoid creating a mishmash of weights, sizes, forms and indents. Resist the temptation to use all your techniques at once, and remember, you do not always have to shout to be heard.

Type size

Your choice of font, weight of heading or amount of leading all depend on other decisions you have made. The same is true of type size: point size is an absolute measure of how big type is, but the same-sized type can look very different depending on other

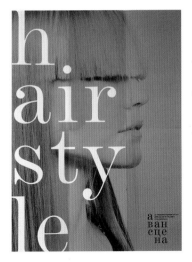

◀ Create contrast
The contrast between background image and large, lowercase, reversed-out text produces an elegant, sensitively handled, and striking design.

Sizing
If you think it should be 10pt, make it 9. It's often the case that when we try to differentiate and create hierarchies through type we overemphasise the importance of size. Try to use space and position before enlarging the size of your type. If anything, keep the type slightly smaller than you think it should be.

SEE ALSO:
FUNDAMENTALS OF COLOUR P92

◀ ▼ Heavy type and space
Simple solutions, such as dramatic use of space, are often more effective than employing many typefaces and filling the page.

factors – the amount of space around it, the relative
size of the text copy, the weight of font used and so on.
The central point about increasing type size is that it
works as a strong form of emphasis, providing a focal
point that attracts the reader's attention.

Headings

Once agreement has been reached about the
different levels of importance in the main text, they
need to be translated into appropriate sizes. If headings
are of varying levels of importance, try to make sure
they are visually segregated. For example, the top level
of heading might be in 48pt, with the next one down
being 24pt. Any closer in size, and readers might have
trouble separating one from another.

There are numerous ways in which you can play with
headings to improve the visual feel of a design.
• Breaking a line or word into different parts, or using
alternating sizes with a heading, can look dynamic. For
example, articles and conjunctions ('a', 'the', 'and', 'or',
etc) could be made smaller to give important words
more stress.
• The names of magazines (known as the masthead),
billboards intended primarily for motorists, newspaper
headlines and posters are all attempting to catch
people's attention, within a short time span, and so
they often need to have large, well-differentiated type
to communicate effectively and quickly. Books, on
the other hand, work in a slower time, and their
typographic presentation can be more subtle.

film scoring stages

"The requirements of a major film score mean
you need enough room to accommodate a large
orchestra, perhaps of 100 players or
more, and a choir too."

Following the flow Different levels of size emphasis, combined with italics, set out three or more levels of information within the text of this book.

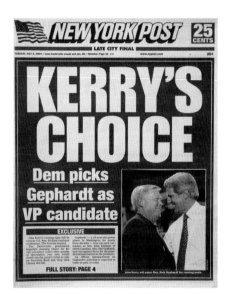

Be organised It's especially important to create a strong emphasis and hierarchy within newspapers and magazines. Typical newspaper style follows the organisational principles of bold headings, which 'speak' clearly and emphatically, and a clear visual structure.

Lively layouts These layouts for *Inmotion* magazine on film scoring (left) and advertising imagery (right), provide clear indications to the reader about informational hierarchies, and order of reading. Good typography will order, contextualise and enrich the reading experience, through varied layouts such as these.

◐ ASSIGNMENT: DESIGNING AN INVITATION CARD

Work with the text below in an A5 (210 x 148mm) landscape or portrait format. Before beginning to design, make sure you have read the copy carefully, and have made some decisions about the main points of emphasis, based on your understanding of the content.

1 Choose only one size of a single typeface, and try at least three of the techniques of typographic emphasis discussed in this module.

2 Now add in the variable of different sizes of type, and do the assignment again.

3 Add a second colour to your design.

You are invited to a private view of the work of graphic design students in their final year at [insert your own college] College of Art on January 12, at the main college campus Victoria Street, [add your city or town], at 8 pm
RSVP
Secretary Design School
[insert your own college] College of Art
[insert address]

PART 1	PRINCIPLES
UNIT 3	FUNDAMENTALS OF TYPOGRAPHY
MODULE 7	**Typographic rules/boxes and ornaments**

Typographic rules and ornaments have been inherited from the letterpress tradition of setting and arranging type matter. The reason they are still invaluable to the designer today is because they serve both functional and aesthetic roles.

Rules draw attention to specific parts of copy and break it into sections. Generally, vertical rules should be used to separate blocks of text only when other means of division are neither possible nor sufficient.

Generally, the weight (thickness) of the rules should match the tonal value of the text to which they relate. Horizontal rules work well for organising information and helping readability. Examples can be found in tabular matter, such as timetables and contents pages, and sometimes between columns of text in newspapers and/ or in books, where they can be used between each entry, and to help direct the eye from item to page number.

Highlighting text

Rules have gained in popularity since the introduction of DTP, in which a single command can underline a word or words. Some designers argue that there are more subtle means available if you want to emphasise typographic elements. Nevertheless, rules can be effectively used to highlight a piece of copy by placing them in the margin alongside the text, or as a dynamic component in the composition of a design. Widths available range from a ½-pt (hairline) rule upwards, and are often measured in points, so that we might use a 4pt or 6pt rule.

Tinted, outlined or solid-coloured panels are popular in newspapers for their ability to provide in-depth focus on a particular editorial theme, while relieving the eye from the potential strain caused by reading column after

column of main text type in a single size. However, rules and boxes can easily overtake a design, particularly when they are used 'decoratively' rather than functionally.

Rules in display type

In display setting, rules can create emphasis by drawing attention. The Constructivist art movement in early 20th-century Russia pioneered the use of rules in this way. Very heavy rules were used, running alongside, or at angles to, the copy. The popularity of the rule is still evident in today's designs.

Ornaments

Ornaments have been in use since the origin of printing, and they give a decorative feel to a layout, and invoke a sense of tradition. They can also separate information, as in the title pages of traditional books. Zapf Dingbats is a well-known digital font made up of ornaments, as is Whirligig, by Zuzana Licko. However, as with rules and boxes or sidebars, over-use of ornaments should generally be avoided.

⊕ SEE ALSO: READABILITY AND LEGIBILITY P80
TYPOGRAPHIC EMPHASIS AND HIERARCHY P84

SEE ALSO: READABILITY AND LEGIBILITY P80 TYPOGRAPHIC EMPHASIS AND HIERARCHY P84

GLOSSARY

Ornaments: Typed characters that embellish the page. Also known as 'flowers'.

Panel: Device used to highlight information. Also known as a 'sidebar'.

Typographic rules: Printed lines that direct the reader's eye.

⌄ ⟩ Digital ornaments
'Whirligig' by Zuzana Licko (for Emigré, 1994), consists of contemporary ornamental elements, produced digitally.

Ordered design The use of rules to reference an underlying grid structure can effectively divide both textual information and imagery, giving a strong sense of order to a design.

Dynamic contrast
Strong diagonal rules contrast well with a lighter weight of sans-serif typography to form a dynamic design.

Break it up Designs such as this are influenced by Russian Constructivism and Dutch design, and use rules as a way to break up the visual surface of the page in dynamic ways.

ASSIGNMENT:
ADDING RULES

Using rules of varying weights and lengths, add a single rule or several rules to a piece of design that previously included only type. This can be a design that you have made yourself, or one that you find. How can your use of rule(s):

- Enhance readability?
- Separate information?
- Create a more dynamic design?

Relieving the strain
The use of rules in traditional newspaper design relieves the eye from the strain of lengthy reading. Long sections of text are broken up by the use of rules placed in the gutters between columns.

Question

Can you find an example of an effective use of ornament(s), from a book printed before 1900, and one after 1900? These might involve different kinds of ornaments (ie traditional/non-traditional).

PART 1	PRINCIPLES
UNIT 3	FUNDAMENTALS OF TYPOGRAPHY
MODULE 8	**Text as image**

Designers have long exploited the fact that type not only communicates specific meaning, but also possesses aesthetically powerful characteristics in its own right. If you think about how many expressive fonts are now available, and the way in which one can apply colour, weight, form and spacing to achieve specific effects, it is possible to see type functioning as an image in its own right. Illustrative, photographic, calligraphic and shaped text are further variations. Working with text as image requires an understanding of both the communicative and aesthetic properties of typography.

Onomatopoeia: In typography, the use of type to suggest the sounds of a spoken language, such as adding a large 'o' to the word 'open'. Marinetti and the Futurists were effective in employing onomatopoeia, in the design of books such as *Zang Tumb Tumb* (see page 40).

⟩ **Layer it up** Many layers of shredded text create the pages of this three-dimensional book, in which the text is overlapping and tactile.

⌃ **Integration** Combining calligraphy with bird shapes creates a lively series of forms in which text and image are fully integrated.

⌃ **Defining the shape** The negative space produced by a series of drawn letterforms defines the shape of the letter 'a'.

Display type is chosen, in part, for mood, and each face has its own characteristics. Just as an artist can create mood through illustration, so can a typographer subtly illustrate meaning by choice of font, type size and weight. This effect of typography is normally seen at its fullest potential when type is used for display (above a certain size, for example 14pt), since smaller type is meant for reading. Display type exploits the specific characteristics of a given typeface.

Symbolisation

Designers can exploit the familiarity of type by carefully manipulating suggestive letterforms so that they become images in their own right. This means that type can actually stand in for objects. For example, two capital 'O's can look like a pair of spectacles or the wheels of a car, a lowercase 'j' resembles a hook and an uppercase 'Z' can look like a flash of lightning. Conversely, images can metamorphose into type: a pair of compasses can form a capital 'A' and tumbling acrobats easily lend themselves to the letter 'D'.

Form matching content

Techniques for using type as illustration are numerous and transcend type as simple objects and vice versa. Certain words, such as verbs indicating action, particularly lend themselves to typography reflecting meaning (imagine 'zoom' with six 'o's instead of four, or 'jump' where the 'm' is lifted off the baseline). There can be word repetition; overlapping of characters; distorting characters to break them up, blur or roughen them; outlining or shadowing type; setting type along a curved path or in a circle; adjusting colour, weight or form – and so on. To be effective, however, positions and forms in type arrangement must reflect meaning, and when working in this way, try to avoid clichés.

To be used effectively, our Latin alphabet, composed basically of straight lines, circles and part circles, has to be resourcefully manipulated. However, calligraphic scripts such as Arabic, which are flowing and organic, lend themselves much more readily to such graphic techniques. The decorative nature of shaped text transforms reading into a visual experience, and advertising and logotype design frequently use these techniques to give text enhanced visual impact to convey a specific message.

⟩ **Drawing attention** Outlines, drop-shadows and multiple colours can transform a word, making it the central focus of a series of pages.

JOHNNY HARDSTAFF

Interview

Using light
Sheet metal with hand-punched lettering utilises light and shadow to convey additional meaning. The piece also operates as a stencil.

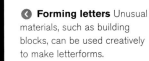

⊙ **Forming letters** Unusual materials, such as building blocks, can be used creatively to make letterforms.

⊙ ASSIGNMENT: **TEXT AS IMAGE**

Experiment with text as image, to create alternative typographic designs. Choose a short text, poem or something you have written yourself. Consider carefully the meaning of the text, making sketches and notes as part of the initial process. Using only typography, handwritten lettering and/or alternative materials (no images), explore/express the meaning of your text, through approaches which might include the following (but experiment in your own ways):

1 Use abstract/simple geometric shapes only: text set inside or as the contours of circles, triangles, lines, curved lines, to express the meaning of your text.

2 Use alternative materials to create your letterforms: anything but printed material. Think 'outside the box'. Work in three dimensions (see examples to the left).

3 Create a design which relies on handwritten letterforms only. No computer typography.

4 Work only with the abstract shapes of letterforms themselves, including counterforms, internal/external contours, negative/positive spaces and overlapping or separate colour.

⊙ **Question**

Are there specific examples of logotype design that you see employing text-as-image? How effective do you think they are?

⓵ **Design history**

Having a good knowledge of design history enables you to pursue type-as-image concepts in a more informed way. Look at the work of Josef Müller-Brockmann, H. N. Werkman and Philippe Apeloig. Also see examples of calligraphy and shaped text throughout history, and you will see how typographers, artists and designers have exploited type-as-image to enhance meaning.

⊙ **Letters as images** The capital letters 'M' and 'Y', in a light serif font, combine to make a shirt and collar; including a pocket and bow-tie transforms it into a logo.

4 FUNDAMENTALS OF COLOUR

An understanding of colour is essential to the designer's skill set. There are tens of thousands of colours at the designer's disposal – and infinite ways of combining them across many media, from printed inks to screen-based colour, all with their own characteristics.

When choosing which colours to incorporate into your design, you will need to consider issues of contrast and harmony, and how these might affect legibility. The psychology of colour is also important in making sure the colours convey the correct message at an unconscious level and that the chosen colours are suitable for the audience your project is intended to reach.

PART 1	PRINCIPLES
UNIT 4	FUNDAMENTALS OF COLOUR
MODULE 1	**Colour terminology**

To understand how to choose or assign colour for a specific purpose, the designer must first develop a knowledge of how colour works, how colours are classified and the terms used to describe them.

Colour is differentiated in three main ways: hue, tone and saturation. 'Hue' refers to the colour's generic name, for example, red or blue. A single hue will have many variations ranging from light (tint) to dark (shade). This is referred to as 'tone'. A single hue will also vary according to its 'saturation' or chroma (also known as intensity). Saturation ranges from full intensity to low intensity or from brightness to greyness. Colour can also be described by its temperature and movement; for example, hues in the red spectrum appear warmer and closer to the viewer than hues in the blue spectrum, which appear colder and farther away.

'Complementary' colours, such as red and green, lie opposite each other on the colour wheel, whereas 'analogous' colours, such as green and blue, lie adjacent to each other. The former are associated with contrast; the latter are linked to harmony. This leads to an analysis of how colours affect each other when combined in a scheme.

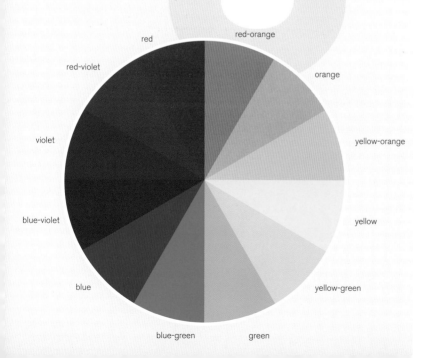

Colour wheel Primary, secondary and tertiary colours of pigment are shown on the wheel. The primary colours are red, yellow and blue. Secondary colours are made by mixing any two primary colours together, producing orange, green and violet. A tertiary colour is produced by mixing a primary colour with the secondary colour nearest to it on the wheel. The tertiary colours here are red-orange, yellow-orange, yellow-green, blue-green, blue-violet and red-violet.

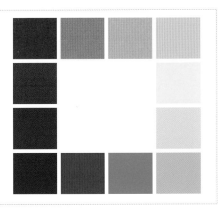

⌃ **Hue** distinguishes one colour from another. It is the generic name of the colour – red, say, as opposed to blue.

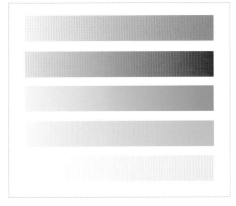

⌃ **Tone** (or value) is the relative lightness or darkness of a colour. A colour with added white is called a tint; a colour with added black is called a shade.

Additive colour: System used on monitors and televisions, based on RGB (red, green, blue). When combined, these form white light.

Analogous colour: Colours, such as blue and green, that lie adjacent to each other on the colour wheel.

CMYK: Cyan, magenta, yellow, key (black): the four colours that make up the full-colour printing process.

Complementary colour: Colours, such as red and green, that lie opposite each other on the colour wheel.

Gamut: The complete range of colours available within one system of reproduction, eg, CMYK gamut or RGB gamut.

Primaries: Red, yellow, blue.

Secondaries: A mix of any two primaries.

Spot colour: Any flat colour, printed as a solid, and not made up of CMYK.

Subtractive colour: System used in printing, based on CMYK colours.

Tertiaries: A mix of any two secondaries.

⊕ **SEE ALSO:** PRINTED COLOUR P128
WORKSPACE, MONITOR AND CALIBRATION P136

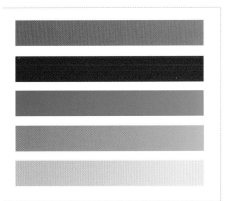

⌃ **Saturation** (or chroma) is roughly equivalent to brightness. A line of high intensity is a bright colour, whereas one of low intensity is a dull colour. Two colours can be of the same line but have different intensities.

Additive and subtractive primaries

To understand how colour works, the most important point to know is that coloured light (additive colours or the RGB system) and coloured pigment (subtractive colours or the CMYK system) do not work in the same way. To put this differently, if you are working with your computer, the colour on your monitor (RGB system) will not be the same as the colour that is printed (CYMK system). This phenomenon creates problems for printed projects, since colours on-screen appear brighter than in print.

With printed matter you will be working with subtractive colour. Here, each colour printed onto a paper stock subtracts from white, and if the three primaries overlap, black results. The colour wheel shows primary colours;

FURTHER READING

http://www.huevaluechroma.com/
Further information on colour.

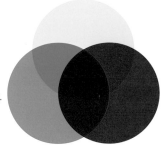

▶ **Printing primaries**
Subtractive primaries and CMYK – cyan, magenta, yellow and key (black) – are the primaries used in printing. When combined, subtractive colours make black.

▶ **On-screen colour**
Additive primaries and RGB light are used to create colours on computers, televisions and monitors. Combined, the additive primaries result in white light.

the subtractive primaries are red, yellow and blue. Secondaries are a mix of any two primaries, resulting in orange, green and violet, and tertiaries are a mix of any two secondaries. The term 'full colour' refers to four-colour printing and to achieve a full range of colours, printers use cyan, yellow, magenta and black (known as CMYK; K = black = key colour).

Pantone

An additional colour used in a layout is called a 'flat colour' or sometimes a 'spot colour'. When selecting colours for this, you should use a universal matching system known as Pantone Matching System (PMS). Pantone colour is mixed from 15 pigments (including black and white) and is primarily used for print colour matching. This system is different to the CMYK system and few colours can be matched between them. For more information see pages 136–137.

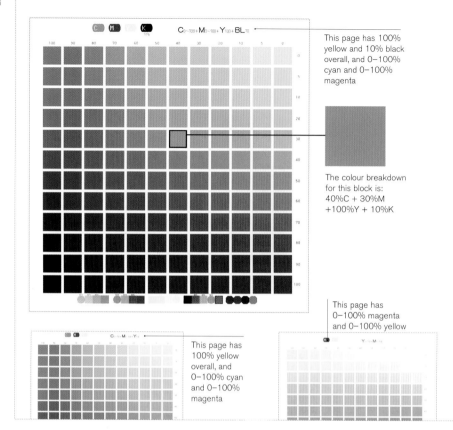

This page has 100% yellow and 10% black overall, and 0–100% cyan and 0–100% magenta

The colour breakdown for this block is: 40%C + 30%M +100%Y + 10%K

This page has 100% yellow overall, and 0–100% cyan and 0–100% magenta

This page has 0–100% magenta and 0–100% yellow

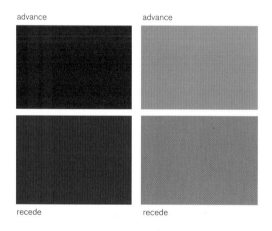

advance

advance

recede

recede

⌃ **Advancing/receding** Some colours appear to advance, while others seem to recede. If you want to make something come towards the viewer, choose warm colours, such as red or orange. Blues and greens seem to recede when set next to red.

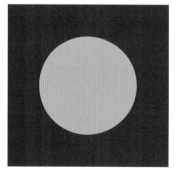

⌃ **Simultaneous contrast** The circle shown in these two images is the same hue, tone and saturation but, when married up to different colours, appears to be different intensities.

▶ **Temperature** Colours appear hotter as yellow diminishes and red increases. Blue is very cold. Green is slightly warmer because of the addition of yellow.

FURTHER READING

http://www.source-promo.com/ PANTONE

Online guide to the Pantone range.

Process charts

When printing in full colour (CMYK) you will find it useful to identify and specify the exact colour that you want to see printed by using a printer's process colour guide. This will show you all of the colours that you can make by specifying and combining different tints of cyan, magenta, yellow and black. Once you have chosen your colour, you can make a new swatch on your document, specifying the different tints. This is the only accurate way to specify the printed colour that you will achieve when ink goes onto paper.

Overlap This design uses overlapping colour in an innovative way, suggesting the transparency of printing inks. The mixture of various colours creates new tones.

Advancing and receding colour: Colours in the red spectrum appear to advance to the human eye, whereas those in the blue spectrum appear to recede.

Simultaneous contrast: The human eye tends to differentiate between two neighbouring colours by emphasising their differences rather than their similarities – background colours affect foreground colours (the image).

Vibration: Complementary colours of equal lightness and high saturation tend to make each other appear more brilliant.

Weight: Colours differ in 'weight'. For example, if a man was to move two large boxes equal in size but one pale green and the other dark brown, he would probably pick up the green one because it appeared lighter. It is generally assumed that blue-greens look lighter whereas reds appear stronger, and therefore heavier.

○ ASSIGNMENT: **DEFINING COLOURS**

This exercise is best tackled in Photoshop, but can also be undertaken in InDesign. Working to a landscape format, set the word 'colour' in lowercase in a sans-serif bold type, such as Helvetica Bold. The size should be such that it occupies at least two-thirds of the width of the format. Centre the word. Now, using the word 'colour', do these experiments, each one on a new page.

• **Advancing colour** Select two different hues, one for the image (the word 'colour') and one for the background in such a way that the image advances.
• **Receding colour** Repeat the above but alter the colours so that the image recedes.
• **Tints** Choosing two tints of a hue, use one for the image and one for the background. Do two variations, one showing good legibility and one poor legibility.
• **Simultaneous contrast** Using the same hue for the image, alter the background hue and note how the appearance of the image changes.
• **Analogous** Select two hues to demonstrate this term.
• **Complementary** Select two hues to demonstrate this term.

Knowledge of the context in which finished work will be viewed is fundamental to use of colour in graphic design. How that colour is perceived – and how legible it is – will vary depending on whether it is viewed on a screen or in a print-based medium. Colour has a dramatic effect on legibility, and needs to be considered carefully. Contrast and harmony are ways in which a design can be further enhanced.

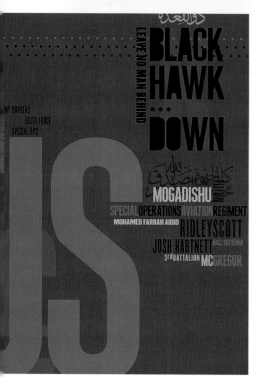

⌃ Multicolour It can be difficult to achieve an effective design with multiple colours, but here they are used harmoniously.

‹ Limits of legibility Coloured in different levels of grey, the larger type allows for lesser contrast whereas the smaller type requires high contrast.

› Colour first Even in the initial research stage, colour is an important consideration. Here, the designer has worked through various options, combinations and palettes.

On-screen you will be working with additive colours (the RGB system). However, as explained in Module 1 problems can occur on translation to print in subtractive colours (the CMYK system), since colours appear brighter on-screen than in print. Both clients and designers can be misled into expecting printed colours to have the same saturation and tonal range as those approved on-screen.

Colour legibility

Legibility refers to how clearly something can be read. Many factors can influence colour perception:
• lighting and viewing conditions in the reading environment, which have a clear effect on the legibility of both print- and screen-based work – compare viewing a monitor in a darkened room and under direct sunlight;
• selection of colours;
• backgrounds on which colours are printed; and
• size and shape of type or image used.
Good colour legibility is achieved when ground and colour are opposites, for example, violet (the colour nearest to black) on a white ground. On this same ground, legibility decreases by moving the image colour towards yellow. Contrast is key to legibility, and this means using your knowledge of the colour wheel. Greatest contrast is a violet image on a yellow ground; poorest legibility results from a red-orange image on a red ground.

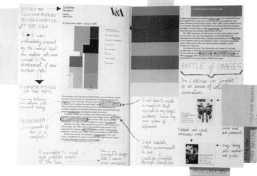

◀ Duotone printing Using half-tones in two different coloured inks to build up a full tonal range is a cost-effective way of creating rich imagery with two colours instead of four.

⊕ **SEE ALSO:** READABILITY AND LEGIBILITY P80

TYPOGRAPHIC EMPHASIS AND HIERARCHY P84

COLOUR TERMINOLOGY P92

PRODUCTION PROCESS AND ISSUES P126

Contrast and harmony

Colour should both contribute to and support the content of a design, and reinforce the ideas you want to give visual form to. Therefore, it is important to understand how colour can work in contrast and in harmony. These are related to legibility and colour associations, and affect both design function and perception.

Colour proportion is a key decision – for example, a small amount of bright red in a complementary scheme can have a bigger impact than equal proportions of red and green. Furthermore, equal amounts of a saturated red and green can result in an unpleasant visual discord, avoided by varying the saturation levels of the hues. By using a greater proportion of green with less saturation and a red with good saturation, the red is given extra emphasis. With analogous schemes, the hues tend to have less vibrancy and therefore similar proportions can be contemplated.

Designers who develop an understanding of the complex and subtle ways in which colours interact will be able to explore new ways to express graphic ideas. Practical needs such as legibility and the requirements of the work should always be considered.

◀ Brought to the fore The darker letters come forwards whereas the lighter-coloured letters recede, reducing legibility while drawing attention to the text.

▶ Backgrounds The simple use of a greyscale image with a bold overlay of red sets up an ease of legibility – the subsequent type dropped out in white is easy to read, whereas the red text recedes into the background.

○ ASSIGNMENT: **LEGIBILITY EXPERIMENTS**

Type the word 'legibility' in landscape format on a white background. Now do these exercises:

1 Set the word 'legibility' in a colour that stands out strongly against the white ground (violet, for example). Now change its colour, gradually moving through the colour wheel from blue, green, red, orange, and finally to yellow. You will see that this is the most difficult colour to read against white.

2 Show the word 'legibility' against a ground of contrasting colours. For example, change the word to yellow on a violet ground, then orange on a blue ground. Continue with increasingly similar colours until you finish with a red-orange word on a red ground – the least legible combination of colours.

● **Traditional meanings** These images show two traditional uses of colour association: red, moving towards maroon, associated with love, passion and Valentine's Day; and lime green on cedar, associated with vegetation, growth and springtime.

PART 1 | PRINCIPLES

UNIT 4 | FUNDAMENTALS OF COLOUR

MODULE 3 | **Colour associations**

Why are certain colours preferred, or seen to be more effective? It is because colours have, throughout history, come to hold particular associations that most likely derive from nature, and have, over time, become rooted in human psychology. They have come to possess cultural, symbolic and often personal associations. To use it well, you need to understand how colour works both as a language and as a system of signs, and how it creates an emotional response.

● **Coloured boxes** The coloured strips on these black boxes have been chosen to enforce the meaning of the text: intense red for sensuality, duck-egg blue for calm wisdom and industrial mid-grey for power.

Intelligence, memory, experience, history, culture: all play a part in colour perception. It is not that each individual perceives colours differently, just that such perceptions have subtly different meanings depending on psychology and cultural background. Colours have symbolic associations in all societies depending on context; different cultures apply different meanings. For example:
• Black is the colour of mourning and death in the industrialised West, whereas in China and India it is white.
• Red does not have the instant conventional association with 'stop' in those countries where automobiles are still rare.
• Green was associated with poison in the 19th century, through its links with arsenic, whereas today it is seen as the colour of spring and environmental awareness.
• Blue is associated with postage in the US – whereas in Sweden or Britain you would look for the colour red. These examples show that colour meaning changes over time and across different cultures. If you are designing in international markets, you should be particularly aware of such differences.

● **Muted palette** The neutrals used in these packaging designs are associated with history and a 'nature' aesthetic.

○ **Question**

Why do some colours change their 'associations' over time, and why do others stay relatively the same? What factors are involved?

◉ ASSIGNMENT: **ASSOCIATION COLLECTION**

1 Consider colours of red, green, yellow and blue and explore your associations with each. Some of your associations will be universal (shared with other people); others subjective (highly personal).

2 Research meanings, associations and connotations of each colour in different situations, such as road signs, clothing, different cultures. Try to find as many different/unusual ways of viewing the colour as possible – for example, a colour may have different meanings in different time periods.

3 Keep a note of these findings, and compile a sketchbook of colour references and information.

Colour in emotion and language

While colour associations are highly subjective, despite local differences, colours and hues may have some universal characteristics. Reds, oranges and yellows stimulate the senses and tend to be perceived as 'warm' – capable of exciting feelings of cheeriness, good health or aggression; opposite on the colour wheel, blues and greens are seen as 'cool', with connotations of calmness, peace, safety and/or depression. On a visual level, reds advance towards the viewer, whereas blues recede.

Other dimensions also influence perception. Compositions close in value seem hazy, vague or introspective, whereas dark designs are evocative of night, fear or mystery. High colour intensities are dynamic and create a feeling of movement. Clearly, colours are rooted in psychology, as they are used figuratively to describe feelings, for example: 'He turned purple with rage', 'I'm feeling blue', 'She turned green with envy'.

COLOUR THEORISTS

Josef Albers (1888–1967) proposed that colours are never stationary; that is, they are constantly changing in relation to the colours surrounding them.

Johannes Itten (1888–1967) created colour experiments based on contrasts such as temperature or hue, and associations based on seasons.

Wassily Kandinsky (1866–1944) developed his colour usage in terms of spiritual moods and relations to musical instruments and sounds. His paintings are a synthetic colour expression of sound.

Wilhelm Ostwald (1853–1932) set up an order of colours based around the concepts of harmony and disharmony.

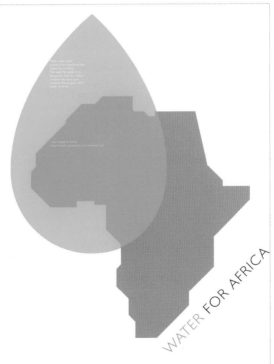

WATER FOR AFRICA

⊕ **SEE ALSO:** COLOUR TERMINOLOGY P92

⊗ **In the mix** The mixture of vibrant colours suggests the mix of contemporary music sounds.

◄ **A message in colour** This simple use of colour tells a story we immediately see: the life-giving blue water over the sand-coloured shape of Africa turns the land green, or fertile.

❯ **Design classic** The London Underground map is based on the 1931 design by Harry Beck. The design has undergone many changes, moving from an accurately spaced to a schematic design, but the colours of the lines have changed little from its first inception. Different colours for different lines enable passengers to trace easily the line that they need to travel on.

➕ **SEE ALSO:** TYPOGRAPHIC EMPHASIS AND HIERARCHY P84

COLOUR ASSOCIATIONS P98

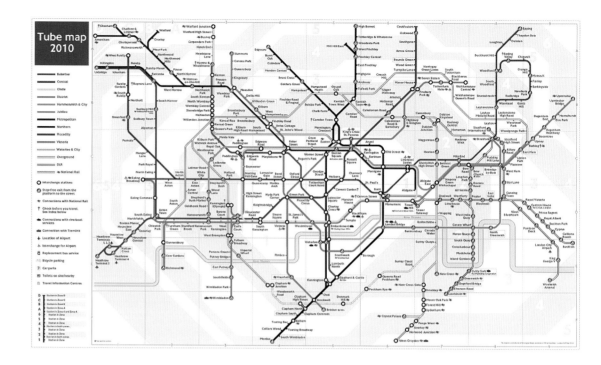

PART 1 | PRINCIPLES

UNIT 4 | FUNDAMENTALS OF COLOUR

MODULE 4 | **Colour as information**

Colour is a powerful tool, especially in information design, where it is used to help the designer organise data into various structures, and to aid the experience of 'reading' a design. Psychologists have proved that the colour of an object is seen before its shape and details. Because colour works at this basic level, it is very good at keeping things delineated, reinforcing informational hierarchies, guiding the eye through complex systems and data and aiding navigation through physical spaces.

Systems are anything that contain a flow of complex information – maps, signage, sections, structures, web pages. Colour helps to categorise that information.

• Complex buildings, such as hospitals and airports, need excellent signage systems to help people negotiate through large, complicated architectural spaces. Colour is an obvious means to correct paths. Many shopping malls are so large that parking zones are now colour coded – a memorable way to help you find your vehicle.

• The London Underground map, developed by engineer Harry Beck, is one of the most famous maps in city transport. Beck used colour to differentiate lines, so that people could readily identify the right route. The map is schematic: it is a simplified diagram that uses abstract graphic elements (lines) to represent a complex real-world situation. This most original of designs is a model copied in various forms throughout the world, including the Paris and New York City metro systems.

❯ **Colour as symbolism**
The colour of a symbol can suggest and enhance the information it conveys.

• In finance, colour has traditionally been used in many ways. Debits in balance sheets would be in red to denote arrears, hence the phrase 'in the red'. This custom is still in use to separate trading figures from year to year.

• Charts apply colour to quantitative and statistical information, where differing quantities of data need to be reinforced.

• Catalogues and books often have different colour-coded sections to aid navigation through pages. Penguin Books introduced the first paperbacks in Britain in the 1930s using a bright orange background. This colour quickly became fused with the books' identity. Later, the same publisher introduced another imprint, called Pelican, whose books were given a blue background. Customers quickly came to recognise the differences through the use of colour. Such visual associations can also help to delineate sections within a body of text and highlight a number of different levels of importance. The designer can set crucial parts in a bold typeface and use a different colour from the rest of the text. The eye picks up this difference very quickly.

• Web designers use colour to help people navigate through the structure of a site.

Clarity In the chaos of an airport, white, yellow and blue stand out on a black background, and the gates are attractively colour coded.

Colour and symbolism Internationally recognised, the red cross is easily seen and clearly marks the entrance to the emergency unit.

◉ ASSIGNMENT: MAP-MAKING

Design a simple map, showing your journey from home to the nearest library or railway station. Annotate the map with as many different types of labels as you wish; these could be street names, bus stops, churches, shops, etc. Use only black and white in your first version. Then repeat the design, this time using colour to differentiate the labels. From this small experiment you should see how important colour is to the information designer. Be aware that colours such as yellow do not stand out on a white background as sharply as a bright red, so you should think carefully about which colours you use and how they are 'read'.

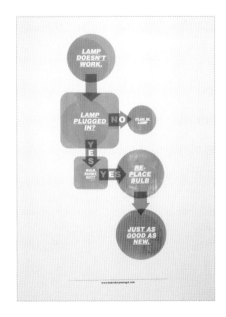

Go with the flow This advertising design emulates a flowchart and uses colour to differentiate between the delineation of questions (red) and directional devices (blue arrows).

Practice

By now, you should have a good grasp of the fundamental skills, attitudes, research, conceptual, contextual, and formal concerns of design, all of which come together to form the 'language' of design. In the second half of the book, you will be introduced to the extended tools and techniques of design, which form a key group of skills for professional practice in any field in which you choose to specialise. Theory and practice are not divorced from one another, and a thorough understanding of each, and of their relationship, is crucial. At the same time, no designer can ignore the requirements of technology, and while you may use these powerful tools regularly in the production of work, it is essential that you familiarise yourself with the industry-standard technologies that designers utilise.

However, these tools cannot generate the idea, nor can they execute the design for you, and the kinds of conceptual, intellectual and formal skills you bring are what will differentiate you from other designers. In short, you need both an excellent understanding of principles, alongside outstanding technical skills, in order to work as a designer in any aspect of the industry. Being able to design formally and/or conceptually eloquent and innovative work is only half the story, since you then need to get the work into print, on screen, in three-dimensions or across multiple browsers, etc. 'Design is the battle, but printing is the war', perfectly captures the problems designers face when getting a design from the sketch stage, to a final, printed piece of work.

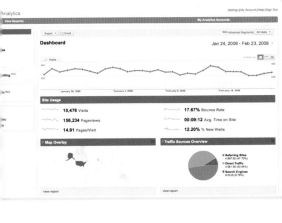

Unit 5 introduces basic image-making and sourcing, followed by an overview of the key technical and software skills used in design today, including Photoshop and InDesign. In Unit 6, various production issues, including colour for print, PDFs, paper stocks and press checks are introduced. Unit 7 is dedicated to web design, and summarises the specific technical skills, tools and languages it requires. Unit 8 overviews seven of the key areas of design, including editorial design, web design and motion graphics. These "tasters" aim to give a sense of the key skills and aptitudes needed to work in each field, the highs and lows of each profession and provide pointers to additional resources, including 'Best in the business', which highlights some of the most influential practitioners in that area of design.

5 TOOLS AND TECHNOLOGIES

The emergence of digital technologies has revolutionised graphic design practice. Where previously typographers would set type, pre-press production would be undertaken by specialists within a printing house and designers would commission a photographer, now one person can do all of these jobs on a computer, under the gamut of desktop publishing (DTP).

This unit introduces you to the software applications and tools that are most commonly used in the graphic design industry today. Each module focuses on a specific medium, such as photography, or a specific software application, such as Photoshop, grounding you in its unique tools, history and terminology, giving you the opportunity to explore further.

PART 2	PRACTICE
UNIT 5	TOOLS AND TECHNOLOGIES
MODULE 1	**Photography basics and image sourcing**

Photography and image-making/sourcing are key elements for a graphic designer. Even if the designer does not specialise in photography, or even if this is not a secondary skill, knowledge and understanding of this discipline are invaluable: to help work out rough proportions, to understand composition and as research for drawing and/or digital illustration.

There are four broad categories of photography and image production that are relevant to designers.
1 Objects and products
2 Portraits and images of people
3 Landscapes and buildings
4 Ephemera and texture

The skill lies in ensuring the qualities of the image fit the purpose. For example, product images are generally brightly lit, sharp and clear, whereas landscapes and portraits have a variety of styles. Your designs will be more powerful if you learn how to spot an effective, well-composed picture, with a good tonal range, which combines effectively with typography, tints and other illustrations. There are many reasons why one image will capture your imagination but another will make you turn the page without stopping to look. It helps if a picture is in focus, correctly exposed, placed where it is shown off at its best and has some interesting content. For an image to work well it must make you stop and think, forcing you to reassess the familiar.

◀ **Dramatic diagonals** Add drama to any photograph by creating a tension within the standard rectilinear format.

⬇ **Long lines** The connection of foreground with background creates a visual pathway for the viewer.

⬇ **Striking light and shadow** The contrast in this image creates a striking, playful shot.

⬇ **Symmetrical compositions** Symmetry evokes feelings of calm, serenity and harmony.

Which camera?

With improvements in digital cameras, high-quality, high-resolution images are easy to create instantly, which has led to fewer people using traditional film cameras. Briefly, digital cameras are more versatile and are capable of taking quality images in poor lighting conditions, with more storage space. You can also select and delete unwanted images immediately. To take a good picture you will need a decent camera. If possible, beginners should use at least a 6 megapixel digital SLR with a 22–80mm zoom range and a viewfinder or viewing screen. These allow you to shoot what you see, and choose where to focus the image and exactly how to compose it. Automatic digital cameras calculate lighting, focal distance and aperture settings with no input from the photographer, setting up a point-and-click attitude, with reasonable results. For manual digital photography, knowledge and understanding of how the camera works means that the photographer will have more control and can adjust the image to create unorthodox and striking results.

⬆ **Asymmetrical compositions** Positioning the focal point off-centre can add dynamism.

◀ **Abstraction** High contrast in image-making, also termed 'chiaroscuro', can be used in photography to produce abstract images.

Unusual image shapes
Just because your camera makes rectangular images, there's no reason why you can't stretch them into panoramic shots or crop them to a square format.

Crop and zoom
Dramatic effects can be achieved by cropping and zooming in.

Orientation Some landscape photos have a greater impact when cropped to portrait format, a technique that can also be used to get rid of unwanted background.

Light and colour, composition and cropping

When producing photographs for illustration work you should try to get as much detail, clarity and balanced lighting as possible in the initial picture, since further effects can be added if desired. You can always return to a clear image, whereas a blurred image will have little use. Consider what you need from the photo, for example high saturated colour, black and white or sepia; however, always shoot in colour then produce different colours in post-production. Also consider the lighting: direct bright sunlight may bleach out the image, whereas overcast conditions will flatten the contrast. Most cameras have a light meter; when taking your shot try to make sure that it is as close to the centre of the contrast range as possible.

To crop an image is to select a part of the shot. Often cropping is used to take out an unwanted part of the picture (the side of a stranger's head, etc); it is a useful tool to get rid of superfluous information and strengthen the image. Remember that a sharp, clear image is versatile and can be altered; a bad, blurred image cannot be corrected with post-production techniques.

Archiving your images

Storage of digital images needs care. It is not enough to have them saved only on a computer; they also need to be backed up on portable external hard drives, USB memory sticks or burnt onto CDs or DVDs. If a negative is scratched, it can still be printed and retouched, but the failure of a hard drive will result in complete loss of all images.

SEE ALSO: FUNDAMENTALS OF COMPOSITION P34
FUNDAMENTALS OF COLOUR P92

ASSIGNMENT: **CHOOSING PHOTOGRAPHS**

For this assignment you will need to produce three to five photographs of your friends, family or relatives.

1 Use the following key words and ideas to inform your decision of what to take.

- Dancing
- Playing a sport
- Engaging in a hobby
- Portrait

These photographs will be used for the Photoshop and Photomontage assignments, so it is important to make sure that the images are clear, focused and have an even contrast. They also need to have as much potential information and versatility as possible, so try to get their entire body in shot. Cropping can be done later in Photoshop if required.

2 Spend one hour walking around your neighbourhood, university or college town or city with your camera. You will need to produce three to five photographs of each of these:

- Buildings or landscapes
- Textures such as grass, stonework or walls.

The aim here is to make sure that each photograph is focused and well lit. Use the examples of the photographs in this section as inspiration for yours.

3 Remember to save these images on a computer or memory stick for use later.

Sourcing images

While working to a deadline graphic designers must make decisions about the images that they will use. The principal point to consider is: does the brief, timescale and fee allow or justify producing an image from scratch, or is it necessary to source a ready-made image from elsewhere?

The internet provides the quickest way to source stock images, from websites such as iStockphoto and Dreamstime. These images can be purchased on a royalty-free basis, with most websites using a credit system. For example, on some sites a picture of a tent can be purchased for 1 credit for a 72dpi image, which would be acceptable for a web-based illustration, or for 5 credits as a 300dpi image, which can be used for a print-based illustration.

Images can be bought either for specific time periods or outright; however, a drawback with purchasing a temporary license is that there is no guarantee that other designers will not use the same picture in their designs. Your client may wish that you purchase the picture outright, which will undoubtedly cost more.

ASSIGNMENT: **SOURCING STOCK IMAGES**

This assignment shows you how to source images from internet stock agencies. It is not necessary to purchase these, but to get an idea of how to use the search functions.

Go to either the iStockphoto or the Dreamstime website. Each has a search function on the front page. Enter the following words in combinations of four into the search facility and see what images you can find.

- Red Tent Book Dog
- Blue Tree Car Horse
- Gray House Light Group
- Orange Coat Dark Stairs

GLOSSARY

Depth of field: Distance between the object of focus and where the focus starts to blur. For example, a photographer may want a product to be in sharp, clear focus but the background to be blurred, so would choose a smaller aperture (f22), a slower film speed (ISO 100) for higher resolution, and have extra lighting and external flashes set up.

F stop/focal length and aperture: Size of aperture or 'iris' inside a camera, which controls the amount of light that hits the film or pixel sensor; the range on a general camera is f4 (large aperture) to f22 (small aperture). A large aperture (f2, for example) brings more light into the camera and results in a softer image; a small aperture (f16, for example) allows less light into the camera but gives a sharper image.

Filter: Plates of glass or plastic attached to the front of the lens in order to accentuate different qualities. For example, a polarising filter cuts down light glare; a colour filter enhances different colours.

ISO: International Organization for Standardization. This sets a standard range for virtual film speeds in digital cameras: ISO 100, for example, works best in good lighting conditions for stationary objects; ISO 1600 works best in poor lighting conditions and for mobile objects.

Lens: Different lenses extend the capabilities of the camera.

- A normal lens on a digital or film SLR is 35mm, considered to be near enough to human vision.
- A macro lens captures sharp, extreme close-ups of objects.
- A wide-angle lens captures a wider vision, but with perspective distortion.
- A telephoto lens captures objects at distance.

Resolution: The resulting output from a digital camera. General camera phones have a low resolution output, therefore the resulting image is pixellated and of low quality; digital cameras and some top-of-the-range camera phones have up to ten megapixel sensors and can produce less pixellated, sharper and higher quality images.

SLR: Single Lens Reflex. These types of camera use a viewfinder and mirrors so that the photographer's sightline goes through the main lens and results in a what-you-see-is-what-you-get image.

PART 2	PRACTICE
UNIT 5	TOOLS AND TECHNOLOGIES
MODULE 2	**Photoshop**

Photoshop is the industry standard software package for raster graphics editing and manipulation and is frequently used for images, to select elements for montage or photo retouching. However, text can also be incorporated into designs, allowing for the seamless integration of text and image within a single digital environment.

Photoshop replaces and enhances darkroom techniques such as retouching and editing brightness and contrast, and allows for ease of cropping while providing a cleaner, 'dry', chemical-free environment for editing. Common tools used in Photoshop are the Brush, Eraser and Healing tools. These allow the editor to remove imperfections and unwanted objects.

Photoshop's major advantage is that imported images can be moved, edited and layered over a potentially infinite canvas both in size and in layers without loss of information, quality or resolution. Any Photoshop graphic artist must have knowledge of all the selection tools on offer and an understanding of layering options.

GLOSSARY

Canvas: The virtual 'ground' that images are placed onto in Photoshop.

DPI: Dots Per (square) Inch; the common form of resolution measurement. Designers typically use 72dpi-sized images for web images, and 300dpi-sized images for photo-realistic prints.

Pixel: The smallest element of a computer screen or printed image. The word 'pixel' is an amalgamation of picture (pix-) and element (-el).

Raster: Assemblages of pixels on a 2D grid system that can be viewed on computer screens or print media.

Resolution: The clarity of a digital image. A low resolution image (30dpi, for example) will have clearly visible pixels; a high resolution image (300dpi, for example) will not.

Work area

This section shows the general layout of Photoshop. Additional pullouts can be accessed through the 'Window' menu on the header bar.

❯ Main toolbar
This bar has easy icon access to all of the main tools, some of which also have keyboard shortcuts.

Foreground/background colour selection. Clicking on the squares selects the colour, whereas the 'X' key swaps them over.

These icons toggle between Quick Mask and Standard Editing

USEFUL TOOLS AND FEATURES

There are four main tools that enable you to edit an isolated area of pixels without altering the rest of the image. Each of these can be accessed through the main toolbar. The Brush tool is versatile and has many options to master.

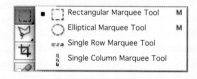

1 Marquee Tool Selects an area or sets up a boundary within the layer that is being worked on. Different Marquee Tools can select rectangles and ovals, and, when holding down the Shift key, geometric circles and squares can be selected. This tool also allows you to select a one-pixel-width line down or across the entire layer. This is useful when making a striped page pattern or creating a boundary line.

2 Magic Wand Tool Selects pixels of the same colour with the Tolerance option set to 1, but within a range of colour with Tolerance set to more than 1. If the Contiguous box is unchecked, the tool will select all the pixels in the entire document that are of the same colour value regardless if they are joined together. Use the Shift key to add pixels to the selection and the Alt key to subtract.

Main toolbar

Filters can be accessed through the header bar

The canvas

Secondary toolbars

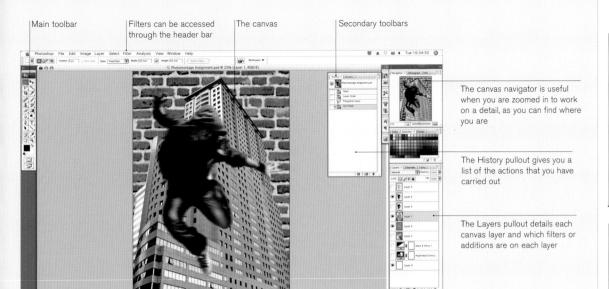

The canvas navigator is useful when you are zoomed in to work on a detail, as you can find where you are

The History pullout gives you a list of the actions that you have carried out

The Layers pullout details each canvas layer and which filters or additions are on each layer

Shortcuts

These keyboard shortcuts are helpful and save time:

- ctrl or ⌘___C   Copy
- ctrl or ⌘___V   Paste
- ctrl or ⌘___Z   Undo
- ctrl or ⌘___T   Free Transform

- Space key + mouse movement: move canvas around in window. '[' or ']' keys make brush size smaller or larger.

Alternatives

Other similar programs that allow for pixel-based image editing:
- CorelDRAW
- ImageReady
- GIMP

Colour editor The Photoshop Colour editor, currently set to the CMYK (cyan, magenta, yellow, key/black) range that is used for print colour. The RGB (red, green, blue) colour editor is used when designing for the web/television. Each range has different effects on the colour usage.

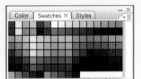

Preset colour swatches The swatches are used as a standard range of colours, for example black, white, 10%, 20% and 50% greys. If you have mixed your own standard swatch, or have been set a range in a brief, you can save and keep it to select when working on a design.

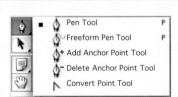

Pen Tool	P
Freeform Pen Tool	P
Add Anchor Point Tool	
Delete Anchor Point Tool	
Convert Point Tool	

3 Pen Tool Creates vector-based lines and curves with control points (see Illustrator, p118). These points can be dragged over the layer for a better fit, converting them from fixed points. An area enclosed by the Pen Tool boundary can be filled with colour by the Paint Tool.

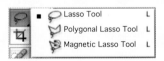

Lasso Tool	L
Polygonal Lasso Tool	L
Magnetic Lasso Tool	L

4 Lasso Tool Draws and selects freehand shapes. Use the Shift key to add a new selection or the Alt key to subtract. The Polygonal Lasso draws straight-line sections. Use the Alt key to toggle between the Lasso and the Polygonal Lasso Tool, and the Shift key to draw perpendicular or 45° angles. The Magnetic Lasso outlines a shape by adhering to the pixel edge.

Brush Tool	B
Pencil Tool	B
Color Replacement Tool	B

5 Brush Tool Its size, shape and colour can be changed, as can its hardness and scatter range. Alter the brush's flow rate or opacity to achieve different effects for use in retouching, adding texture or digital painting. The Brush Tool options can be found by the F5 key and under the header bar.

Pixels

The best way to describe a pixel is as a tiny square in a grid of squares on the monitor screen. Each square is lit by different intensities of red, green or blue light (RGB) to form the entire gamut of colours. These pixels can be modified either on their own or as a group. If these pixels are tiny enough, they merge together to form a smooth picture. Another name for this is a raster image.

ⓘ Scanning

One way to import images into Photoshop for modification and incorporation into a design is to scan them. To do this, go to File > Import and choose the scanner, then follow the scanner's instructions. For example, cartoonists would scan in pencil and pen drawings either as line art, or full-colour at 300dpi. This can be set on a layer, with the blending option set to Multiply. Further layers can then be added to render highlights, mid-tones and shadows with the Brush Tool.

Layering

Photoshop can layer different images and elements so that each can be worked on separately without altering the rest of the image. The following can be accessed through the Layer options bar to the right of the canvas:

Opacity Changes how translucent each layer is.
Presets Adds colour styles and textures to the layer.
Layer styles Adds effects such as shadows, strokes, glowing edges and textures to the layer.
Blending options Changes the properties of the layer.

The following can be accessed through the main header:
Layer > Merge/Flatten Merges all or some of the layers together.
Filter Applies effects such as blur, sharpen, lighting and textures.

Use these to adjust the size, resolution, colour values and white balance of each layer:
Image > Adjustments >
Hue/Saturation
Brightness/Contrast
Image size/Resolution
Canvas size

Click and hold on a layer to drag it to different positions, bringing it to the front or moving it behind other layers.

Resolution

Image resolution is a key area of knowledge for a graphic designer. The most common measurement of resolution is dots per inch, or DPI. At 25dpi an image is heavily pixellated; at 72dpi (used for all web-based imagery) it is clearer but not a high enough quality for print. The standard resolution for photo quality and print images is 300dpi, or for large posters, 600dpi.

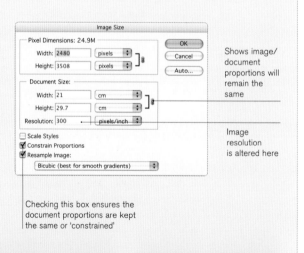

Shows image/document proportions will remain the same

Image resolution is altered here

Checking this box ensures the document proportions are kept the same or 'constrained'

25 dpi

72 dpi

300 dpi

Each layer is on a separate bar

Layer thumbnail

Hides the layer or makes it visible

Layer mask, which covers all the image in the black area for that layer

Adds new layers

Delete layers by dragging them here

MASKS

Quick Mask Selects and masks out an area that needs to be protected from editing. Using a selection tool, outline the area you want to edit. Then select the Quick Mask option from the left-hand main toolbar. To add to the selection, paint in black; to subtract, paint in white. When you select the Standard Editing mode, the selection will reflect the edits made in the Quick Mask mode.

Layer Mask Creates a new layer on top of the existing image to which effects can be added.

Channel Mask Selects and masks all areas within a specific colour range.

● ASSIGNMENT: **Cutting out photographs**

This assignment takes one of the photographs you produced in Module 1 and shows you how to cut out an element, such as a person or an object, so that it is separated from the background.

1 Import your chosen picture into Photoshop and select the Pen Tool. This is the most effective tool for cutting, giving you more control of the process so that less is left to chance. Select the option 'Create a new work path'.

2 Set up as many control points as you need, making sure that areas with more detail have more curves. You will be able to add or subtract the control points later if needed.

3 Once the entire outline of the person or object has been covered with control points, zoom in to the image and, using the Convert option, make sure that the lines have a tight fit against the outline. Aim for a 'best fit' approach, because some outlines may be indistinct.

4 After you have made all the adjustments select the 'Make selection' option. Now you can cut and paste the element of your image to a new document. Save the image as a PSD file called 'Element'.

● **Removing the background (4)**
Once the image has been cut out, you can paste it into a new document.

● **Creating a path (2)**
You can see the beginning of the path created by the Pen Tool.

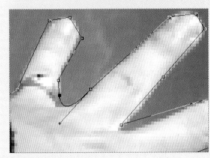

▲ **Zooming in (3)** Straight lines may need to be changed to curves for a tighter fit.

PART 2	PRACTICE
UNIT 5	TOOLS AND TECHNOLOGIES
MODULE 3	**Photomontage/collage**

Photomontage and collage are historical artistic methods, where fragments of photographs, images, elements, textures and typography are brought together to create new meanings and new images. Photoshop extends this process by making it possible to hide the methods of assembly, creating a seamless picture.

Photomontage is a process concerned with manipulation of photographs and is historically associated with graphic artists such as Hannah Höch and John Heartfield, as well as contemporary illustrators, such as Dave McKean. The process pulls in and reassembles fragments to construct images that appear seamless or that leave the edges exposed for different aesthetic purposes. The aesthetics of punk are a good example of this process: the idea of a handmade and edgy look and feel to make the image stand out.

Collage is a process more concerned with the assemblage of ephemera, textures and typography, and can be seen in the work of artists Kurt Schwitters and Romare Bearden. Many of these images are based on found objects or materials and result in abstract assemblages and patterns, where the emphasis is placed more on texture and aesthetic qualities than on conveying any particular meaning.

Abstract lines This assemblage of fragmented photographs with added lines creates an abstract image.

Simple montage This book jacket is an excellent example of how simple photomontage can be an effective graphic process.

Question

In contemporary photomontage work, do you think the technique has become divorced from its political roots (eg Höch, Heartfield) and become largely aesthetic? Has the digitisation of photomontage as a technique changed what is possible in this medium?

⦿ ASSIGNMENT: **PHOTOMONTAGE WITH PHOTOSHOP**

The previous unit showed you how to cut out elements of your images to reassemble them. This assignment takes you through the basics of combining all of these in Photoshop to create a new image. Once you've worked your way through this assignment, experiment by using more layers. From other assignments in this module you should have the following:

- Three to five photographs of your friends or relatives with one of them cut out in Photoshop
- Three to five photographs of buildings, landscapes and/or textures

1 Open up a blank Photoshop document, select the A4/8½ x 11in size, and name it 'Photomontage Assignment'. Select Background and change it to 'Layer 0'. Now import your images, either by dragging and dropping them from the desktop onto the Photoshop icon/application, or by the Open option. Move the textures, buildings and landscapes into the Photomontage Assignment document by dragging and dropping using the Move Tool. Each should now appear as a separate layer. Use the Free Transform option (Edit > Free Transform) to make each element fit the screen. Hold down Shift so that the image does not warp. Do not worry if your images go off the page or that you have white margins, because you will crop the image later.

⊕ **SEE ALSO:**
PHOTOSHOP P108

2 Now you can use the different filters and image adjustments to change the look of the different layers to make different effects like these examples.

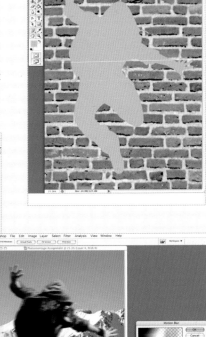

3 Move the cut-out selection of your friend or relative into the document by the same method, or by Copy and Paste from the Element document. Use one of your landscape or building images as the background or bottom layer and move the Element selection until you are satisfied with the composition.

4 Once you have found the combination of textures, filters and backgrounds that you like, flatten the layers, then crop the image.

PART 2	PRACTICE
UNIT 5	TOOLS AND TECHNOLOGIES
MODULE 4	**DTP applications**

Desktop publishing (DTP) applications are where all your lessons in composition, page layout, contrast and typography come into play. In these applications the elements you create in vector software or the imagery you edit in raster-based applications merge with your content. Using this WYSIWYG (What You See Is What You Get) layout-generating word processor, you can string text and image together to create brochures, booklets, one-page flyers or multi-volume novels.

Although Adobe InDesign may be the industry standard, at some point somebody will probably email you a .qxd file. Whereas Quark is similar to InDesign, just a bit less agile and less featured, it's the differences in how they handle file types from image-making programs that may cause problems. As native products, Adobe files work between programs without filtering; however an Adobe Illustrator or Photoshop image brought to QuarkXpress will always need to be exported to an EPS, JPG or TIFF. Each file type has their own 'Quarky' characteristic, but none have the same full-on editability that Illustrator/Photoshop-to-InDesign provides.

GLOSSARY

Crop mark: Vertical and horizontal lines at the corners of an image or page to indicate to a vendor where to trim off the bleed area.

FPO: For Position Only; the use of a temporary placeholder or low resolution image in place of the high quality counterpart during the design process.

Gutter: The inside margins or blank space between two facing pages in a publication. Used to accommodate binding, the amount of gutter needed changes depending on how the project will be bound.

Margin: The usually blank space to the top, bottom and sides of a page between the trim and the live printing area. Headers, footers and page numbers are traditionally placed within this area.

✚ **SEE ALSO:**
BASIC PRINCIPLES OF
LAYOUT P42

Work area

The main toolbar sits to the left of the screen, the canvas in the centre and the secondary toolbars to the right.

❯ **Main toolbar**
InDesign localises its main tools into one long toolbox. Mirroring many of the functions found in Illustrator, Photoshop and Quark, the tools in this panel can be accessed by clicking the icons or utilising the keystrokes assigned to each item, such as 'V' for the Selection Tool, 'P' for the Pen Tool and 'G' for the Gradient Tool. Notice that some of the items with a small arrow also reveal other fly-out tools such as Rounded Frames, the Fill Tool and the Measure Tool.

USEFUL TOOLS
AND FEATURES

InDesign has many tools chock full of features and functions to help create amazing compositions. Here are some of the more basic yet powerful tools that are the mainstays of any InDesign user.

1 Selection Tool Selects the entire shape or line, which can then be stretched, rotated or moved anywhere on the canvas.

2 Direct Selection Tool Selects and manipulates specific lines, path points or handle ends distinctly to change the position of individual lines, points or curves of a shape.

3 Pen Tool Enables you to create straight or curved lines by selecting two points on the page and 'bending' to your desired shape. By clicking the Pen Tool you can reveal the Add Anchor Point, Delete Anchor Point and Convert Direction Point Tools to manipulate the points that make up curves and lines.

The Control Panel can be docked at the top or bottom of the screen, as well as float freely, like all of the panels

Master pages are the page templates upon which you can program elements such as grids, header and footer elements and automatic page numbering.

Swatches Panel This is where all the colours used in a document are located.

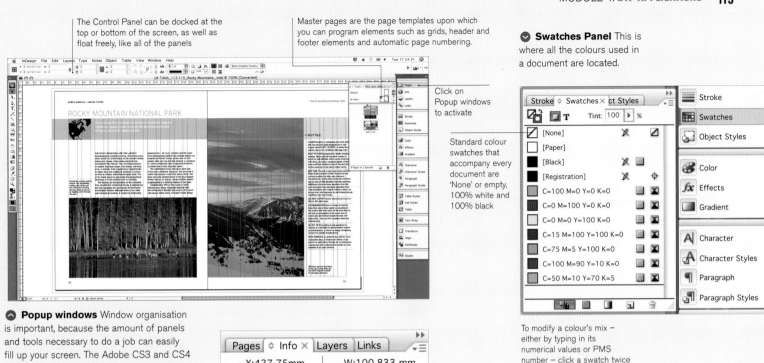

Click on Popup windows to activate

Standard colour swatches that accompany every document are 'None' or empty, 100% white and 100% black

 Popup windows Window organisation is important, because the amount of panels and tools necessary to do a job can easily fill up your screen. The Adobe CS3 and CS4 applications help reclaim screen real-estate by allowing users to 'dock' and minimise panels as they see fit. With a variety of options available under Window > Workspace, you can select one of the pre-organised panel arrangements or create your own.

Pages | Info × | Layers | Links

X: 427.75mm   W: 100.833 mm
Y: 110mm   H: 62.4mm
D:

Type: Portable N...ics (PNG)
Actual ppi: 72x72
Effective ppi: 425x425
Color Space: RGB
ICC Profile: sRGB IEC61966-2.1

To modify a colour's mix – either by typing in its numerical values or PMS number – click a swatch twice to reveal the Colour Mixer

Info panel Displays layout information for the document or selected objects including values for position, colour, size, text and rotation. For viewing only – you cannot enter or edit the information in the panel, but you can ascertain many qualities of an on-page object by hovering over it with your cursor.

4 Type Tool Used in the creation of text boxes and edits the type within them. By working in conjunction with the Control Panel and Type Panels, this tool will allow you to select and modify text to create headlines, paragraph blocks and captions.

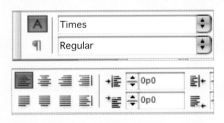

Times
Regular

The Control Panel Provides a customisable array of functions for the Type Tool in relation to choosing font, leading, tracking, text weight and style, paragraph alignment, column count and margin spacing.

5 Frame Tool and Shapes Tool Both create rectangular, polygon and rounded forms: the Frame Tool creates frames to insert graphics and imagery into; the Shapes Tool is for drawing shapes to fill or outline with colour. Precise adjustments can be made to size and position with the Transform Panel.

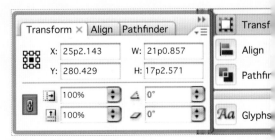

Transform × | Align | Pathfinder

X: 25p2.143   W: 21p0.857
Y: 280.429   H: 17p2.571

100%   0°
100%   0°

Page layout concepts

Beyond the ability to draw boxes and size imagery, the designer can use DTP to express content meaning with maximum typographic control. Through the splitting up and flowing of text from multiple columns to multiple pages, hierarchy and information organisation is achieved. Proper composition and text layout is handled by the manipulation of page items that usually causes countless ragging and adjusting – get used to it. Magazines and newspapers everywhere use DTP for one purpose: to get as many words as is comfortably legible and aesthetically pleasing on a page, with grids, layouts, templates and columns to make it happen.

Master Pages and Style Sheets help you to create almost any composition and project. Successful export for proofing – such as with PDFs – and file preparation for publishing – such as with an outside vendor – are important details usually handled well by DTP, but you should know what you are looking for. Proper embedding in a PDF or exported package to a service bureau should include the updated document file, PDF for proofing, folder of imagery, as well as a folder of all fonts used.

Page layout

Layout creation utilises different on-page items such as text boxes and image boxes to help place imagery, content and colour in compositions on a generated pasteboard. These compositions can be sorted into a virtual pagination structure, for example 2, 10 or 50 pages. The program also manages issues such as page size, orientation and output. The following tools are standard:

▶ Guides Imaginary rules are pulled over the page and viewed upon request. They do not print, but help in creating layouts and grids and lining up items. Usually gutters and margins are set with guides in the Master Pages.

❗ Bleed
When preparing imagery, remember to compensate for the bleed. If any of your pictures go to the edge of the page, remember to add about .3175cm (⅛in) to that side of the image to be clipped off at press-time. This goes for background colours and lines as well.

Reoccurring graphics can be set up in the Master Pages

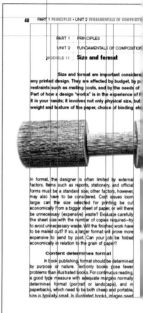

Object styles can be assigned to objects, groups and frames to modify the stroke, colour, fill, drop shadows, transparency, text wrap and more

Character styles are formatting attributes that can be applied to selected items of text, such as size, weight, tracking and italics

In paragraph styles, character and paragraph formatting attributes that can be applied to a paragraph or series of paragraphs to adjust overall spacing, leading and style

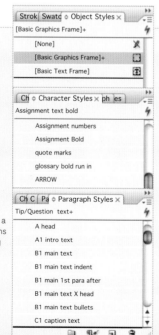

◀ Style Sheets Design and typographic styles such as colour, size, leading, position and decoration may be applied to text automatically with Style Sheets. Selections of text may be tagged with certain pre-defined meta-information at the click of a button. By naming a series of elements Headline, you can globally affect the styles and attributes of each selection.

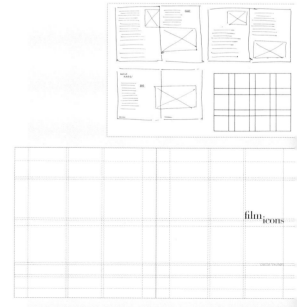

film:icons

Page numbers and running heads are set in the Master Pages

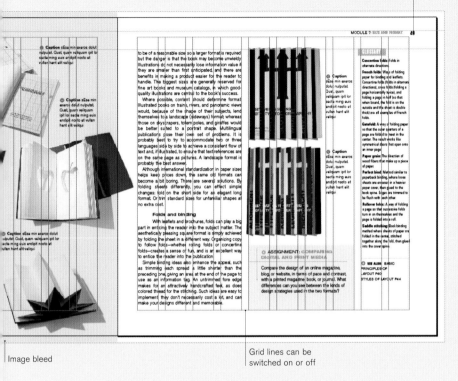

Image bleed

Grid lines can be switched on or off

Master Pages

These template pages, upon which pre-defined pages mimic grid elements and on-page template elements such as text block items, header and footer elements and automatic page numbering, are usually found at the top of the Pages or Page Layout panel. These pre-styled layouts help in creating uniform changes throughout a large document, but can be specifically changed on a per-page basis when necessary.

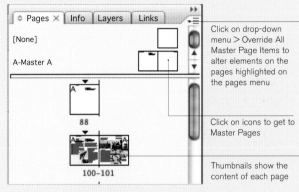

Click on drop-down menu > Override All Master Page Items to alter elements on the pages highlighted on the pages menu

Click on icons to get to Master Pages

Thumbnails show the content of each page

Page numbering

When on a Master Page create a Text Box and go to Type > Insert Special Character > Markers – Current Page Number. Now, that same text block on each page will reflect the appropriate page number.

ASSIGNMENT: CREATING A FILM BOOK

This brief was set for students on a typography course. The example was designed by Clarice Trevisan.

Brief Design one of a series of books on 'icons'. These books are intended as serious biographies, so the emphasis is on text rather than pictures. The books should be 240 pages in length and of a similar visual style. For the presentation of your solution produce a series of rough designs showing your working process (see above left), a grid to support various levels of information and images (see lower left), a few final spreads (see right), covers and a full-size blank dummy.

Concept Create a template for a double-page spread flexible enough to accommodate the different 'icons' without losing the identity of each one of the individual subjects. Now design, as the first in the series, a book about Pedro Almodóvar, the acclaimed Spanish film-maker, that parallels through format, space and typography the director's points of view as represented in his films.

The way in which the pictures meet in the corner echoes the typographic treatment of headings in the design

Adobe Illustrator is a vector-based package used for illustrative, logo and page layout design because of its shape-rendering and text-editing capabilities. Its linear handling complements Photoshop's pixel-based format, and most designers have knowledge of both programs.

Illustrator's main advantage is the resizing of images without loss of detail, from its 'point and line' function. For example, at billboard size a raster image becomes pixellated and loose, whereas a vector image retains design by angle geometry and proportion. Similar in many respects to Photoshop, Illustrator is focused on the logo developer, cartoonist, T-shirt artist, billboard designer or decal cutter, to name a few.

For the graphic designer, Illustrator offers a clean, crisp edge to the produced objects and brushes, and mapped along 'paths' can be moved, edited and recoloured with an ease not found in Photoshop. As well as the ability to work purely in vectors, Illustrator facilitates working over raster images, for example adding text or symbols for a poster, building up a complex layered image.

GLOSSARY

Anchor point: A point on or at the end of a curve or line that can be 'grabbed' by the cursor and moved around the canvas, either to change the curve shape or to move the entire curve.

Canvas: Like Photoshop, the virtual 'ground' into which images are placed.

Handle: Anchor points connected to the main vector path by tangential lines which can be manipulated to change the shape of the curve.

Path: A drawn line, mathematically determined; also called a vector.

Creative curves
Illustrator can create wonderfully smooth, flowing artwork to embellish a layout.

Artistic possibilities
This image shows how versatile Illustrator can be, from smooth transitions of layered colour on the hair traced with a Pen Tool, to the textures used on the clothes.

USEFUL TOOLS AND FEATURES

Many of the tools found in Photoshop are duplicated across the Adobe range, such as the Selection Tools, Lassos and Pen Tools. Here are four that are unique to Illustrator.

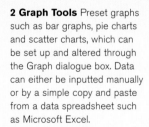

1 Warp Tools Change the geometry of vector objects. Warp Tool: drags a specific area of an object. Twirl Tool: changes the local geometry/colour into a spiral. Crystallise Tool: changes the local geometry/colour to splines.

2 Graph Tools Preset graphs such as bar graphs, pie charts and scatter charts, which can be set up and altered through the Graph dialogue box. Data can either be inputted manually or by a simple copy and paste from a data spreadsheet such as Microsoft Excel.

3 Mesh Tool Creates colour graduations within a 2D vector object. For example, making a star with the Star Tool, and clicking within the shape with the Mesh Tool sets up a gradient, which can then be edited.

Work area

The main toolbar sits to the left of the screen, the canvas in the centre, and the secondary toolbars to the right.

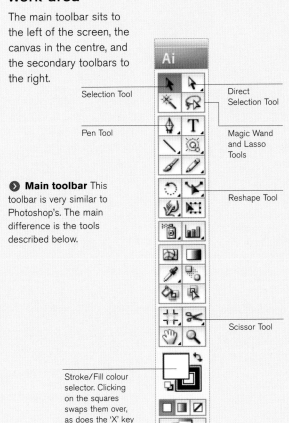

Selection Tool

Direct Selection Tool

Pen Tool

Magic Wand and Lasso Tools

Reshape Tool

Scissor Tool

Stroke/Fill colour selector. Clicking on the squares swaps them over, as does the 'X' key

❯ Main toolbar This toolbar is very similar to Photoshop's. The main difference is the tools described below.

Main toolbar   Header bar   Palettes, including Swatches and Layers

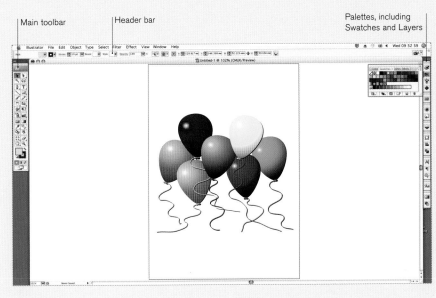

❯ Pathfinder Use these boxes to transform simple shapes into more complex ones, through merging, overlapping and subtracting parts.

❯ Align Clicking on these options will realign selected objects into the formations shown or add space evenly between objects as desired.

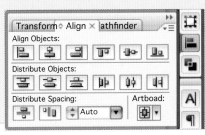

4 Symbol Sprayer Similar to Photoshop's Brush Tool but will alter the local positioning of previous symbols and make room for the new, resulting in minimal layering or overlap.

◉ ASSIGNMENT: USING THE TOOLS

Familiarise yourself with the three line editing tools.

• Scissor Tool: Cut a line or curve in two – each end now has a new anchor point.

• Reshape Tool: Select and manipulate anchor points and lines, and insert an anchor point within a straight line, pulling the line into a curve without the use of handles.

• Stroke Options: Change line thickness, the mitre shape at the end of a line and a line to dotted or dashed.

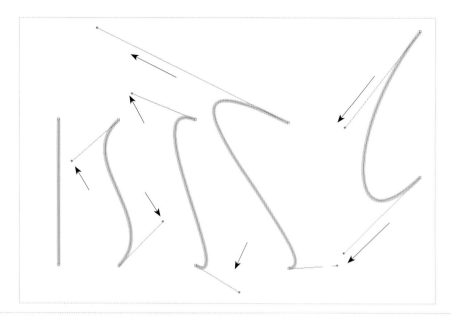

Vectors

Bézier curves are mathematically determined paths or vectors created between two points, which can be manipulated by handles at either end. These curves, popularised by Pierre Bézier in 1962 from Paul de Casteljau's algorithms, provide the backbone of objects produced in Illustrator, and are found in the Adobe range as paths created by the Pen Tool, lines, objects and type guides in InDesign. They are also the basis for digital type used in 'what you see is what you get' (WYSIWYG) publishing, text editing software and 3D software programs.

The Bézier curve in Illustrator with anchor points at either end and handles (straight blue lines) that control the curve.

This detail shows how the spirals are being made from Bézier curves

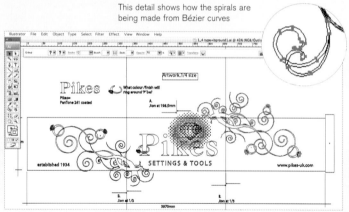

This screengrab shows the individual elements as they are created

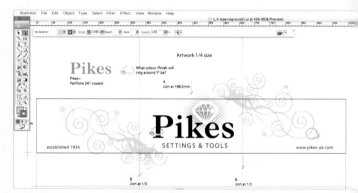

The design is now uploaded to the company website

Here, the spirals have been printed on frosted glass panels for the business frontage, keeping the pattern running throughout

⊙ ASSIGNMENT: CREATING A LEAF

1 Select the Arc Tool and make four lines as shown. Make sure that the two outside lines, the inside lines that create the 'stem' and the other end of the leaf all end at the same point. You will need to use the White Selection arrow to move the anchor points into place as well as move the handles on each of the lines.

2 Select the two inner lines by holding down the Shift key and clicking on each of them with the Black Selection tool. Then give the lines a mid-green colour or C80 M15 Y100 K5. Next select the topmost line and give it a yellow colour or C5 M0 Y100 K0. Finally select the bottommost line and give it a rust colour or C40 M70 Y85 K35.

3 Select the bottom two lines with the Black Selection arrow. Go to Object > Blend > Blend Options, choose the Smooth Colour option, and press OK. Next press Alt + B and either ⌘ (Mac) or ctrl (PC). The bottom half of the leaf should now be filled.

4 Select the top two lines and repeat stage 3. The whole leaf should now be filled. Finally, select both sides of the leaf and go to Object > Group. The leaf is now one object.

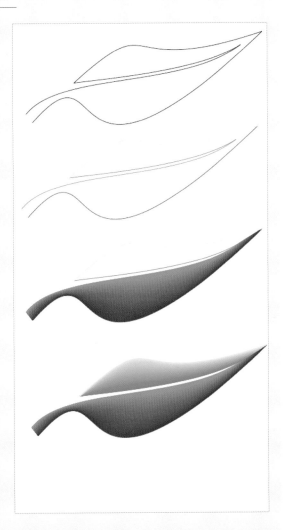

PRINCIPLES AND COMPONENTS

• Curves are never fixed with the finished image. A composite image/shape can be manipulated in size, colour, stroke, gradient and layer without affecting nearby shapes, and fragments. More complex shapes and images can be built up by layering lines and the many standard shape tools such as the rectangle, circle and pentagon.

• Superior text-editing abilities, such as kerning, leading, stroke, font size and typeface options, are on the secondary toolbars to the right of the work page.

⊙ File types

There are three main file types: PDF (Portable Document Format); EPS (Encapsulated PostScript); and AI (Adobe Illustrator Artwork). Generally, PDF format is used for final images sent for print or submission, whereas EPS and AI are file formats kept in-house.

⊙ CMYK

Illustrator documents need initially to be set to CMYK four-colour basis in preparation for the output to be delivered to print.

⊕ SEE ALSO:
PHOTOSHOP P108

3D GRAPHICS P122

FLASH/AFTER EFFECTS P124

◄ **Application of Illustrator** The example at left shows how fundamental and versatile Illustrator can be in establishing a corporate identity. The Illustrator logo at right is displayed on the shop frontage and the company website.

STAGES IN RENDERING AN OBJECT

1 Starting modelling There are two main ways to start modelling an object. The first is to generate a 'primitive' object, such as a cube or sphere, and manipulate it by surface tools or control point manipulation to the form desired. The second is to import an image or drawing into the viewport, map lines onto the drawing and use the Lathe Tool to generate a 3D form.

2 Surfaces, textures, bump mapping Once the wireframe model is complete, the next stage is to work on the surface. Images can be mapped onto the surface, and bump mapping adds texture along with options such as surface transparency and gloss.

3 Lighting The final stage in producing a rendered image or 'render' of the finished object is to set the lighting situation. 3ds Max has a full complement of lighting options, including spotlights, daylight simulators and diffuse shadows.

GLOSSARY

Control Point: Similar to Illustrator, the points that can be selected and moved three-dimensionally, manipulating the surface.

NURBS: NonUniform Rational B(Bézier)-splines — mathematically determined and generated curves and surfaces first developed by Pierre Bézier to model freeform surfaces.

Order: Higher orders of control points give more flexibility to manipulation of a curve or surface.

Polygon count: The higher the count, the more Polygons are generated on the surface and the smoother the surface becomes.

Polygon mesh: A modelling system that divides surfaces into triangles or polygons, enabling complex surfaces to be determined with flat faces and straight lines between three or more points on an x, y, z 3D coordinate system.

Render: The image produced where surfaces and textures are mapped onto the wireframe.

Wireframe: A way to see the entire structure of the object represented in lines.

> Isometric This example of typography uses an isometric view of complex letterforms in rendered and wireframe examples.

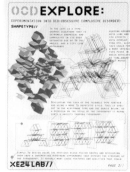

PART 2	PRACTICE
UNIT 5	TOOLS AND TECHNOLOGIES
MODULE 6	**3D graphics**

3D graphics are becoming more prevalent in graphic design, especially for product design and rapid prototyping. 3ds Max is one of the most versatile programs since it supports modelling in NURBS and Polygons with rendering and animation capabilities.

NURBS and Polygons are different systems of representing complex freeform surfaces accurately in three dimensions in 3ds Max. Both have advantages and disadvantages — for example, NURBS surfaces are generally smoother when rendered because the system is based on curves; sharp or flat forms are harder to model. Polygon meshes are generally less smooth, unless the Polygon count is high, which results in smoother curves. You can translate NURBS to Polygons and vice versa with conversion functions within 3ds Max.

USEFUL TOOLS AND FEATURES

3ds Max is similar to Illustrator, with tools that rely on control points and vectors. It is a complex program but has some key features that you should familiarize yourself with.

1 Objects, Shapes, and Compounds Objects (see panel at left) are 3D Standard or Extended Primitives, which are the basic building blocks from cones, spheres, and cubes to more complex objects such as prisms and spindles. Shapes are 2D line variations, or splines such as arcs or circles. Text can also be generated as 2D splines. Compounds are a group of functions that generate or morph objects together, such as a 3D contoured landscape out of a 2D map.

2 Modifier panel When complex objects are built, they are altered from primitives by increasing the polygon count, using surface editing tools and Boolean unions/subtractions. Some of the tools found in 3ds Max behave like those in Photoshop such as Bend, Taper, Skew, and Stretch. The Loft function can be used to generate 3D objects out of a 2D shape. The Lathe function can be used to generate 3D objects out of a 2D shape.

ASSIGNMENT: CREATING A BOWL IN 3DS MAX

1 From the Primitives menu on the right of the workspace choose the Line Tool (as highlighted in the first picture), then draw six lines (Spline) as you would in Illustrator. When prompted, select Yes to close the splines into one object.

2a Bring up the options for the shape (Ctrl click [Mac] or Right click [PC]) and choose the Bezier Corners option. **2b** You can now change the shape of each line by moving the control points and the handles (green circle) as you would do in Illustrator.

3 Once you have the shape as you want it, switch the right toolbar to the Modify tab and select Lathe from the Modifier drop-down list. This will give you an object similar to the bottom right-hand panel in the picture.

4 Select Min from the Parameters options on the right-hand toolbar. This will give you the fully formed bowl shape.

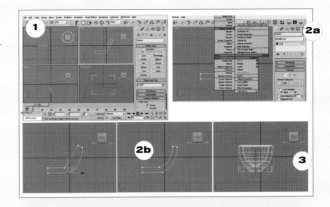

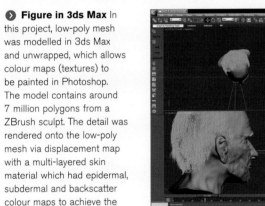
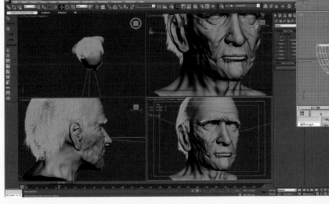

▶ Figure in 3ds Max In this project, low-poly mesh was modelled in 3ds Max and unwrapped, which allows colour maps (textures) to be painted in Photoshop. The model contains around 7 million polygons from a ZBrush sculpt. The detail was rendered onto the low-poly mesh via displacement map with a multi-layered skin material which had epidermal, subdermal and backscatter colour maps to achieve the veiny layered look and colour of the character.

3 Space Warps and Particle Tools Space Warp Tools (see left) are used with animations to deform objects as if they are under real conditions such as Ripples or Wind effects, or if the objects are under stress such as Twist, Bend, and Stretch. Particles Tools are used to create systems of particulate behavior from Rain, Snow, and Spray generators to insect swarms.

4 Object Hierarchies Setting up objects and shapes in hierarchies enables objects to respond to the movement of their related or linked objects. You can determine how the object moves in relation to its neighbors, by twisting, pivoting, rotating, or changing size.

3D Packages

There are many industry standard 3D graphics packages, each with their exponents and specialisations. The four main programs are (name, structure, abilities, industry):

- 3ds Max: Modelling, animation, rendering
  NURBS, Polygons
  Games, character design
- Maya: Modelling, animation, rendering
  NURBS, Polygons, SubDivs
  Films, rapid prototyping
- AutoCAD: Modelling
  Lines, vectors
  Product design, architecture
- Rhinoceros 3D: Modelling, rendering
  NURBS, Polygons
  Product design, architecture

PART 2	PRACTICE
UNIT 5	TOOLS AND TECHNOLOGIES
MODULE 7	**Flash/After Effects**

Adobe Flash and Adobe After Effects are two of the main software packages for creation of time-based presentation. Both compose 'moving imagery' for screen or web, use timelines and keyframes to order workspace and incorporate both pixel and vector graphics. They differ in how material is rendered in the program and how it is delivered to the audience.

Flash excels with vector graphics, and is used for interactive web-based applications and animation, with a range of features.
• Illustrator images can be imported then animated, or created in the design stage.
• Complex animations, such as an acorn growing into a shoot, require each seminal stage of the animation to be drawn, called a 'keyframe'. 'Tweening' then creates transitions between two keyframes. A higher number of frames per minute ('frame rate') creates a smoother transition. Unlike After Effects, transitions between different scenes or forms need to be built in by hand.
• Animations within the main animation can be set up, for instance a leaf circling as it drops.
• Flash supports ActionScript, a scripting language that creates computer-generated geometry and timing for complex animations.

• There are open source community libraries of script for assembling into the desired forms, and Flash is prevalent on the internet, in the form of animations, navigation, and video, due to its discreet file size.

After Effects excels with raster graphics, from either stills or video clips imported from Photoshop, video cameras or animation packages, and is used primarily as a post-production effects and compositing tool. As a stand-alone product for viewing (.mpeg or .qt [Quicktime] file formats), clips and stills are organised on tracks similar to audio editing programs. Transitions and fades can be drag-and-dropped between tracks that will then automatically render. After Effects also has many filters and effects, such as film scratches or blurring, to give a mood or tone to your project.

◉ E-cards Greetings cards produced in Flash are easily emailed and are effective in quickly delivering a message, such as 'Bon Voyage' in this example from Cartoon Salon.

ⓘ Less is more
Keep banner advertisements simple; a few well-judged movements and transitions in text and image will be more effective than trying to be complex. With both After Effects and Flash the same theories of composition apply: keep it legible and make it striking.

USEFUL TOOLS
AND FEATURES

The Flash interface is set up in a similar way to most of the Adobe software. The After Effects interface is less similar to the Adobe range, which reflects its use as a film compositor. Here are some tools and resources that stand out from both programs.

1 Flash: Bone Tool One of the developments in the CS4 version of Flash, the Bone Tool can be used for inverse kinematics (IK). In other words, they can be used to link several elements on the canvas with armatures, so that movement of one element will translate back through the link and respond as if the elements are connected by bones.

2 Flash: online tools and applications Visit www.swftools.com for tools to convert Powerpoint to Flash, 3D tools, and animated map tools. Check whether the license on the tool or application that you want to use is freeware, open source, or commercial. Action Script at www.actionscript.org has tutorials, libraries of scripts, and forums.

3 After Effects: Cartoon Effect Create a cartoon aesthetic similar to *A Scanner Darkly* and other rotoscoped films. Simply import the live footage into the work environment, go to the Effects and Presets menu, and select "Cartoon." Tweaking the presets and using the Blur options flattens the colors, removes some of the detail, and creates a cartoon effect.

GLOSSARY

Clip: The name for a sequence of images or length of developed film or video.

FLA: The uncompressed and editable file format from Flash. Make sure to keep your master copy safe.

FLV: Flash Video, the file extension format for displaying video on the internet supported by YouTube and news feed streaming.

Keyframe: Either the frame of an animation at a key stage or a frame in a clip where a transition is due to start.

SWF: ShockWave Flash, the file extension format for displaying animated vector files on the web.

Timeline: The linear timeline in both Flash and After Effects in which keyframes can be fixed in order to designate animated milestones in a production.

⊕ **SEE ALSO:** ILLUSTRATOR P118

○ ASSIGNMENT: **FLASH TUTORIAL**

1 Open a new Flash file, in which you should see a single Layer called 'Layer 1' in the timeline at the top of the page.

2 Select the first frame. Import the leaf image you created in the Adobe Illustrator section on page 121 on to the stage. You can easily do this by going to File > Import > Import to Stage. If you have not completed the Adobe Illustrator leaf tutorial you can import another image or even make your own using the drawing tools.

3 Now select your object on the stage and go to Modify > Convert To Symbol in the menu (or press F8) to convert this image to a Symbol. When the Convert to Symbol window opens name your symbol whatever you like. Select Graphic behaviour and press OK.

4 At this point your symbol is in Frame 1 of Layer 1. Select Frame 30 and go to Insert > Timeline > Keyframe in the menu (or press F6) to insert a new keyframe.

5 While still keeping playhead (the red vertical line) on Frame 30, move your image to any other position on the page other than where it's at now.

6 Select any frame between 2 to 29 and select Motion from the tween pop-up menu in the Property Inspector, usually found at the bottom of the screen (if you don't have the Property Inspector activated, go to Window > Properties > Properties).

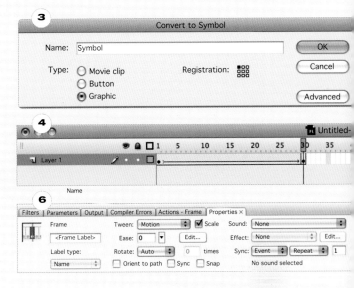

7 Go to File > Publish Preview to preview the results. You can also modify the easing, rotation and sound effects of the object by adjusting the settings found in the Property Inspector.

① **Making changes**

By selecting Frame 30 and clicking directly on the image, you can see the Property Inspector will allow you to modify the end result's brightness, opacity and tint using the Colour drop-down. After adjusting these settings, previewing again will show the animation change colour and opacity from start to finish depending on the parameters you set.

4 After Effects: Mocha

Enables you to motion-track objects within a film so that words, images, or symbols can be spliced into the film, even if the film tracks fast or is blurred. For example, you could track a different billboard image onto a billboard as a car passes and the camera pans to follow the car.

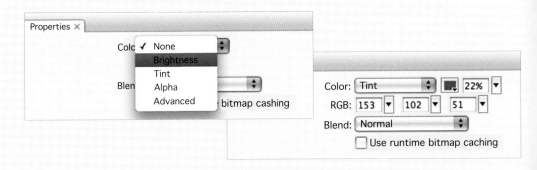

6 PRODUCTION PROCESS AND ISSUES

It could be said that 'design is the battle, but printing is the war', as a variety of complex factors must be taken into account throughout. Print production is the last stage in the design process; it can be the first to be overlooked by the junior designer focusing intently on 'design'.

However, familiarity with print-production issues is vital to ensure the final printed job looks and feels the way it was intended. The use of a special-effect ink, stock or particular finish will only be achievable if you have a thorough (and up-to-date) understanding of the print-production process.

PART 2	PRACTICE
UNIT 6	PRODUCTION PROCESS AND ISSUES
MODULE 1	**Lithography**

In all traditional printing methods (ie, everything except digital printing) your digital artwork needs to be separated into the constituent colours in which it will be printed. This allows the printer to make plates.

Most work will probably be printed using offset lithography; other methods include:
• Screen-printing for T-shirts, billboards, hoardings and some packaging. Normally associated with smaller print-runs.
• Flexography for certain types of packaging and plastic bags.
• Gravure, generally for long runs such as magazines and catalogues.
• Digital printing for short-run full-colour work.

The offset lithography principle

This printing process is based on the principle that water and oil do not mix. The digitally produced printing plate is treated chemically so that the image

The principle in action
This press diagram shows an exposed plate wrapped around the rotating plate cylinder, where the image is dampened and inked before being transferred onto the blanket cylinder.

On a roll Most presses feed one sheet of paper through at a time, but larger web presses, which are used for long runs, draw paper from a roll.

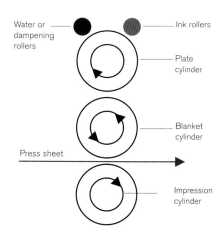

Water or dampening rollers — Ink rollers

Plate cylinder

Blanket cylinder

Press sheet

Impression cylinder

◀ **Printing in CMYK**
This concertina brochure shows strong use of flat and gradient tints obtained from a full-colour print run.

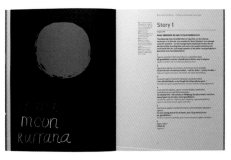

will accept ink and reject water. The simplified diagram below left shows an exposed plate wrapped around the rotating plate cylinder, where the image is dampened and inked. The inked image on the plate is then transferred onto the blanket cylinder. The rubber blanket transfers the image onto the stock, which has been carried around the impression cylinder (adjusted depending on the stock used). This planographic process is rapid, and the plate is inked on each rotation.

▶ **Spot colours** This book is a good example of printing using only two Pantone colours, which creates a varied, powerful and striking design.

GLOSSARY

Digital printing: Method of printing that uses a plateless computer-controlled press.

Flexography: Method of printing that uses rubber relief plates.

Gravure: Method of printing that uses plates with recessed cells of varying depths.

Offset lithography: The digitally produced printing plate is treated chemically so that the image will accept ink and reject water.

Planographic: A printing process that does not use a raised surface.

Plates: Enable the printing of separate colours.

Relief: A printing process that uses a raised surface, such as letterpress.

Screen printing: Method of printing that uses stencils.

◉ ASSIGNMENT: IDENTIFYING PRINT TYPES

Look through your post, newspapers and magazines to find examples of full-colour and spot-colour prints. Many one- and two-colour pieces arrive in the form of business letters and flyers, whereas full-colour pieces may be supermarket circulars, magazine ads and high-volume newspapers.

Using the naked eye or a loupe, have a look at the different dot patterns used to create the imagery.
• Is it a fine field of smaller dots making a clear image?
• Is it a rugged terrain of large dots?
• Or is it a flat, solid tone?

OFFSET ADVANTAGES

• High-quality images can be achieved by providing a higher resolution print.
• Works on a wide range of print media such as paper, fabric, plastic, wood, metal, leather and glass.
• Cost per printed piece decreases as quantity increases.
• Quality, cost-effectiveness, and finishing are fully controllable in large-run jobs.
• Modern offset presses use computer-to-plate technology, increasing economy and quality.

PART 2 | PRACTICE

UNIT 6 | PRODUCTION PROCESS AND ISSUES

MODULE 2 | **Printed colour**

Various factors determine how many colours you choose to produce a job. Aspects such as aesthetics, budget and branding come into play as you begin to select the best printing colour.

Any printed image we see is an illusion of light, paper and patterns of ink that rely on the visual cortex 'blending' the information our retinas perceive into a logical image that our brains can understand. Many different kinds of printing types have been created in order to mass-produce this 'illusion' over the decades.

Single- (monotone-) colour printing can be used when there are budget constraints or when there is a particular colour to be adhered to – for instance, most companies specify a particular Pantone ink for consistency across all their printed work.

Two- and three-colour printing allows for interesting mixtures of Pantones: overprinting two inks can generate a third colour, and printing black-and-white images in two colours (duotone) and three colours (tritone) can enhance their effect.

Full-colour printing uses cyan (C), magenta (M), yellow (Y) and black (K) inks specified in percentage tints to create a huge variety of other colours. This more popular method is used for reproducing full-colour imagery, photographs or flat colours.

Styles of printed colour and shade

⬆ **CMYK** When a full-colour image is needed for print it must be generated as a CMYK file.

⬆ **Greyscale/monotone** Used for a range of tones and in a single colour, such as with newsprint or high-resolution photocopying.

⬆ **Duotone** Here a cyan and black duotone can enhance a monochromatic image or equalise images of varying qualities, in both two- and full-colour jobs.

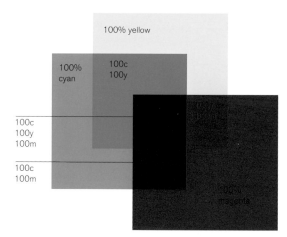

100% yellow

100% cyan

100c 100y

100c 100y 100m

100c 100m

100c 100m 100y

100% magenta

⌃ Full-colour printing
CMYK is the most popular form of print used daily in book and magazine production.

⊕ SEE ALSO:
FUNDAMENTALS OF COLOUR P92

ⓘ Black
Many designers and printers prefer the 'mega-black' or 'super-black' formula for large areas of black. This formula, at 60C, 40M, 40Y, 100K, should be used in imagery, not text and provides a much richer interpretation over 100K alone to create black.

RGB TO CMYK
Printers often insist that you give final image files converted to a CMYK format. Generally, it's best to keep images in RGB format until you are ready to send the file to the printer, since image manipulation programs such as Adobe Photoshop work best with RGB files for correction and effects. Printers recommend the Edit > Convert to Profile function to change an image from RGB to CMYK.

Color Settings...	⇧⌘K
Assign Profile...	
Convert to Profile...	
keyboard Shortcuts...	⌥⇧⌘K
Menus...	⌥⇧⌘M

ⓞ ASSIGNMENT: COMPARING PRINT TYPES
Align the samples you gathered from the Assignment on page 107 with the types of printing processes below. Find any types that are missing. If you have more than one sample for each, organise them by the quality of the printed imagery by considering the 'tightness' of the dot pattern and how successfully it renders the image. Think about the different impressions each printing style yields for the message conveyed.

- Do the lower-quality prints come across as cheaper?
- Do the monotone or duotone images offer an emotional response?
- Do the styles work for or against the message?

⌃ **Resolution** For full-colour, duotone and grey-scale images, image size is reproduced and digital file resolution should be twice the lines per inch (lpi). The standard for high-resolution print is 300 dpi.

⌃ **Halftone** Many periodicals and screen-printers use a halftone pattern to mimic the detail and gradients in a one-colour printed image.

⌃ **Line art** Used when you wish to reproduce an image in black and white, with no intermediate tones, for effect or low-resolution photocopying. At reproduction size, digital file resolution should be eight times the lpi.

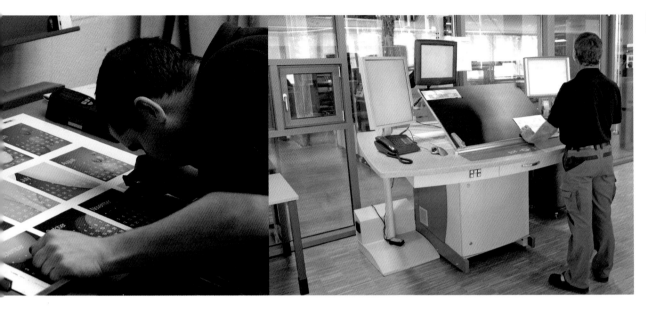

⬆ **Instant proofing** When dealing with digital printing, the proof at the beginning is exactly what you should receive at the end, in terms of colour, quality and stock. If there is a problem with the proof, it takes seconds to produce another. In offset, if there is a change to the plate, add another 15 minutes to make another plate, plus the time to set up and run off another test print.

⬆ **Digital printing** The reproduction of digital images on a physical surface, mostly using toner instead of ink, is known as digital printing. It is generally used for quick, short print runs and for the customisation of print media.

PART 2	PRACTICE
UNIT 6	PRODUCTION PROCESS AND ISSUES
MODULE 3	**Digital printing**

With conventional offset lithography almost a century old, digital presses – emerging in the early 1990s with the ability to create print directly from a digital file – have opened up new frontiers. Forward-thinking printers have embraced any technology that enables them to provide more options for their customers. Different from traditional offset, from speed to price to flexibility, digital printing has worked its way into the workflow of many designers and print houses as clients' needs, wants and timeframes accelerate with the changing times.

Digital presses reproduce documents through a process of toner-based electro-photography – a technology inherent in the common desktop laser printer. This not only speeds up the process but also removes a variety of margins for error.

Generally used for print runs of fewer than 1,000 pieces for economy, digital printing also opens up per-piece customisation for direct mailing, variable data jobs and frequently updated publications, such as newsletters. Personalised printing and printing-on-demand are therefore growing industries, allowing for short-run books and other items of varying printed details, page quantities and binding techniques.

Users include online-and-on-demand service bureaus, traditional sheet-fed and web offset printers, screen printers, sign manufacturers and point-of-purchase display producers. Working with a newer technology, allow yourself and these agencies a margin for error in production stages as you prepare and oversee your digitally printed project.

Ink versus toner

In digital printing, the toner does not permeate the paper, as does conventional ink, but forms a thin layer on the surface. The consensus among designers and printers is that digitally printed colour can appear a bit more 'saturated'. This happens due to lack of light absorption by the paper when ink 'sinks in', as in traditionally printed items. It is not necessarily a bad thing, because 'more saturated' to a printer can also mean 'more vibrant' to a client. Make sure to discuss project adjustments to match intended output more closely, since some newer presses use a combination of toner and ink to achieve more exact colour values.

Digital presses that use toner are notorious for producing large areas of solid colour with banding and blending problems. If a design has a few square centimetres or more of solid colour it's best to add a subtle pattern into those fields to reduce the possibility of banding. When in doubt, ask your printer to run samples, so you can review what may or may not work.

Timeframe

Digital printing cannot be beaten for production timing, since there is no set-up and clean-up of the press for each job. Some offset print houses are now offering shorter print-timing by utilising such techniques as gang-run printing or shift-scheduling.

Personalisation

Database-driven variable data printing allows digital printing to offer the most economical way to customise marketing materials, direct mail pieces, newsletters, etc with different information or designs on each individual printed piece. Finally, all that information that companies have been collecting for years can be easily used in print!

○ ASSIGNMENT: **CLOSE-UP**

Look at any printed piece you may have run-off your home desktop printer or a colour printer at college and compare it to, say, the printed images in this book under a magnifying glass or a loupe. Do you see the difference?

A digitally printed piece employs a much different type of dot-pattern to create its imagery: notice that it is usually less uniform and the dots are more like specks that may use inks beyond the traditional CMYK.

DIGITAL OR OFFSET OPTIONS

• **Quantity** Short-run jobs can prove more cost-effective with digital printing; larger quantities are likely to have a lower per unit cost with offset printing. The rule of thumb is: over 1,000 pieces – go to offset.

• **Colour** Digital presses are like large four-colour process (CMYK) desktop printers. With monotone or duotone printing, offset printing may offer a more cost-effective solution. If Pantone colours are needed, traditional offset is the only way. However, digital printing may offer economical and scheduling advantages when it comes to full-colour pieces.

• **Paper and finishing** Special paper, finishes, surfaces and unique size options are increasing every year for digital, but offset printing still offers more flexibility because the overall sheet size is larger (digital presses can only handle 30 × 45cm [12 × 18in] sheets, whereas offset goes up to 100 × 70cm [40 × 28in]).

• **Proofs** Digital offers more accurate proofs since you receive a sample of the final printed piece, using the exact process and paper that will be used for the intended final run. In offset printing, proofs are generally being produced by digital printers.

◀ **Information age**
Captured data can now be used in tandem with digital presses to create individualised printed items that reference a recipient's name, region or interests for a higher response at a much more affordable rate than in the past.

PART 1	PRACTICE
UNIT 6	PRODUCTION PROCESS AND ISSUES
MODULE 4	**File preparation and sending**

It is best practice to ensure that the need to tidy up files just before sending them is kept to an absolute minimum. By this stage, your bleeds should be set, your colours checked against samples and swatches, all photography should have been purchased/prepared, page items should be aligned, ragging adjusted and the spell check complete. Creating a positive workflow, from design stage to finished product, will help ensure a successful outcome every time. A true measure of a designer is in both your conceptual design and typographic skills, and your handling of the process, from start to finish, which involves preparing and sending out a lot of files to service bureaus and print vendors.

The Preflight check tells you if images or fonts are missing or incorrectly saved. Make sure that everything is correct before you package

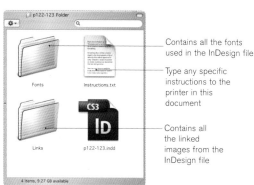

⌃ ⌄ Collecting files Adobe InDesign will collect and sort all the files you need to produce a printed piece at the click of a mouse, as long as you have everything linked in the file.

Contains all the fonts used in the InDesign file

Type any specific instructions to the printer in this document

Contains all the linked images from the InDesign file

⌄ Production ready
By using such functions as guides, the magnifying glass, spell check and Preflight, you can assure your job will be ready for production.

After a final proof is signed off by the client many issues often remain before work can be printed. Remind yourself that because every piece of design work is unique, it creates a unique set of problems: this stage is your last chance to check your work before handing it over to a printer.
• Be meticulous. It is your responsibility to check everything from tint specifications and image colour spaces to tidying up unused colours, style sheets, unintentional indents on justified edges and missing fonts. Programs such as InDesign have spell check and Preflight capabilities.
• Printers are often sent postscript or PDF files – locked documents including all fonts and images – thereby reducing the potential for error. PDFs play a big role these days in near-instant proofing, and are the primary format to send files to periodicals.
• Understand what you are trying to achieve and make sure you are in complete accordance with the printer or producer on such things as paper, folds, die-cuts, enclosure sizes on envelopes, price and timing. Have a clear idea of what is needed to get the job done.

What to send

When collecting a project for output, essentially you are mirroring requisite elements that make up the design: fonts, images and page layouts. However, you are also augmenting these with as many items as possible to help translate to your vendor what you are trying to achieve in production. You can do this by including a satisfactory printout to be used as a guide.

Traditionally, elements such as images and fonts were strung together in page layout programs such as InDesign and Quark; naturally, these included a suite of Preflight and packaging capabilities to check and collect everything for output. To send a file electronically, you must include:
• Your final approved document (InDesign: .indd; Quark: .qxd);
• A folder of all linked images (.psd, .ai, .eps, .tif, .jpg, .pdf), entitled either 'links' or 'images';
• A folder of all fonts (PostScript, True type, Open Type);
• Printer instructions and profiles (automatically included by a lot of programs).
You can also include:
• A printout or a low-resolution PDF for the printer to use as a guide, clearly labelled as such to avoid confusion;
• A note to the vendor that may include specific instructions, a copy of any relevant correspondence, and job numbers; and
• Phone call or email information reiterating agreed-upon specifications with the files attached or a notice of online upload.

◎ Question

What are the key ingredients you need to supply to the print house so that they can create a printed piece?

◎ ASSIGNMENT: PACKAGING FILES

Create a layout in InDesign, with a solid colour background, an image and a short body of text. If you do not have any text on hand, go to Type > Fill with Placeholder Text, which will insert dummy Latin text. Upon completion, package the file by going to File > Package and follow the steps. Familiarise yourself with the way it has automatically organised the requisite job files.

Common errors

On the receiving end of hundreds of designers' production workflows, printers worldwide can tell you there are three things that tend to be overlooked when a project is handed to them.

1 Bleeds With imagery and colour reaching the end of the paper, an actual section of that colour 'bleeds' into the outer margin of the larger print sheet. Printers ask for at least about .3175cm (⅛in) around the page. When preparing imagery, remember to compensate for the bleed by cropping more to the side of the image that is later cut off to make the finished size.

2 Fonts Include all used fonts with the final files, checking that you have the licences. Do not assume that printers have the same fonts. Fonts of the same name come in different versions and from different foundries, and so can have minor characteristic changes. In Illustrator-rendered pieces, you can outline text to reduce file requisites and retain consistency.

3 Resolution A common problem at printing stage is bitmapped pictures due to low-resolution imagery. The standard dots-per-inch resolution for printed imagery is 300dpi, which is much higher than what you see on your computer screens (a mere 72dpi, which translates to 72 rows of 72 dots). The 300dpi rule goes for photography as well as images and illustrations.

PART 2	PRACTICE
UNIT 6	PRODUCTION PROCESS AND ISSUES
MODULE 5	**File types and compression**

Different applications store and compress data in various ways. Misunderstand or misuse these formats and you are heading for trouble. For example, you might spend hours scanning-in files and creating artwork for a magazine only to save your hard work in the wrong format. At best, this will cost you hours; at worst, the job. A working knowledge of file formats and the process of compression could go a long way in preventing this scenario.

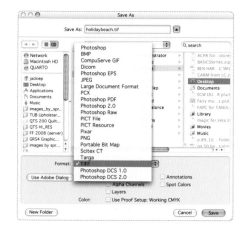

▲ **Adobe Photoshop** This program offers a wide variety of formats for saving files natively in its Save and Save As… functions, whereas other programs may have certain formats hidden in their Export dialogue, such as Adobe Illustrator.

Key graphic file formats

PSD and **AI** are the file formats for Adobe Photoshop and Adobe Illustrator used for image creation.
Compatible with: Photoshop, Illustrator and InDesign with minor restrictions.
Tip: Make sure to always save an unflattened, master version of your Photoshop files to fall back on, and for Illustrator files with unoutlined text.

➕ **SEE ALSO:** ELECTRONIC MEDIA PRODUCTION P146

EPS used to be the most widely used file format in artwork preparation for print. It can contain either vector or bitmap information and is best used when dealing with logos and illustrations as well as vinyl printing and one- and two-colour jobs.
Compatible with: Adobe Illustrator for edits; QuarkXpress and InDesign for layout.
Tip: EPSes themselves can contain font data that may need to be backed up with a font file at the collection stage, or font outlines can be created.

TIFF creates one of the largest files because it saves an alpha channel in the file, which allows for transparency at the art's edge, not at the pasteboard's edge. Best when dealing with monotone, greyscale or watermarks for colour toning, TIFF is the highest-quality image format for full-colour photography as well.
Compatible with: Photoshop for editing; QuarkXpress and InDesign for layout.
Tip: Make sure to check with your printer as to whether they accept files with LZW compression, which is an option while saving.

JPEG is a format that uses 'lossy' compression – meaning that a certain amount of the image quality is lost during the saving process. With a complex photographic image, this would usually remain unnoticed (unless the image is over-compressed).
Compatible with: Photoshop for editing; QuarkXpress and InDesign for layout.
Tip: Nowadays, most digital cameras save as large jpegs, which can be resaved as high-quality images for print due to advances in image resampling and printing.

Electronic files appear to travel many distances around the city or around the globe, when in fact one computer is just copying from another. During this process, corruption can occur, especially to page layout and font files. Compressing files before sending via email or FTP is an effective way of preventing this. Most files that are not native application formats can include some sort of compression to facilitate use in other programs or transmission via the internet. The amount and type of compression, especially with imagery, video and audio projects, can affect the quality and performance of your final file.

.ZIP and .SIT compression file types reduce the number of bytes by removing the redundant areas of underlying code that make up every file. These repeated and replaceable areas are put back into the file using a program such as WinZip or Stuffit to 'unzip' or 'unstuff' the file back to its original format. The final, expanded file is identical to the original before it was compressed. Macs and PCs natively create and open ZIP files, whereas Stuffit file creation and expansion needs a separate program.

Sometimes called 'archives', these compression formats are in all walks of design and production because they speed up and simplify data transmission across the internet. Used primarily to send large files within emails, many studios and companies utilise a File Transfer Protocol (FTP) set-up on their web server to easily transfer files online.

Close	⌘W
Close All	⌥⌘W
Close and Go To Bridge...	⇧⌘W
Save	⌘S
Save As...	⇧⌘S
Check In...	
Save for Web & Devices...	⌥⇧⌘S
Revert	F12

FILE NAMING

• Do not put any spaces in the name or extension; if you need to separate words, use an underscore: 'my_file.jpg'.

• Use lowercase and NOT UPPERCASE characters.

• Use only alpha (abc) or numeric (123) characters. Avoid characters such as @%^&*(), and use a full stop (.) to separate name and extension.

• Try to keep the file name to within eight characters, and remember to add the file extension.

◎ ASSIGNMENT: AVOIDING COMMON ERRORS

If you haven't already, complete the assignment in the previous module. Pull the bleeds off the solid colour background .3175cm (⅛in) of the page on all sides and resave the file. Double check manually that all fonts and imagery are collected, and that the image is of print-quality resolution, or 300dpi, at the size the image will print. Get used to this routine and make it a habit.

⌃ Errors The image directly above is an example of a low-resolution image and with no bleeds pulled. Does that headline look ugly? Many printer programs will simply replace an intended yet not provided font with a standard font like Courier, ruining the design. The intended version is shown at the top of the page, complete with high-resolution image.

⌃ Keep saving Either by going to File > Save or by using speed keystrokes (Ctrl+S for Windows, ⌘+S for Macs) you can avoid the loss of hours of work by making sure you have the latest version of your file secure from program or computer crashes. Also, use Save As to create a back-up file just in case!

❗ Play it safe When working on a large project over time, make an extra copy of your file periodically for safe-keeping since corruption can occur.

⊕ SEE ALSO: FILE PREPARATION AND SENDING P128

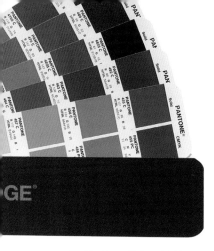

The key to consistent colour is to work in a well-lit room with a calibrated monitor; using colour conventions such as the Pantone Matching System (PMS) and composing colours using CMYK breaks help you achieve correct colour from screen to press. When in doubt, do it by the numbers.

With colour you can mix cyan, magenta, yellow and black in any image-making program or by selecting colours from an image. This approach mimics the pioneer press person's experimentation with inks that forged the path for printing today. However, PMS is a more reliable way to ensure you are going to get the colour you choose.

PMS

The internationally used Pantone Matching System consists of colour reference manuals used for selection and input, either by 'PMS number' or by precise CMYK formulas. Printers have these books and the corresponding matching inks.

Pantone colours, or spot colours, have different types since colour reacts differently with different printing processes and surfaces. To help approximate this, PMS swatch books come in many versions, made for different papers such as coated and matt, and in solid or process colours.

⌃ Pantone Colour Bridge
This not only shows you what a particular solid PMS colour will look like, but also its full-colour printed counterpart, while giving the CMYK, RGB and hexidecimal formulas for typing it in.

⌄ A PMS book Keep one of these books on hand when designing, attending client meetings and going on press check as a guide to help choose and validate colour.

Calibration: Colour settings that should be set to show colour on-screen as it will be in print.

Colourimeter: Hardware that attaches to or hangs in front of your screen, allowing you to calibrate and profile your monitor.

CMYK break: The computed percentages of C, M, Y and K ink that make up a colour.

Pantone Matching System (PMS): An international system to ensure reliable colour selection, specification and control.

PMS BOOK CHOICES

• **Solid** Over 1,000 PMS spot colours are contained in either the fan guide or the chip book, with some speciality versions for metallic colours, pastels or tints.

• **Process** Over 3,000 Pantone Process Colours with their CMYK percentages are contained in these books.

• **Colour Bridge** Formerly known as the Solid to Process Guide, this book provides a larger colour swatch and tint comparison showing how solid colours will look in CMYK, and gives print and web formulas.

PANTONE BOOK PAPER CHOICES

• **Coated** This book contains PMS numbers followed by a C, indicating that a colour can only be matched by printing on a coated (glossy) surface.

• **Uncoated** This book contains PMS numbers followed by a U, indicating an uncoated (matt) surface.

Monitors

The best place to begin a successful colour workflow is with the monitor. Correct calibration and profile usage ensure what you see on-screen is what turns out in print. Reliable translation of material from scanner or camera to monitor then printer means proper communication from one device to the next.

Although brand choices and preferences can be wide and far-reaching, all good monitors allow you to make adjustments to their White Point Temperature and Gamma:
• White Point Temperature controls the overall tint that the colour white on the screen will have. Traditionally, 6500 Kelvin has always been recommended for computer monitors to simulate normal white.
• Gamma, on the other hand, dictates overall contrast and usually runs at a value of 1.8 for Apple-based systems and 2.2 for Windows-based systems, due to the inherent differences between platforms.

Colourimeters

Many modern monitors come with presets and programs to help you get basic values, but in recent years colourimeters have become readily available to ensure every colour point and setting is consistently and dependably adjusted to standard. Colourimeters cycle through a series of modes to read the current state of display and adjust the video card correctly, creating a new profile, called an ICC profile, for the monitor to create colour from.

ICC profiles

Every device has its own set of specifications known as ICC profiles. Set up by the International Color Consortium, these standards facilitate the translation of colour information of an image from one device to the next. When a screen, scanner or camera is recalibrated, each is given a new profile and the image produced picks up that profile. Images opened in Photoshop can be reviewed; if a profile setting is different or missing, then the working profile of the monitor is used.

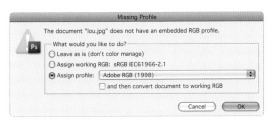

⊕ **SEE ALSO:** THE FUNDAMENTALS OF COLOUR P92

◀ **Image missing** Best practice says to leave a profile as is if it is already embedded, or to give an image one (the one your screen is working in) if it is missing.

◉ ASSIGNMENT: **PRINTER PROFILES**

Printer profiles can be tricky because they deal with the translation of colour information from screen to vendor. Dealing mostly with grey balance and percentages of CMY and K inks to approximate colour, printer profiles remain region-specific, with SWOP in some areas and FOGRA in others, for example.

To adjust your Colour Settings for Photoshop, Illustrator and InDesign choose Edit > Colour Settings from the menu. When there you can modify your presets and working spaces for print and web. Find out if you are using the correct colour space for your region and experiment with how modifying these settings changes the way your monitor represents the colour.

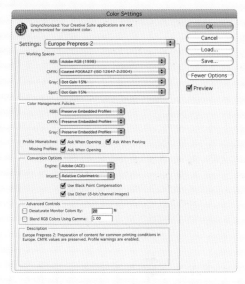

ℹ **Global standard**
GRACOL is currently the standard colour profile, but before you start your project, ask your service bureau which profile they may prefer you to work with — they may even have created their own.

◀ **Colour calibration** Many factors such as time, usage and heat cause a monitor to go out of calibration, so many professional yet consumer-grade colourimeters, such as the Spyder, are available to re-calibrate a monitor.

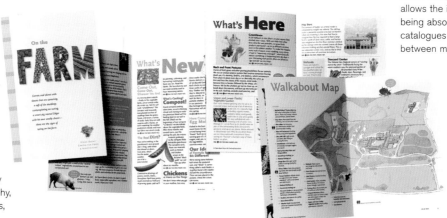

◄ **Coated** Gloss or matt, coated stock has a hard, nonporous surface, which allows the ink to sit on the paper without being absorbed. Many brochures and catalogues use satin, which is somewhere between matt and gloss.

🛈 **Going green** Concerns about sustainability in recent years mean that many designers now use recycled papers, or ones made from cotton, not wood pulp. This is not the only concern for sustainable design, but an important consideration when choosing paper.

▲ **High gloss** Frequently used for fashion photography, and especially in magazines, gloss stock is used when sharp, highly contrasted images are required.

▼ **Matt** Generally dull and absorbent, matt stock is used for books, newspapers, brochures and stationery. This example shows how the dull quality of the paper matches the 'earthy' content. Paper choices can reinforce content.

↘ **Stationery** In stationery design, laid or wove paper is frequently used. Both are matt, absorbent and take ink well. All can be laser and inkjet printed.

PART 2	PRACTICE
UNIT 6	PRODUCTION PROCESS AND ISSUES
MODULE 7	**Paper stocks and finishing**

Paper is often the most costly item in a printing job. It is manufactured in a large assortment of weights, colours, textures and finishes, and selecting the correct one is critical to the success of the finished product. Sampling is the ideal way to determine whether or not a particular stock will work for you. You should also be aware of the common terms used to describe paper, including the various attributes and how they apply to a particular job.

Paper is produced from pressed pulped wood, cotton or recycled paper. Seven standard attributes describe different characteristics.

1 Weight describes density of fibres that make up the sheet, and is measured in grams per square metre, or g/m^2, or gsm. Heavier weights are usually of better quality and last longer.

2 Thickness is measured in caliper (inches) or millimetres; however, greater thickness does not mean better quality.

3 Texture depends on the size or quality of wood fibres and the method of construction. Tightly pressed, fine fibres result in a smoother paper normally used for writing or printing; less pressed, bigger fibres form board and fibrous card.

4 Strength (tension and resilience) is affected by texture, density, weight and thickness; for example, tissue paper and paperboard are both used for packaging, but in different contexts.

5 Opacity depends on density and thickness, and refers to how much text or image on the overleaf page can be masked. Tracing paper is highly translucent and is made by immersing good-quality paper in acid, which alters the fibres.

6 Brightness depends on how much the paper has been bleached before it is pressed. Brighter stock reflects more light and results in a 'fresher' look to a page. Environmental concerns have resulted in a return to unbleached paper in recent years.

7 Colour is produced by dyeing the fibre pulp before it is pressed. Coloured stocks are more expensive than white stock.

Matt, satin and gloss

Different paper qualities affect the intensity of printed ink – there is a stark difference between printed matt and gloss surfaces. When ink adheres to matt paper it is absorbed and appears dull. This quality is normally used for printed word texts such as newspapers and books. However, ink printed onto gloss paper stays on the surface, so that more light hits the paper below and bounces off, giving a deeper, more intense colour. This quality is used for covers, magazines and brochures. Satin paper comes somewhere between the two, giving a slightly less intense colour than gloss but without the shiny surface.

Finishes and coatings

Finishes and coatings are added either to protect printed ink, or in patches to emphasise an area of ink. There are four main kinds.

1 Varnishes are coatings applied 'on-press' either with other inks or as a separate run, and can be matt, stain or gloss, and tinted with added pigment.

2 UV coatings are spread on as a liquid then hardened with ultraviolet light. They can be matt or gloss, and applied accurately in spot form or as complete coverage.

3 Aqueous coatings – matt, satin and gloss – are relatively expensive and are laid at the end of a run. As such they cannot be controlled to be put in specific areas, only as a complete coat.

4 Laminates are layers of sheet plastic or clear liquids that bind into the paper to protect it.

Paper can also be embossed to emphasise lettering or an image, or laser cut or die cut to expose the page underneath. Debossing or embossing are, however, expensive techniques, along with die-cutting, therefore need to be used sparingly.

⬆ **Visual effect** Debossing creates an indented image below the surface of the paper.

⬆ **Shades of white** Sample swatches are provided free by paper companies and enable you to make informed decisions about paper by comparing the various qualities. For example, white is a variable colour in terms of paper, and you'll find that there can be big differences between 'bright', 'fluorescent', 'dull' and 'off-white'.

⬤ ASSIGNMENT: **PAPER SAMPLES**

Collect as many samples of different paper as you can. Whenever you find a new quality of paper, in either a newspaper, magazine, offcut or brochure, cut out a 10 x 3cm (4 x 1.2in) strip and punch a hole in the centre of one end. The samples can be loosely tied together to give you an idea of different textures, weights and thicknesses. Also try to find your nearest large print/copy/binding shop. Speak to one of the employees and find out if they have any paper samples you can take away with you.

PART 2	PRACTICE
UNIT 6	PRODUCTION PROCESS AND ISSUES
MODULE 8	**The role of PDFs**

The Adobe Portable Document Format (PDF) has come a long way from the aim of the 'paperless office' and is now a means to instantaneously review in-progress drafts and final sign-offs, or 'soft proofs', with clients, vendors and colleagues. Like a high-resolution, electronic fax machine, the PDF has become the standard for version editing, as well as submitting ads and media to newspaper and periodical publishers; the final output for the printer is itself a 'high-res' PDF.

In creating PDFs using Acrobat, InDesign or Illustrator, you should start the press optimisation process using predefined settings in either the Save As or Adobe PDF Presets menus, unless you were provided with specific settings from your service bureau.

Many programs create reliable PDFs automatically, ensuring correct colour profiles as well as final images and fonts are properly linked. Always double check the PDF in Acrobat to make sure everything is correct.

Photoshop can be a different animal when it comes to PDFs, and a great way of ensuring consistency is to flatten all layers, although this creates a file that can, at times, be impervious to compression.

Errors Mistakes are often caught after PDFs and review, both from different views, and from zooming up images, up to 1,600 percent, for proofing the slightest text incongruities and alignment anomalies.

GLOSSARY

Adobe Acrobat: The family of Adobe programs that create and manage PDFs.

Downsampling: A form of compression that lowers the resolution of images by eliminating unnecessary pixel data.

Embedding: A PDF removes the need for multiple requisite files by including fonts and compressed imagery into one file.

PDF ADVANTAGES

• **Highly compressed files** can be generated – with optimised imagery and fonts embedded – to create a very close copy to the original working document. This condensed and mobile format can be easily emailed en masse to clients and co-workers for feedback, with edits and mistakes more easily caught during the production process.

• **To print**, the recipient needs only the free Adobe Acrobat Reader download. Many systems have this pre-installed, but it is best to get the latest version.

• **Newspaper and magazine publishers** often receive ads as high-resolution PDFs only, with properly embedded fonts and images at correct resolution and profile. Advanced tools in Adobe Acrobat Professional such as Preflight, optimiser and fix-ups can be key to achieving a successful run.

• **Email and internet creators** can link files to web pages for online viewing or attach files to emails.

Downsize The PDF process saves precious kilobytes by removing repetitive algorithms, creating vector shapes from elements, compressing imagery and embedding fonts.

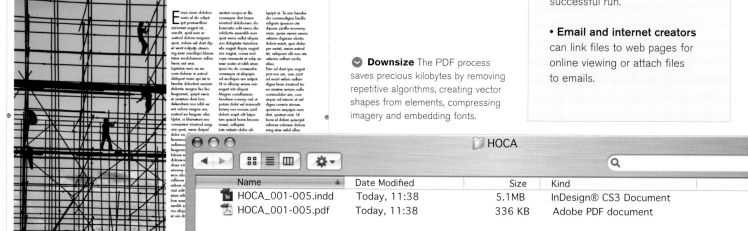

Name	Date Modified	Size	Kind
HOCA_001-005.indd	Today, 11:38	5.1MB	InDesign® CS3 Document
HOCA_001-005.pdf	Today, 11:38	336 KB	Adobe PDF document

◀ **Adobe Acrobat's**
Preflight This tool checks your document's validity against agreed-upon printing standards such as proper font embedding, CMYK colour conversion, image resolution and other factors that may inhibit the file from producing the intended design.

◀ **Editing** Much client and inter-office editing is done electronically directly to the PDF using a variety of comment, call-out and highlighting tools to make suggestions, spot spelling errors and give feedback on a concept or choice of imagery.

⊙ ASSIGNMENT:
PREFLIGHT OPTIONS

The Preflight Tool identifies issues with colours, fonts, imagery, resolution, compatibility and more, and can apply 'fix-ups' to correct certain errors.

1 Create a PDF using InDesign, open it in Adobe Acrobat and select Preflight from the Advanced menu.

2 Look through the list and run different profile tests to see what comes up in the results.

3 Undo any fix-ups that may have been applied as you go through the different tests and try to understand what information the results are giving you and how this applies to how the file that generated the PDF was created.

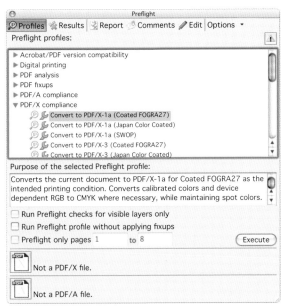

Font embedding

When a font is not embedded it is usually because it is missing or has vendor restrictions; when opened or printed a generic typeface can be substituted. Nothing is worse than opening an ad book with your client's advertisement – a masterpiece in Gill Sans, say – and being greeted with a horror dripping in Courier. Proper embedding at creation time prevents font substitution at viewing stage, and ensures that vendors reprint the text in its intended font. Preflighting tools in InDesign and Illustrator usually help you steer clear of errors before reaching PDFs, and you can always check Properties when viewing PDFs to check that fonts are embedded.

PDF/X

When Preflighting, you can bring your PDF to PDF/X and PDF/A standards. These file types, defined by the International Organization for Standardization (ISO), adhere to standards that facilitate reliable PDF transmission. They apply the wills and will-nots of a file. Using a PDF-X1a file generated from Acrobat Preflight is considered the best way to ensure that your file is correct and secure.

PDF OPTIONS

• **PDF optimiser** Compresses large PDFs by auditing file size through downsampling imagery, flattening transparencies and outlining fonts.

• **Comments** A variety of tools to help illustrate edits such as notes and arrows to mark up the PDF.

• **Review** Many offices utilise the sign-off, meeting and version features of Acrobat to handle edits and reviews.

• **Interactivity** Although not print-specific, PDFs have multimedia and interactive capabilities for presentations and e-zines.

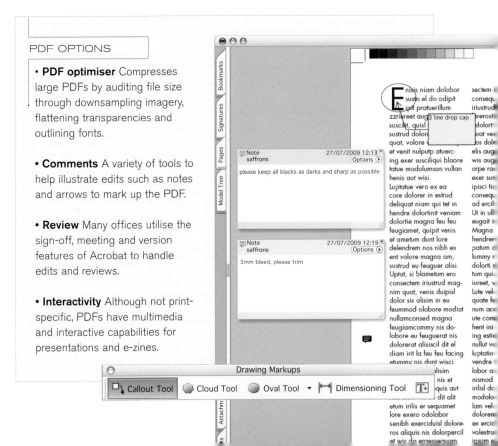

PART 2	PRACTICE
UNIT 6	PRODUCTION PROCESS AND ISSUES
MODULE 9	**Correcting colour proofs**

The arrival of colour proofs is second only to the arrival of a finished printed piece of work you have created. However, at colour proof stage, it is still possible to correct any flaws in photography, both digital and conventional.

Transparency viewer (lightbox)

These are available in various sizes, but what is more important is that the lighting conforms to ISO 3664:2000. This international standard defines colour and intensity in the light source; most transparency viewers used by colour-separation houses and printers conform to it.

Linen tester (loupe)

This is the type of magnifying glass used by colour-separation houses and printers to view both colour transparencies and proofs. The folding stand means that the lens is the correct distance from the subject and hands are left free (see below).

➕ **SEE ALSO:**
PRINTED COLOUR P128
PRESS CHECK P144

❗ **Flopping**
When a picture appears reversed left to right in a colour proof, it should be marked 'flop'. This correction is not simply a matter of the colour house turning the film over, since the emulsion would be on the wrong side and therefore out of contact with the plate. Instead, a new contact film has to be made so that the emulsion is on the right side.

❗ **Fit**
If the register marks fit but you can see colours sticking out from the edge of the picture, the job has been planned out of fit.

The colour control strip tells the designer whether the proof is faithful to the film being proofed. For example, if the proofreader has used too much yellow ink, so that the proof looks too yellow when the film is correct, the colour bar will help to show this

Check registration marks to see if the job has been proofed in register. If it is correct, all you will see is black. If it is out of register, one or more colours will show next to the black

Greyscale density patches are printed in steps from no tint through to black. They are used to check black-and-white photography and black text in a similar way to that of a colour control strip

Check trim marks for position and that the bleed allowance is correct

1st Proof

BACKGROUNDS

If a common special colour or tint background is required for several pages in a publication, the designer should be aware of problems the printer might have in maintaining consistency between pages. For example, if a buff background is used, consisting of a percentage tint of process yellow, and there are some pages that require a heavy weight of yellow to be run for the pictures, the tints on those pages will be heavier than on the other pages. The use of a special fifth colour (a Pantone colour, for example) for the backgrounds only should prevent this problem. But remember that it is more expensive to run five colours than four.

◉ ASSIGNMENT: **QUICK PROOFING CHECKLIST**

Memorise this list for points you should always check. Add more, and create your own personalised list of things to watch out for.

- Register
- Trim and bleed
- Type – broken, missing, illegible, too fine
- Colour – check the colour bar
- Flopped subjects
- Artwork overlays
- Tints
- Special colours
- Gutter

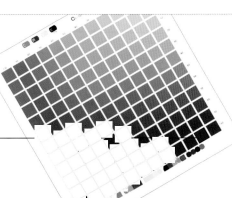

On first specifying a tint, always give percentages of the process colours, obtainable from a tint chart, rather than a Pantone colour swatch or reference number to match, because many special colours cannot be achieved from the four-colour process. The tint on the proof can then be checked against the tint chart. Watch out for mottled tints, which can be caused by the film or plate being exposed out of contact

PART 2	PRACTICE
UNIT 6	PRODUCTION PROCESS AND ISSUES
MODULE 10	**Press check**

Printers are usually very receptive to clients overseeing their jobs at the beginning of the press run; this almost always turns into a learning experience. It is especially helpful when aesthetic judgment is needed, for example in adjustment of print by increasing or decreasing ink intensity to match intended colour. The press person will pull a sheet of press for you to review, approve and sign off on. At this point you should take your time, pay attention, ask questions and have a checklist to keep you focused.

◉ **Hot off the press** By the time a job hits the press, errors should have already been caught and corrected, so that the focus can be on the colour and finish of the overall job.

At a press check time is expensive – egregious errors such as misspelt words and unaligned edges should have been handled at proof stages. This will help to avoid any extra correction costs, set-up charges and rescheduling for you and your client. When you are 'on the floor' in the press room, you should focus on overall aesthetic considerations, although a keen eye is always on the hunt for an errant inch-mark instead of an apostrophe, or random double space.

⊙ ASSIGNMENT: **TEST SHEET**

Take a test sheet and cut the press paper with a pair of scissors. Lay the cut press sheet up against the hard proof you signed off on to make sure colours match and margins align. No home monitor nor inkjet printout can approximate the press – not even the hard proof! When you are finally holding a test sheet in your hands, make the following assessments.

• Is the overall tone of the piece as intended?
• Is the colour dominance of the piece correct as is, or is there a colour cast?
• Are the colours printing to registration (printer marks and a linen tester can be of service here)?
• Check the paper stock. Is it the correct paper? Is it the correct weight and free from imperfections?
• Does the paper colour affect the final print?
• Are all page elements, text and fonts present and accounted for?
• How are the images printing in terms of resolution, colour and tone?
• When trimmed and folded, are all live area elements sound and correctly aligning?

A closer look A loupe can be used to pick up on detail that might not be visible to the naked eye, but that is vital in the overall quality of the printed product.

PRESS CHECK CHECKLIST

Be prepared; bring these with you.

• **An extra copy of electronic files** or, even better, a laptop you can work directly from (with requisite fonts and imagery installed).

• **The Pantone book** (coated/uncoated, or spot or process). See page 136.

• **The colour proof** that you signed off on, although many vendors may want this back – be sure to ask for it again at press time.

• **A linen tester or loupe** – a type of magnifying glass used to check for such things as registration, dot bleed, dot gain, and font-clarity. It usually has a folding stand to hold the lens at the correct distance from the page.

GLOSSARY

Dot gain: A printed dot that becomes bigger than intended due to spreading, causing a darkening of screened images, mid-tones and textures. Varies with different paper stock, such as newsprint.

Quality control strip: Usually incorporated in printed sheets outside the grid to monitor the quality of plate-making, inking and registration. Checking black sections helps point out colour casting.

Registration mark: Hairline mark at the corner of a printed page to help ensure plates are lined up correctly and designate what will be cropped off at finishing time.

Question

Have you ever come across a printed piece with an obvious printing error: the colours are off-register, the fonts are obviously wrong a word is misspelt, or an image is too low in resolution? How could these errors have been avoided at the press check and proofing stages?

Quality control strip
Printed sheets usually incorporate a control strip outside the grid to monitor the quality of plate-making, inking, registration, dot grain, etc.

CMY 75% 50% 25%   B 75% 50% 25%   C 75% 50% 25%   M 75% 50% 25%   75% 50% 25%   SLUR   EXPOSURE   PaperC+Y C+M Y+M

The press room floor
The floor is a busy place, with projects being scheduled and waiting in queue for their turn for production, as press people manage and maintain the quality of the presses and the printed pieces they create. Many print houses work in shifts, allowing them to continue printing into the night and on weekends to keep up with client demands and timeframes.

SEE ALSO: FILE PREPARATION AND SENDING P132

WORKSPACE, MONITOR AND CALIBRATION P136

CORRECTING COLOUR PROOFS P142

PART 2	PRACTICE
UNIT 6	PRODUCTION PROCESS AND ISSUES
MODULE 11	**Electronic media production**

The production process and issues related to electronic media (audio, visual, animation and imagery) could bring you into contact with other issues relating to film, video, sound, animation and web formats, to name a few. Various projects leading to a more multimedia solution can start with your basic pen and paper, or Illustrator or Photoshop document, but quickly become entrenched with specific file types, compatibility factors and production considerations that must be mastered.

Although there are many file types, each specific to their discipline, some main players are utilised across the board. As a designer, you will time and again be faced with new file types and applications, so a basic understanding of what is standard so far in electronic production can help prepare you for any future situations. Most of the file types described here rest in a more web-based arena, as the web has quickly become a main conduit for the public to access animation, motion and video-based designs. However, a mastery of these formats will be crucial as you move to more specific applications focusing on motion and video editing, animation and audio.

⊙ ASSIGNMENT: TEST SHEET

Find two images: a photograph and an illustration (preferably one with only a few colours, like a logo).
1 Open the photo in Photoshop and go to Save For Web and Devices in the File menu. You will see the image with a variety of controls to the right.
2 Explore the drop-down selectors, choose between JPG and GIF, and modify the settings for each format to see how the image is re-rendered. Watch the file size change in the lower left as you make adjustments.
3 Repeat the process with the illustration and make a note of which option best suits each image.

⊕ **SEE ALSO:** FILE PREPARATION AND SENDING P132

FILE TYPES AND COMPRESSION P134

THE ROLE OF PDFS P140

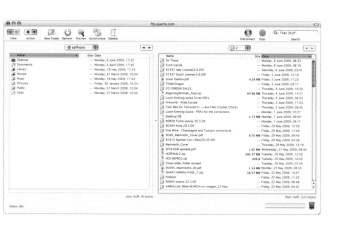

◀ **Panic's Transmit** A popular Mac FTP application, Transmit is simple to use, by just dragging a file from your desktop to the window designated as the server. Many vendors have FTPs set up on their servers for file collection, and may provide a username, password and folder for your job.

▶ **Artifacting** Seen in JPEGs mostly, 'artifacting' is a large, unclear area of a lossy-compressed image that can mimic pixellation due to the blurred areas being contained in blocks. Careful compression values can lessen this effect.

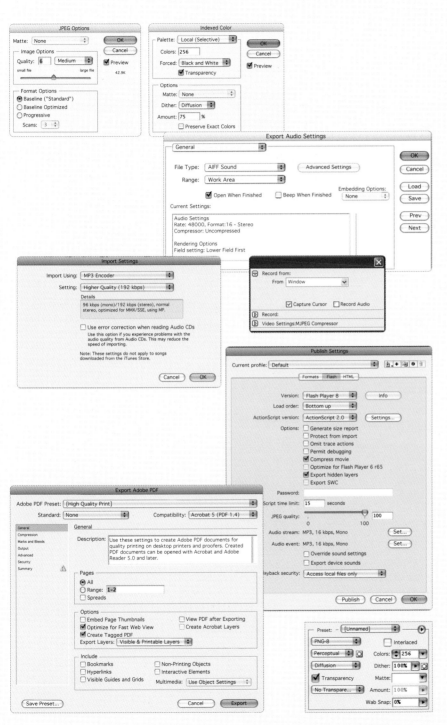

Key audiovisual file formats

JPEG uses 'lossy' compression – some image quality is lost during the saving process. With a complex photographic image, this should go unnoticed; if you save an image with large areas of solid colour you will get distorted areas.

GIF can only hold up to 256 colours. They are good for flat graphic images, can retain transparency and be animated to create rotating images.

AIFF is used for storing uncompressed sound files on the Macintosh platform. These files are larger than MP3 format, but are often used for mobile-phone ringtones.

MOV stores Apple Quicktime movie and audio files. Quicktime Player is needed to view the files.

MPEG and MP3 are compression formats for movie and audio files. MPEG files are smaller than other formats at the same quality. MP3 and MPEG4 are popular for portable and online players.

SWF (ShockWave Flash) delivers vector graphics and animation over the internet. It is most commonly used in animation and interactivity design, and requires a Flash Player to load and play the file.

FLV is a similar format to the SWF but deals with online video playback.

PDF is a highly compressed format suited to emailing large files, linking files to web pages and even printing directly from, as long as the PDF and images within it are suitably high-resolution and the fonts are properly embedded.

PNG (Portable Network Graphic) is an alternative to GIF, and offers a wider range of transparency options.

7 WEB DESIGN BASICS

Designing for the web has become a fast-developing field in which a designer must honour and yet at times reinterpret design basics and principles to meet the ever-evolving capabilities of technology. While incorporating such areas as visual information design, aesthetics and composition, a web designer must also demonstrate an encompassing understanding of more modern technological considerations such as coding, user interaction and online trends.

The most direct route to creating a site that is both usable and well designed is to understand the limitations and freedoms inherent in the technology involved, and how these interplay with the expectations of client and audience. Such things as the end user's screen resolution, cross-browsing differences, personal user settings and age of a user's computer play a large role in determining how a web designer prepares for a project.

The practices of understanding basic visual aesthetics, interface ergonomics and good typography will aid you in steering your traffic effectively. All of this is done through a visual graphic concept generated near-instantly by pure transmitted computer code.

PART 2	PRACTICE
UNIT 7	WEB DESIGN BASICS
MODULE 1	**Visual design and coding**

To look more closely at the limitations and opportunities that exist within web design, we must first examine what is being limited and how these opportunities reveal themselves.

With a fair amount of time spent in 'design mode', and such key aspects as composition, colour and message coming in to play with web design, this presentation then becomes an interpretation of an underlying body of code. This coding is the stream of instructions that detail how a browser will piece together content and imagery into the visual representation the user sees when typing in a web address. Web developers and coders have expanded this 'language of the internet' to create a wide range of possibilities, including such innovations as Flash animation, dynamic interaction, instant communication and on-page information processing.

Conveying the message

Many web designers work from Photoshop mock-ups. They create templates in perfect proportion to how they should render work onscreen, then snip out the imagery they need and stitch it together in code. Others work directly with code, and create a layout with <div>s and other structural elements, then design from there. Either way, it is the information and how the intended audience best digests it that should always be paramount, as a site is only a vehicle for messages to receivers. With good design principles, some creativity and a basic understanding of both coding and semantics, as well as common contemporary conventions (such as browser differences, web standards and best font sizes), you'll be ready to start breaking down your site's information into the language of the internet: Hypertext Mark-up Language (HTML).

◀ **Initial sketch** Creating a site from thumbnail sketches through designing to coding and launch has always proved a successful approach.

▼ **Source** The information that a browser uses to render a site is nothing more than a page of instructional code of tags and scripts.

Separation of content and presentation

When the internet was young, sites were mostly created using complex grids made of tables, much like a spreadsheet, with a piece of an image within each cell. The entire grid would come together to form one big image, which would be your site. Most of the text was trapped within the flattened images or surrounded by complex code, making it inaccessible and search-engine invisible, and it took forever to download a page. Especially when all that was available was 56k dial-up!

This came to a quick end in 2001 when the World Wide Web Consortium (the regulatory committee that maintains the web's best practices, standards and language drafts) updated HTML to XHTML and adopted Cascading Style Sheets (CSS), which allowed the user to separate presentational mark-up (such as images, colours and layout instructions) from the main document and move them to a separately loaded document. This allowed the designer to tag the main content semantically, speed up download timing and style the visual outcome purely using CSS. Not only did this create a wide variety of design applications and possibilities, but it also allowed for more thorough and pointed search engine penetration, and opened up the internet for wider accessibility for the visually and motor impaired.

With a mindset for the web's future, or its 'extensibility', the major reason to separate presentation from content is that the isolation of content helps secure future browser compatibility by reducing complexity of the on-page structural content, which also leads to easier updates while retaining a consistent presentation. This sets the stage for future concepts, such as more meaningful, or semantic, web and search options, and eases the support and integration of upcoming technologies and features.

Doctype prepares the browser for the kind of code to be rendered and how

Scripts and links load other pages of code for the browser to use when called upon

Meta-information gives search engines important data on the site's content and audience

Divisions group together sections of tags to be styled and positioned graphically

Lists are used when creating the navigation of a site due to the styling options available to the tag

```
<!DOCTYPE html PUBLIC "-//W3C//DTD XHTML 1.0 Transitional//EN"
   http://www.w3.org/TR/xhtml1/DTD/xhtml1-transitional.dtd>
<html xmlns=http://www.w3.org/1999/xhtml xml:lang="">
      <head>
         <meta http-equiv="content-type content="text/html; charset=utf-8" />
         <title>Bella Vista Trattoria & Pizzeria</title>
<link href="css/style.css" rel="stylesheet" type="text/css" />
<script src="scripts/mootools.v1.11.js" type="text/javascript"></script>
         <script src="scripts/jd.gallery.js" type="text/javascript"></script>
         <script src="scripts/jd.gallery.transitions.js" type="text/javascript"></script>
         <link rel="stylesheet" href="css/slideshow.css" type="text/css" media="screen" />

<!--[if IE]>
<link rel="stylesheet" type="text/css" href=css/ie.css"/>
<![endif]-->

         <meta http-equiv="Content-Type" content="text/html; charset=iso-8859-1" />
</head>
<body id="indexpage">
<div id="headerMain">
<div id="header">

<div id="address">Mon&ndash;Thu 11am-9pm, Fri&ndash;Sat 11am-10pm<br />
5337B Limestone Road Wilmington, DE 19808<br /><a href="directions.html">directions</a></div>
<ul class="top">
<li><a href="index.html" class="about">home</a></li>
<li><a href="pdfs/bellavistamenu.pdf" class="about">menu</a></li>
<li><a href="contact.html" class="contact">contact</a></li>
</ul>
<ul class="nav">
<li><a href="menu.html">Menu</a></li>
<li><a href="catering.html">Catering Services</a></li>
<li><a href="freshingredients.html">Our Ingredients</a></li>
<li><a href="news.html">News &amp; Events</a></li>
<li><a href="comments.html">Comments &amp; Reviews</a></li>
</ul>
</div>
```

Variously styled instructions and images turn a list of links into an inviting and functional navigation bar

◀ **Following the grid** Conventions for headers, footers, sidebars and navigation menus make the internet easy to use.

▷ **Advanced technology** Faster and less-expensive bandwidth allows sites to have complex imagery and motion graphic elements such as Flash.

PART 2	PRACTICE
UNIT 7	WEB DESIGN BASICS
MODULE 2	**The languages of the internet**

Websites and web pages can be written in numerous languages, but HTML is a good place to start. Hypertext Mark-up Language is the most popular language used on the internet and with it you can build documents (web pages) with text, images, sounds and links to other pages – in short, a website.

The web comprises multiple languages that 'mark-up' or create upon another language a new informational, or 'meta', hierarchy. This hierarchy is used logically and graphically to create visual sites out of lines of text. This text is processed each time it is sent to a browser, and the browser follows its instructions the best it can, whether to load an image from one server or to send a form to another.

Making up the bulk of the internet as we know it, Hypertext Mark-up Language is a semantic computer language that is used widely due to its compatibility with other languages and innovations such as CSS, PHP, Javascript, AJAX, Java and image types such as .jpg, .tif, .png and .swf. Created in 1991 by Tim Berners-Lee, HTML is now in its fourth draft, called HTML 4.0, and is regulated by the World Wide Web Consortium (www.wc3.org). A newer, stricter version, XHTML, has become more popular due to its forward-thinking, clean coding, and higher compatibility with CSS, AJAX and other technologies.

The syntax of an HTML or XHTML document is composed of tags that create the structure and layout of the document, and appoint function and hierarchy to on-page elements. This tag hierarchy sets up a semantic structure for information, and is a way to localise an on-page element and apply style to it, like a wrapper. This tag surrounds text, imagery and objects, allowing designers to style, position and correlate elements together, such as lists (the <ul> and <li> tags). The tag consists of two parts: a start and end tag. The start tag always has some sort of HTML element, be it 'a' for 'anchor' or 'p' for 'paragraph', and is bracketed by a '<' and a '>'. Often, a start tag may contain one or more different attributes, such as 'id' or 'class' for CSS referencing, and each attribute usually has a value. These elements are symbols that tell a browser what to display, and the element's attributes are instructions to the browser on how to display them.

Static versus dynamic

One major development in many modern websites is that they are dynamic rather than static. The principal difference is that in a dynamic site, the web server creates the page on demand. Amazon.com is a good example. When you search for a book on Amazon the page delivered is generated on the fly, based on your search criteria. Text and images are pulled into a pre-programmed template, delivering the relevant information. Compare this with a static website, in which each page must be designed and exist on the server before the information for a particular book can be presented.

Content-rich A Flash-based website can utilise abstract layouts, animation, 3D motion graphics and alternative navigation.

Make it easy Many sites use a combination of AJAX and dynamic HTML to simplify user experience.

Dynamic rendering Amazon.com is a great example of a site that is rendered dynamically. Can you imagine someone creating all of those thousands of pages by hand?

Language class

The many languages of the web are best classified by their inherent qualities, and all have a level of complexity and mastery. Whole industries and careers are built upon the languages listed below; these languages are what make up the face of the internet as we see it today.

• **Structure and content** HTML is an internet standard used by all browsers to provide instructions on how to visually display or process information retrieved from the net. Its syntax comprises a list of tags that describe the structure of text-based information in a document by denoting certain blocks of copy as headings, paragraphs, links, lists, as well as interactive forms, embedded images and other scripting objects. XHTML is the latest, and more strictly written, draft of HTML.

• **Style and layout** CSS describes the stylistic presentation of a structured document written in HTML or XHTML. With its own language and syntax structure, it works with HTML elements and attributes predominantly to define colours, fonts, layout and other document characteristics, and was designed primarily to enable the separation of document structure (HTML) from document presentation (CSS).

• **On-the-fly templated page creation** PHP, or PHP Hypertext Preprocessor, is a general-purpose server side-scripting language. It allows web developers to create dynamic content that interacts with databases such as MySQL. PHP is used to build large-scale complex installations such as catalogue sites, e-commerce sites, news media sites and blogs by populating generated content into templated layouts. Its final output is usually HTML and the like.

• **Element activity and motion** JavaScript is a cross-platform, client-side, object-based scripting language. It allows dynamic behaviour to elements and is used on web pages to add interactivity and dynamic content such as image rotation, mouse-overs and creation of pop-up windows. When combined with XML, CSS and the XMLHttpRequest, it becomes Asynchronous JavaScript and XML (AJAX), as a set of techniques to allow interaction without reloading the entire page, allowing a more responsive experience without interruption.

• **Animation and interaction** Flash is used to create animation, advertisements and various websites and web-page components such as video, and more recently to develop rich internet applications. The program allows the user to manipulate and animate vector and raster graphics by employing a scripting language called ActionScript, and create motion and effects using a frame-by-frame approach similar to video.

GLOSSARY

Anchor: Signified by a singular 'a' in a start and end tag, this creates a hyperlink.

Href: The hypertext reference attribute in a tag is the active participle that instructs the browser of the intended jump location.

URL: The Uniform Resource Locator is the basic address of any website.

Start tag | Content | End tag

`<a href="http://www.websitenametogohere.com" id="gds4link">Learn More!<a>`

Attribute | Uniform resource locator | Value

○ ASSIGNMENT: GATHERING INFORMATION

The best way to learn how to design effectively for the internet is to use the multitude of sites that focus solely on web creation and culture.

• www.w3schools.com
• www.alistapart.com
• www.smashingmagazine.com
• www.digital-web.com
• www.456bereastreet.com
• www.stylegala.com
• www.webtypography.net

⊙ The hyperlink The main connective tissue of the internet, a hyperlink is a hypertext reference in a hypermedia document to another document available on the web. As the primary navigation element on any web page, linking is the transmission point of web-based information and so is a source of revenue for online industries through banner advertising, search engines and search engine optimisation. In the link above, the different pieces of code are spliced together, with the different shades highlighting the pieces of code that perform the same function.

PART 2	PRINCIPLES
UNIT 7	WEB DESIGN BASICS
MODULE 3	**The building blocks of a web page**

A web page constructed using HTML must adhere to an essential structure in order to assure proper rendering by the browser. A series of tags nested inside one another, with attributes and built-in qualities of their own, join together to form a working document. By retaining the basic syntax that all browsers understand, you can build upon its conventions to create visuals and interactions that go beyond the conventional.

```
<!DOCTYPE html PUBLIC "-//W3C//DTD XHTML 1.0 Strict//EN" "http://
www.w3.org/TR/xhtml1/DTD/xhtml1-strict.dtd">
<html xmlns="http://www.w3.org/1999/xhtml" xml:lang="en">
<head>
<meta http-equiv="content-type" content="text/html; charset=utf-8" />
<title>Lorem Ipsum</title>
<meta name="Description" content="Lorem Ipsum dolor sit amet" />
</head>
<body>
<div id="content">
<h1>Lorem Ipsum</h1>
<h2>Lorem Ipsum</h2>
<ul>
<li>dolor sit amet</li>
<li>dolor sit amet</li>
<li>dolor sit amet</li>
</ul>
<p>Lorem ipsum dolor sit amet, <a href="elit.html">consectetur
adipisicing elit</a>, sed do eiusmod tempor incididunt. </p>
</div>
</body>
</html>
```

JPEG When modifying the settings of a JPEG, the Quality slider will downsample the visual accuracy of an image to reduce its file size.

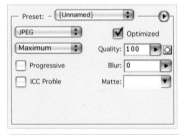

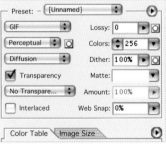

GIF When trying to minimise GIF file size while retaining clarity, the amount of colours used, dithering, transparency and matting all come into play.

Starting from the initial <html> element, the content of a page is split into two sections, the head and the body. The <head> section invisibly contains instructions on how to title, categorise and apply styles and interactivity to the page. The <body> section contains almost all the viewable content formatted with HTML in conjunction with CSS, Javascript and Flash, etc.

In the example above, you can see a variety of tags that make up a web document beyond the main page tags (<html>, <head>, <body>). Elements such as a <doctype>, <meta> tag informtation, <div> tags, an <h1>, an <h2> and a list (<ul><li>), as well as paragraph (<p>) tags, all form the basic items on a web page.

With a working knowledge of HTML, you can apply many design principles covered earlier in this book, such as composition, colour and typography to the skeletal structure of a web document to create a variety of functional and usable web interfaces. Concepts such as aesthetics, market appeal and customer satisfaction are skills that come with time and experience.

Image formats: JPEGs, GIFs, PNGs

Various image formats are available; the most widely used are JPEGs and GIFs. A major consideration in choosing the file type is the type of information you are saving. JPEG files can contain millions of colours and are therefore good for saving photographic

A basic HTML document The web page created by this code has a doctype, meta-information, and links to the CSS document in the head (see page 156).

information. Some loss of quality is inevitable when saving, because colour information is reduced in order to make the file size smaller. GIF files have a reduced colour palette by comparison and so are good for recording solid areas of colour information such as single-colour logos or buttons. GIFs can also be used to record transparency and animation sequences. PNG is a bitmapped image format that employs lossless data compression with a lot of possibility. PNG supports palette-based (palettes of 24-bit RGB colours), greyscale, and RGB images, and was created to improve upon and replace GIF while gaining wider support by all browsers.

It is important to keep file size to a minimum, but much of this depends on audience. If you are designing a site that will be accessed by a wide variety of people from all over the world, you will need to consider that not everyone will be on a high-speed internet connection using the latest PC or Mac. Using the Photoshop Save for web option is a good way to visualise the final image quality and anticipated download time for a variety of internet connection speeds. Generally, images should be saved at 72dpi at the final pixel dimension. Try not to resize an image at the code level.

WEB-SAFE FONTS

The internet retains a speedy load-time, even on the slowest computers, because all the fonts that the website uses are not included as it loads each site. The fonts used are rendered from a set of files that are already found within every computer system, and as such it has become commonplace to utilise these most widely available font faces for content. This is a limitation that has existed since the earliest days of the internet, and as such has inspired countless designers to use this limited set of fonts to achieve highly successful and visually stunning sites.

Arial

Courier

Georgia

Times New Roman

Verdana

Trebuchet MS

Comic Sans

Lucida

Impact

Tahoma

Colour and the internet

A wide range of colour values to select for your site's palette is displayable by monitors. Final output varies due to each individual's specific monitor settings, and these colour values approximate a tone generated by hexadecimal colour coding, which allows a web designer to choose from among potentially 16 million colour definitions. The hexadecimal colour code is a six-digit code preceded by a '#' using any number from 0 to 9 or any letter from 'a' through 'f'. The code applies the three primary colours of projected light using the RGB colour system, where the first two digits signify the amount of red, the second two digits signify the green and the last two digits signify blue. For example, with '0' denoting no light, a colour value of #000000 equates to black. Using online colour generators and palettes, or even those in Photoshop, you can create a variety of colours beyond the traditional 216 web-safe colours. Example colour values: #ffffff = white, #ff0000 = bright red, #00ff00 = bright green and #0000ff = bright blue.

ⓘ New rules

A website is really a compositional ballet of textual content, colour and image. But contrary to its predecessor print design, certain rules and conventions are flipped, in that lower image file sizes are sought after, and your font choices are limited. Colour is much more subjective since the web designer is specifying an approximate colour choice that will render slightly differently on every screen.

◀ **Choosing colour** Many online sites have a variety of ways to choose colours and themes, such as www.kuler. com, or you could always use the Photoshop colour palette.

◉ ASSIGNMENT: PREPARING TO DESIGN A SITE

Organising a website's assets from content through imagery to hosting needs to be planned. Imagine you are creating a website for a small boutique specialising in designer sunglasses. Using the questions below, create a proposal on what will be necessary for you to complete the job and what you will need to get from the client.

• What must the website do? What is the goal?
• How many levels will the site have? How will the content be organised?
• What navigation conventions will you need to ensure that the user can easily move between pages?
• What images and techniques will need to be generated?
• Consider domain registration and hosting of the site, since this may affect how you build it.
• Do you have access to all relevant content to build your site? How much content will the client/ you generate?
• Who is the audience, and on what size screen will the site need to be seen? Widescreen HD or mobile?
• Does the client want Flash or Javascript-based motion?
• Are there any special requirements for larger font sizes?
• Consider the target audience and the browsers from which they will most likely be visiting the site.
• How will client information and purchases be collected? How will they contact the vendor?

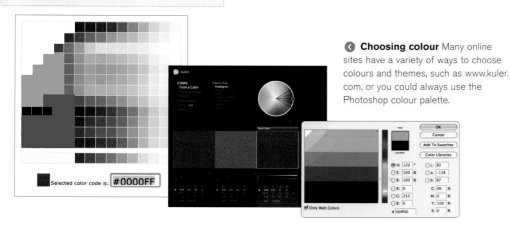

Selected color code is: #0000FF

PART 2 | PRINCIPLES

UNIT 7 | WEB DESIGN BASICS

MODULE 4 | # The graphical user interface

⌃ **Horizontal menu** On the Apple website (www. apple.com) the menu bar runs along the top of the page.

Designing for the web is not the same as designing for print. Web pages not only have to look great, but must also work across a range of devices and browsers; they must also be straightforward to navigate and instantly intuitive – that is, you should know what to click on and where to look without being told. This is where the interface design becomes vital and you, the designer, can make a big difference.

A standard feature within most sites is the menu, normally presented as either a row across the top of the page (www.apple.com) or a column down the side of the page (www.wikipedia.org). Either way, it must be prominent, and making your page layouts consistent will help the user navigate through your site. Navigation menus should always be in the same place and follow the same format: basically, do not relocate the steering wheel every time the driver turns a corner. It is important to create a site that is an invisible utility, with the most necessary and poignant features for your goal obvious and findable, and other content and features available for discovery. Periodical content, blogs and entertainment sites thrive on returning traffic due to updating content and ease of use.

Be aware of contemporary conventions such as column layouts and box styles, since this not only keeps your work up to date and offers the most functionality; but also saves you from overlapping with conventions that already exist: underlining, for example, is frequently used to indicate a link, so it would not be a good idea to use underlined text for decorative reasons.

When dealing with a newer medium like the internet, leaning towards interactive simplicity is best – from both aesthetic and practical standpoints. You do not want to lose customers because you are blowing up their browser with your heavily Javascripted, multi-level animated navigation menu.

Sitemaps

Web design is no different from any other design process: the more organised you are, the more successful you will be. As careful planning will save you considerable time, your first step should be to plan your site out in a sitemap. The main purpose of this is to carefully plan out the site's architecture for you and your client to review. By understanding how the site will allow the user to move around the site, you can then anticipate and influence how the user might like to navigate through the content. An easy-to-navigate site is essential to this success.

⌄ **Vertical menu** The Wikipedia website (www.wikipedia.org) employs a menu running down the left edge of the screen.

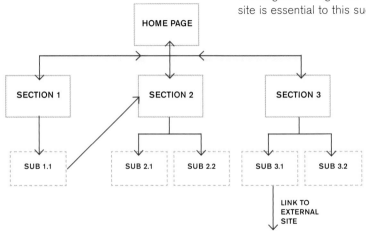

⌃ **Website map** This map shows website sections, main subsections and navigation routes between pages. So, for example, you can see it is possible to travel from subsection 1.1 to section 2, but not from section 2 to subsection 1.1.

⌃⌄ ▶ Banner ads

Marketing is another field that many web designers find themselves having a hand in, using static imagery, animated GIFs and Flash to create highly effective campaigns.

⊙ ASSIGNMENT: USER SCENARIOS

Following these steps will help to ensure your site meets client and audience needs.

1 Test how many clicks deep a feature is or how easy it is to find a goal page. You could ask friends or your study group to try out the site, too.

2 Consider goals from the onset. For example:

• Why are users here?
• Where do you want them to go?
• What do you want them to do – sign up for your newsletter or buy your latest sale item?

3 Test that your goals are clear and follow up after launching the site with an analytics program, such as Google Analytics, Mint or StatCounter, to help you tailor the site towards its audience and raise the return on investment for your client.

❝ The key to any successful website has to be understanding your audience and the content that the site wraps itself around. All too often websites showcase a designer's software skills and cutting-edge graphics, with precious little thought to which people are using the site and how best to get the information across. There is nothing wrong with pushing those boundaries, just don't forget to consider the end user: design for the audience, design for the content, do not solely design for yourself ❞

Chris Jones

Trends and standards

Technology has one evolutionary timetable: fast. In both form and capability, the internet is a technological medium in which cutting-edge design ideas and concepts find forums. But as with all trends, one day the hippest convention will turn cliché as it gives way to a newer, more innovative standard. As a jumpstart to help you stay ahead of the trends, here is a list of popular user conventions that have withstood the test of time.

• Contact forms
• Pop-ups
• Lightboxes and galleries
• Drop-down menus
• Rounded corners
• Drop shadows
• Polls
• Blogs
• Banner ads
• Tags
• Categories
• Sitemaps
• Flash animation
• Links
• Message boards

ART   MUSIC

the sites | the designs | the blo

⌃ **Tabs** The use of tabs is a commonplace visual navigational tool.

◀ **Forms** Gathering user information is made simple with the use of forms.

Please enter your name and address:

First name: *

Last Name: *

E-mail address: *

I'd like to set up an appointment for a free consultation.

Home:

Work:

Best time to call:

How did you hear about the practice?

Questions and Comments

Your Message:

PART 2	PRACTICE
UNIT 7	WEB DESIGN BASICS
MODULE 5	**CSS**

Cascading Style Sheets (CSS) is a major feature in web development since it entails a set of instructions that tells the web browser how to present a page, either inline with the HTML code or, preferably, in a separate, linked document. Style sheets control many elements of site design including font display, image positioning and page object creation, and do so utilising CSS, a language with its own syntax and conceptual structure.

An easy way to understand CSS is to think of clothing. The main document tree of a web page is composed of a head and a body. The naked form can take only so many shapes, and to properly decorate and illustrate the body with visual meaning, one option is to clothe it. CSS is the coding analogue for choosing how you dress a site. Will you dress to impress? To excite? Are you political in your attire? Punk rock? Goth? Cute? Every element helps to create a visual message through daily presentation. CSS acts in the same way. Does my header have a certain background, but my body content another? (Do I wear a hat and a T-shirt?) Shall I float this image to the right or have it to the left? (Does this pin go on my jacket or on my bag?)

Advantages

CSS allows flexibility and speed by not having to mess too much with the underlying document tree. By reducing on-page coding to standard elements, CSS can rely on certain unobtrusive tags to do its heavy lifting, although all HTML elements can be styled. The <div> and the <span> are two presentational

The paper doll analogy

CSS decides where an element appears on the page, how it is colored, and how its contents are styled. Take this paper doll as an example: while imagining her entire form as the web page, she can be easily sectioned out into divisions (<div>), each given the IDs of #header, #content, and #footer.

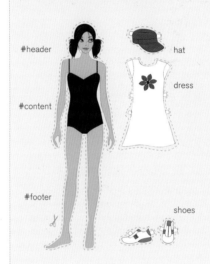

The HTML code for her would be:
```
<html>
<body>
<div id="header">face and hair</div>
<div id="content">torso and arms</div>
<div id="footer">legs and feet</div>
</body>
</html>
```

To get her dressed, we can use CSS to apply styles and background imagery to the correct divisions:
```
#header{
background: "hat";
color: gray;
}
#content{
background: "dress";
color: white;
}
#footer{
background: "shoes";
color: white;
}
```

elements that CSS hooks to with great control since these do not break into the document flow with pre-defined characteristics, such as the <p> or the <li>. CSS can override inherent layout rules of any tag, but it's best to use styling tags to create your layout.

CSS empowers you to enact global changes to all similar elements with one instruction. You need instruct only once to colour all your text black but all of your bold words purple, instead of hand colouring each time. 'Cascading' is the way in which defined characteristics shower down to tags within tags, and how hierarchy governs. This gives great flexibility and predictability on how one or more elements can be targeted for styling throughout an entire site.

Block-level: Starts a new line; can have width, height and position.

Class: A group of elements sharing common styling rules; can appear multiple times on a page; prefixed by a full stop (.).

ID: Unique identity of an element; can only be used once on a page; denoted by hash (#).

Inline: Used for visual styling; provide no structure to a document but apply effects to text.

Cascading

The 'cascade' aspect of CSS means a rule only needs to be instructed once to affect many elements in a site simultaneously, saving not only creative time for the developer but also download time for the browser. In the example below, due to the cascade, all <p> elements within the <div>, unless later instructed, will be grey.

```
<div id="box">
<p> This is grey. </p>
<p> This is also grey.> </p>
</div>
```

```
#box p {
        color:
gray;
        }
```

=

This is grey.
This is also grey.

CSS specifies a priority schema to decide which rules apply if more than one style rule matches against a particular element. These priorities, or weights, are calculated and pre-assigned so that the results are predictable and standard. Using the example above, a <p> tag, once closed, will always start a new paragraph line. Hence the <p> tag is short for 'paragraph'. Built-in rules such as these enable frameworks to be created as elements become pre-defined, positionable objects, suitable for layout purposes.

KEY CONCEPTS

• Sites using CSS 'degrade gracefully' in browsers unable to display graphical content, and allows for easier redesigns and updates by localising all your styling instructions.

• CSS allows the user to choose defined styles (such as enlarge all text on the page for easier viewing) by removing all non-essential presentational items from the main document.

• CSS also allows the same mark-up page to be presented in different styles for different rendering methods, such as on-screen, mobile, in print or from simulated voice, by keeping the main content separate and fluid from the design.

◉ ASSIGNMENT: TERMINOLOGY

Many tricks and clever solutions create widely successful design with the best that CSS has to offer. Research and understand these key terms:

• Floats and clears
• CSS shorthand
• The box model
• The sliding doors technique
• Background images
• Conditional comments
• Z-index
• CSS frameworks

CSS Zen Garden

The CSS Zen Garden was created in 2003 by Dave Shea, a web designer and author from Vancouver, as a demonstrational and educational space of what can be accomplished visually through valid CSS-based design. By retaining a locked and uneditable HTML document tree as a base to work on, designers and developers globally have contributed numerous designs to visually format the inherent site code. By demonstrating the enormous flexibility and power of CSS and the skill of the designers, more than 700 contributions, ie style sheets, can be viewed through the site's navigation. By clicking each entry, the browser reloads what appears to be a completely different web page visually, but the HTML content is the same. By reviewing the code of the different style sheets you can learn a lot about how to properly organise the elements of a page, utilise correct web typography or create visual effects by using advanced CSS.

> **Explore the possibilities** Take a stroll through the Zen Garden at http://www.csszengarden.com to see the extent of the design potential of CSS.

PART 2 | PRACTICE

UNIT 7 | WEB DESIGN BASICS

MODULE 6 | **Web standards, validation, Doctype and SEO**

Proper coding semantics has been a key term that refers to which tags you select for your information and how they are used. An 'information about information' revolution in web design developed as HTML and XHTML iterations evolved and emphasis was placed on the incorporation of meta-information, alternate tagging, proper tag and syntax usage and the replacement of old tags for more expressive ones. With widespread interest in validation for cross-browser compatibility and code cleanliness, this review of how web spaces 'should be' made paved the way not only for higher forms of accessibility and functionality, but also for a better understanding of a site's content by search engines.

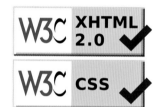

Successful and valid documents are achieved by creating grammatically correct coding, with guidelines set up and maintained by the World Wide Web Consortium (WC3). Against these standards designers can have their site's coding tested using the WC3's well-known Validator site. A passing grade means a site's HTML and CSS validate to fulfil standards set up by its <doctype> and should render equally on all current and future standardised browsers.

🔺 **Display of affiliation**
Web badges have become a popular phenomenon. Many sites are proud to sport the WC3's Valid XHTML and CSS badges, available by passing the Validator test.

Doctypes
Document Type Definition (DTD) defines rendering modes a browser should take and which elements and attributes can be used. This is placed before the head in your HTML document, helping to define how CSS styling works and how elements behave, either with leniency (transitional) or by making you stick to the rules (strict). These two modes were made to ease HTML 4.0 users into XHTML.

🔻 **Doctypes** These examples of the doctype signify to the browser that the web document to be displayed is either written in Strict XHTML, Transitional XHTML or in Transitional or Loose HTML 4.

```
<!DOCTYPE html PUBLIC "-//W3C//DTD XHTML 1.0 Strict//EN"
        "http://www.w3.org/TR/xhtml1/DTD/xhtml1-strict.dtd">
<html xmlns="http://www.w3.org/1999/xhtml" xml:lang="">

<!DOCTYPE html PUBLIC "-//W3C//DTD XHTML 1.0 Transitional//EN"
        "http://www.w3.org/TR/xhtml1/DTD/xhtml1-transitional.dtd">
<html xmlns="http://www.w3.org/1999/xhtml" xml:lang="">

<!DOCTYPE HTML PUBLIC "-//W3C//DTD HTML 4.01 Transitional//EN"
        "http://www.w3.org/TR/html4/loose.dtd">
```

◀ **Quality control**
Webstandards.org is one of many projects maintained by members that work to create a better web by enforcing and educating designers and technology developers on the importance of validation, standards and accessibility.

Search engines

Search Engine Optimisation (SEO) The SEO industry works with designers and copywriters to discover and expertly utilise the most relevant and popular keywords for a site. By boosting on-page content, in-bound links, as well as meta- and alt-tag information, agencies globally help connect content with audience. Although many SEO practices are officially frowned upon by Google, Yahoo and MSN – with some that will get your site banned completely from their search indexes – the search engines do offer various pay-per-click and keyword advertising options to elevate incoming traffic.

Meta-information Search engines explore a website the way a person might a very dimly lit room: feel out the important sections, familiarise yourself with the layout, know the exits. As a search engine 'crawls' a site it downloads and indexes various amounts of data from each page, such as navigation and the prevalence and position of certain keywords. The semantic weight for specific keywords (be they main headings or plain text) is calculated, as well as any and all links the page has to and from other pages and sites. From this a search engine deduces your site's importance on a topic and relation it may have to certain keyword phrases.

With the emergence of Google in 1998 and its PageRank algorithm – which assigned relevance to URLs based on the quantity and strength of in-bound links and meta-information – the search engine industry has become a multi-million-pound market, as businesses and institutions rely more on the internet and its advertising and prospective business potential. Above all, relevant and well-written content displayed using proper web design conventions is the starting point to ready a site for search engine indexing.

Readiness To ensure that your site is fully prepared, certain bits of code must be used correctly. In the <head> of each page exist <meta> tags with descriptive text and keywords, and author information is already stored for the search engines. Within the <body> exists special attributes, such as 'alt' and 'title', that allow more information to be related to imagery and links. Not only does this provide descriptive information for those 'hearing' the internet, but it also gives engines fodder to decide how and where to rank your site.

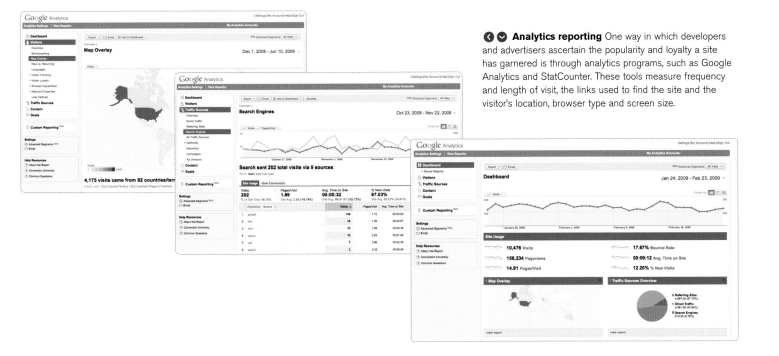

Analytics reporting One way in which developers and advertisers ascertain the popularity and loyalty a site has garnered is through analytics programs, such as Google Analytics and StatCounter. These tools measure frequency and length of visit, the links used to find the site and the visitor's location, browser type and screen size.

PART 2 | PRACTICE

UNIT 7 | WEB DESIGN BASICS

MODULE 7 | # Designing for different browsers and platforms

One of the hardest concepts to grasp for developing web designers entering the field is that, unlike designing for print, designing a web page is never a completely controllable process. Different computers and different browsers will affect how the web page is displayed, due to the opposing ways that vendors interpret how their browser renders the underlying coding that generates the site. The main issues involve differences between how the 'Big Three' browsers (Internet Explorer, Firefox and Safari) handle such things as the width of layout boxes, default character-width size and colour. Ideally, you want your site to work across all browsers and devices, and for the most part, these differences can be handled at coding level.

As well as having a thorough understanding of your intended audience, you should continually check your site as you design it, by viewing it on different browsers (traditionally called 'cross-browser compatibility testing'). While at one time web designers would be running to and fro from home studio to local internet café, to test their sites on public Windows-based computers, advances in computing now allow for designers to afford a separate station or to merge their platforms into one computer (ie the ability to run Windows on a Mac since their Intel chip changeover in 2006). Luckily, there are countless resources from which a designer can now gain better understanding of how to identify and handle various technological idiosyncrasies where designing for the web and technology meet.

Advancements in browsing capabilities and internet connectivity extend possibilities for designers to achieve both their own and their clients' goals more successfully. You must always design for the future; features and layouts can always be updated to meet constantly evolving browser capabilities. Awareness of how browsers compare in usage and popularity will help you greatly in keeping your skill level fresh and content highly accessible. In terms of market share, internet Explorer has beat out Firefox, Safari and Opera for many years; a whole school of thought revolves around how to code correctly for the different ways to view the internet. Organised by such entities as WC3 (www.wc3.org) and the Web Standards Project (www.webstandards.org), and expounded upon at such sites as A List Apart (www.alistapart.com), proper adherence to recommended XHTML and CSS syntax standards helps both to alleviate many cross-browser differences, and to open up your code for future versions and updates. It can be said that if web design were painting, then it would be the frame that creates the final image, and not the painter.

The importance of platform-rendering differences because of technologies – both electronic and physical – must be accounted for, as it is in print and paper. As you must compensate for certain aspects when printing for either two-colour newsprint or full-colour glossy magazines, so must you incorporate additional care for how your site will render on a standards-based browser such as Safari or Firefox, or on a less-than-standards-based browser such as Internet Explorer. Furthermore, you must now compensate for growing screen sizes and mobile devices.

Standardisation

A popular way to standardise proper practices in web design is to use free or premium templates and frameworks to get started, such as the case with the two sites below. Often this is the best way to set up e-commerce solutions, forums and blogs, and using snippets of PHP andJavascript modularly, like widgets and mini-apps, are common as well. Remember, many successful designers are not always master coders but are efficient users of code.

Screen sizes

Different viewers will visit your site using monitors with different screen sizes and resolutions. The most widely available resolutions for today's screen sizes are 1024 x 768 pixels, 1280 x 1024 pixels and 1680 x 1050 pixels. The prevailing screen size of yesteryear was 800 x 600 pixels, so you may find that many sites from the 1990s float very thinly in the middle of the screen because they compensated for a 800-pixel screen width.

With the advent of proper coding standards, DTD selection and CSS, the information at the heart of a website now has a separate and fluid quality that allows designers to easily compensate for the variety of screen sizes without sacrificing message. Mobile viewing of the internet relies on this principle since it is developing better ways to deliver content instantly on a very small screen.

BROWSING SOLUTIONS

One of the main differences between browsers is how they handle instructions on rendering boxes, padding and fonts, which are handled primarily by CSS. These differences wreaked havoc on sites that display perfectly on Firefox or Opera, but miserably in Internet Explorer, for example, and have caused a variety of 'solutions' throughout web history to trick IE into ignoring certain instructions.

In modern times, as most browsers have become more standardised, the common way to handle these rendering issues follows the 'separation of presentation' example by focusing distinct instructions directly to Internet Explorer through conditional style sheets. These override or mix into the main style sheet only for the Internet Explorer version it specifies (5.5, 6, 7 or all). See an example below used in the <head> portion of a web document to apply a conditional style sheet only for Internet Apple Safari 3.1.2 Explorer 7 users:

```
<!--[if IE 7]> <link href="css/ie.css"
rel="stylesheet" type="text/css" />
<![endif]-->
```

BROWSER TESTING

A browser is much like a picture frame for the internet; the main difference is that the browser directly affects the way the web is seen from computer to computer. A popular example is Acid2, published by the Web Standards Project to identify visual and structural page-rendering issues in different browsers. By testing their handling of HTML and CSS layout and styling, a browser that follows WC3 specifications should render the layout correctly.

> **Results** Firefox, Safari and Opera rendered this page correctly (top image), whereas Microsoft Internet Explorer 7 (middle) and 6 (bottom) failed this Acid2 test.

> **Fluid resizing**
The search engine www.google.com is a good illustration of a site viewable by all. With different screen resolutions for different screen formats, you see more or less white space as the point of interest resizes to stay in the middle of the screen. The middle and top images show different computer screen formats, and the bottom image shows a mobile phone interface.

PART 2	PRACTICE
UNIT 7	WEB DESIGN BASICS
MODULE 8	**Web design software**

There are several pieces of software available today with varying degrees of functionality and freedom. Some you have to pay a fee for and others are free; google 'List of HTML Editors' for a complete idea of the choices out there. Either way, learning HTML, CSS, Javascript and the like will be your key selling point as a web designer or developer.

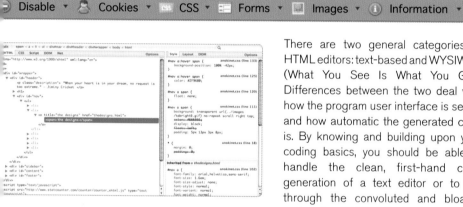

There are two general categories of HTML editors: text-based and WYSIWYG (What You See Is What You Get). Differences between the two deal with how the program user interface is set up and how automatic the generated code is. By knowing and building upon your coding basics, you should be able to handle the clean, first-hand code generation of a text editor or to sift through the convoluted and bloated code of a WYSIWYG. In the realm of HTML editors, convenience in one area can often become inconvenience in another.

Starting out in industry

The world of web design is a varied place occupied by all kinds of artists, designers and programmers. As someone with an interest in web design, try not to be put off by all the jargon and complicated language – you will learn this as you go along, and it is very much a case of learning to crawl, walk and then run.

The industry ranges from large teams of developers and designers, for example looking after the huge BBC Online sites, to individuals wanting to create their own site. Obviously, there is a huge space between these

extremes; skills to develop will be determined by where you want to sit within this range. Assuming you are working on a large site, you may have a very particular role within the team – perhaps editing and uploading images with minor text changes. If this is the case, a basic understanding of software such as a good HTML editor and Photoshop would probably suffice. On the other hand, you might end up developing online shopping applications, in which case a much more extensive knowledge of programming languages would be needed.

Tools and add-ons
Many tools are available to add to your browser's functionality. The Web Developers toolbar for both Firefox and Internet Explorer is a perfect example since it gives you options to turn off styles, outline objects, display layout information, make measurements and more. Downloading Firebug for Firefox will give you an interactive x-ray view of a site's construction.

Sitepoint.com is a news and educational website out of Australia that features a variety of blogs, emailers, tutorials, contests, books, videos and articles about building a better website and a better web.

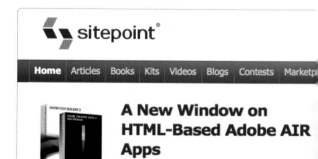

▶ **Notepad** is a great example of a text-based HTML editor for Windows, used by designers and developers worldwide due to its features, customisability and price: free!

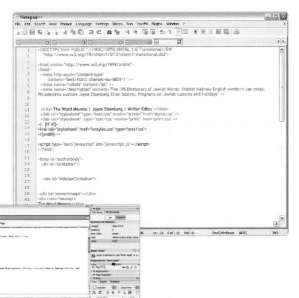

◀ **Dreamweaver** has long been a popular WYSIWYG HTML editor, and allows you to see your work visually and in code view, which is a great way to learn.

TEXT-BASED HTML EDITORS

Text-based HTML editors are souped-up word-processing programs with advancement for code generation such as browser previewing, code auto-completion, code-folding and snippet insertion. 'Hand-coding' is a term associated with these types of editors.

• **Advantage** Dealing directly with the code, you have greater flexibility at code level over content and presentation, as well as code-accuracy and precision.

• **Disadvantage** The design process becomes two tiered as the designer must be not only a competent designer, but well practised at modifying existing code or coding from scratch.

• **Text-based HTML editors of note** BBEdit, Notepad ++, Coda, SkEdit, TextMate.

WYSIWYG HTML EDITORS

WYSIWYG HTML editors are graphical in nature, and allow you to work directly with generated page elements, much like a DTP program like InDesign. Usually coupled with a variety of features and 'plug-ins', these 'suite' programs can also help handle file and image organisation, CSS style sheets and Javascript.

• **Advantage** WYSIWYG editors can be a great help during the transition from print design to web design since they bridge the standard visual tools in traditional publishing with the web.

• **Disadvantage** Generated automatically by the program, the code rendered by WYSIWYG editors tends to be bloated with extra snippets of HTML here and there for structure. Most of the time it is unintentional and unnecessary, which can raise editing issues, extend load time and lower search engine penetration.

• **WYSIWYG HTML editors of note** Dreamweaver, Amaya, Aptana, iWeb, Rapidweaver.

⊙ ASSIGNMENT: **RESEARCH**

Web design is constantly evolving. Explore these sites and collect others in your search for further information.
• www.w3c.org
• www.sitepoint.com
• www.webstandards.org
• www.opera.com/company/education
• www.developer.yahoo.com
• www.cssplay.co.uk
• www.htmldog.com
• www.webmonkey.com

PART 2 | PRACTICE

UNIT 7 | WEB DESIGN BASICS

MODULE 9 | **Web-based self-publishing**

Self-publishing is fast becoming the way for artists and designers to get their work known through forums, blogs, community sites or their own website. Marshall McLuhan's concept of the 'global village' is becoming a reality with the interactivity built into Web 2.0. Not only is there a proliferation of sites and pages to upload your work and research to, but additional matters to consider, such as copyright.

Mutual learning and uploading images to the net can become problematic if others steal your ideas. There are many attitudes to this, with some saying this is all part of the graphic arts world; however, copyright still applies to uploaded work. Whenever you post your work to a site, first check out its policies about authored work, and legal issues pertaining to fair use. There are ongoing legal discussions about internet copyright, and if you are in doubt, find other ways to advertise your work. There are other movements for freedom of knowledge, but this largely has more to do with program code rather than individuals' work. Caution is advised.

⊙ ASSIGNMENT: CREATING GROUP SITES

Choose a group that you are currently a part of. It could be your art/design class or a group of your peers who meet regularly to make work or discuss ideas. Choosing either a wiki, blog or a community host site, make a web presence for your group. Some things to consider are:

• Do you want individual profiles or just the group profile?
• How will you go about setting up examples of everyone's work?
• Will you nominate an editor or is the whole site accessible for all the group?

TYPES OF SITE

• **Community sites** Flickr, DeviantART and YouTube are three examples of community sites that host still images, such as photographs and pictures (Flickr and DeviantART), and animation and video (YouTube) to create online portfolios. Each is free to join, to set up a profile page and start uploading images to. You can subscribe to gain extra features or more storage space. Other users can comment on uploads, give advice and share knowledge.

• **Blogs** Hosts such as Wordpress, Blogger and LiveJournal offer free start-up pages with options to upgrade with better services. Users can embed images and multimedia into posts and pages. Microblogs such as Twitter allow users to post fragments of information and links rather than full posts. Designers educate themselves on the programs that they use, sharing knowledge, tips and tutorials about what they have learned and collaborating in others' education.

• **Wikis** A collection of web pages that can be written and edited by anyone; the best known is Wikipedia.

• **Marketing and link sites** In these sites, artists, graphic or otherwise, are reviewed/critiqued by testimonials and comments from viewers and previous clients. This provides not only community knowledge on who's who, or whose work is 'current', but also information about skills, timeliness in meeting deadlines and good customer service. Del.icio.us shares bookmarks, enabling users to track popular sites and trends. Similarly, Digg users not only share website links, but also comment and vote on stories, increasing or decreasing their popularity.

• **e-portfolios** Many graphic designers will have their own website to present their range of skills to potential employers and to generate interest in their work. Setting up your own means greater creative freedom because you won't be restricted by existing templates or rules that may be in force on hosting sites.

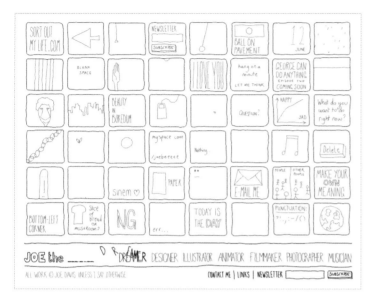

Do it yourself These interactive portfolios enable the visitor to experience all aspects of the designer's skills. The layout and navigation of the sites themselves reflect the creativity of the designer, and the navigator is given the opportunity of seeing existing work, areas of interest, and some background information about the personality and aims of the designer. Although the emphasis is on fun and exploration, the sites also feature clear and easy-to-find contact details – essential in successful self-promotion.

8 | COMMERCIAL APPLICATIONS

This final section combines everything that has been discussed throughout the book and looks at how this will impact on you finding your way into employment as a trained graphic design professional. By now, you should be closer to finding your desired career path and will be interested in discovering what your specific creative field would be like to work in.

Each module examines a different discipline, reviewing the skills needed, assessing the ups and downs you might encounter on the job, giving examples of Best in the Business, and will also provide you with resources and options to help find a career that best suits your skills and aptitudes.

> **❝❝Design is the search for a magical balance between business and art, art and craft, intuition and reason, concept and detail, playfulness and formality, client and designer, designer and printer, and printer and public.❞❞**
>
> *Valerie Petts*

❯ Core/specialist skills The diagram on the right shows how the core design skills covered in the first part of the book relate to all the design career options covered in Unit 8. While each skill may be differently 'weighted' – information designers tend to be more research focused, while editorial design requires a more detailed knowledge of typography and composition – it's important to be well versed in all of the skills indicated, whatever career path you choose. The descriptions give a short overview of the key attributes needed to work each field, while the symbols show which software is essential to those working environments. Note that the diagram design demonstrates the Gestalt Law of Closure, as described on page 39.

AE After Effects	**M** Maya
Ai Adobe Illustrator	**Pp** Powerpoint
AS Action Script	**Ps** Photoshop
Fl Flash	**Q** Quark
FP Final Cut Pro	**3ds** 3ds Max
ID InDesign	

◗ For more detail, The American Institute of Graphic Designers' (AIGA) website has an overview of the different design career options, and what they entail: http://www.aiga.org/content.cfm/guide-designersatwork. The website information is taken from *Graphic Design: A Career Guide and Education Directory* by Sharon Poggenpohl.

Editorial Design
Excellent spatial awareness and composition skills with a love of complexity and layering, a knowledge of design history and a team-focused attitude. ID, Q, Ai, Ps

Motion Graphics
Pace, rhythm and storyboarding skills required, with diplomacy, a client-centred outlook and knowledge of communication strategies and rhetoric. Fl, AS, AE, Ai, Ps, M, 3ds, FP

Information Design
A perfectionist and detail-oriented attitude with a love of systems, problem-solving and a user-centred focus. Ps, Ai, Fl

CORE SKILLS

ANALYSIS   RESEARCH

LAYOUT   TYPOGRAPHY   COMPOSITION

SOFTWARE AND TOOLS

COLOUR THEORY

Web Design
A focus on user interaction with client and cultural sensitivity, with a knowledge of web standards and accessibility. XHTML, CSS, Java, Ajax, PHP, HTML 4.0, Fl

Advertising
First-rate communication skills with cultural sensitivity, audience knowledge and an ability to work under pressure. Q, ID, Fl, AE, Pp, Ai, Ps

Game Design
Speed of image production with a love of virtual physics, a narrative thought process, a team-player attitude and the ability to take criticism. Ps, Ai, Fl, AE, 3ds, M

Logo Design/Branding
Knowledge of traditional and innovative marketing of psychological campaigns, combined with a client focus. Ps, Ai, Fl, AE

HIGHS

- Opportunities for visual creativity, especially for those designers interested in identity, marketing and sales.
- Many accomplished identity developers are independent freelances who have also spent many successful years in agencies and studios, making employment options versatile.
- An interest in marketing, psychology and business can only help the logo designer, who over time will most likely pick up some tenets and lessons of these industries in their career.
- Being the very foundation for all advertising and marketing efforts, it is always gratifying to see a brand you helped develop launch, expand and succeed.

LOWS

- Many have created their 'perfect logo' only to have it modified beyond recognition or trashed by a less-than-thrilled client. Such is the life of a designer.
- Unless you are hired for a full branding development position with a company, you'll need to generate a lot of clients just doing logos and letterheads in order to pay the bills.
- Ultimately, the ability to be completely creatively present for the client yet let go enough to meet their needs, regardless of all your training and better judgment, is a quality that is hard for some. It's called customer service, and remember: you are creating their identity, not yours.

PART 2	PRACTICE
UNIT 8	COMMERCIAL APPLICATIONS
MODULE 1	**Logo design and brand identity**

Based in the realm of symbology and sign, and originating in pre-Neolithic times, the logo, or ideogram, is no stranger to anyone these days. Instantly recognisable and distinctly memorable, a well-designed logo is versatile in multiple ways, from dimensions to application, but resilient enough to retain its identity instantly in the viewer's mind and throughout future evolutions. It is both cornerstone and keystone for brand development. In logo creation, decisions on style, colour, aesthetics and typography set up a 'Rosetta Stone' upon which a client's whole branding and marketing strategy will be based. A designer researches then refracts the essence of an idea into a system of elements showcasing a singular icon and idea, which in turn creates identity.

⊙ **The culture of logos** Logo design has its roots in a long history of 'identifying' marks, related not only to commercial applications (such as branding for companies or organisations), but also personal, tribal, and cultural contexts.

'Company logo', 'corporate identity', 'brand', 'trademark' – no matter how you slice it, these terms all point to the creation of a cohesive defining symbol that represents a client in every piece of communication. Easy and effective translation of goals, values and expertise is vital to build trust with current and potential customers. Nowadays, there are multiple ways to create a public identity: business cards, letterheads, brochures, advertisements, clothing, websites, promotional items. And each stems from the initial identity developed by the identity developer.

By researching and collecting information from a client and their industry, the identity developer utilises creativity and marketing savvy to generate several different ideas from multiple avenues of approach for a client to choose from. Patience and understanding are then needed to survive the editing process as a client mixes, changes

◀ **Erikson Institute** The logo for a graduate school in child development emphasises the importance of adult influence. The logo was modified for a maths curriculum project (bottom), incorporating mathematical symbols into the fun design.

⊕ SKILLS REQUIRED

- A firm, creative understanding and love of fonts, basic typography, visual semiotics, symbolism, illustration, colour theory, brand design and marketing psychology.
- A capable identity developer must be both adept at all pro-level software programs and printing systems, and familiar with a variety of traditional and innovative marketing materials and campaign approaches.
- A patient love of research: Listening to a client at the beginning and through the branding process is the only way to deliver what is needed. Fully researching a client's business, mission and competition is crucial in attempting to create a unique and perfect identity.

and experiments with requests as you work with them to get their logo just right. Always keeping in mind the alternatives for different contexts and consistency across a variety of media, an accomplished identity developer is a paragon of refinement and service so that the client is happy and the brand is beautiful.

Identity and logo designers

A great identity developer should be detail-oriented, flexible and have well-developed design and problem-solving skills that employ clarity, simplicity and scalability. Annually, organisations spend hundreds of thousands of pounds to keep identity and branding fresh, current and innovative, so we know there are clients out there just waiting to find the right talent. Large companies employ in-house designers to develop their logos, but many turn to external graphic design firms, advertising agencies and individuals to develop their brand.

Be prepared: you need a thorough and wide-reaching mind both to always maintain evolution and consistency during the creative process, and to imagine how best these elements should carry the brand.

Whether you decide to work in an advertising agency or a design studio, or go out on your own, you will run across a request for a logo every now and again. Sticking to the concepts of simplicity, clarity, scalability and innovation will provide a starting point for any successful logo. It's been said that if it can be etched in stone or printed in just black and white successfully, you may be onto something!

✱ BEST IN THE BUSINESS

Paul Rand (1914–1996), Pratt Institute graduate, Yale University professor and American graphic designer, who will go down in history for his groundbreaking work with some of the best-known corporate logo designs. A strong proponent of the Swiss style of design, Rand developed the foundation corporate identities for Apple, IBM, UPS, Westinghouse and ABC. He was touted as a consummate salesman who, through explaining the necessity of proper identity creation to clients and students, helped usher in a new era for marketing and design.

Paula Scher Corcoran College of Art and Design doctorate graduate, began as a record cover art director at Atlantic and CBS Records and has developed a career and style that has won many prestigious awards for her work and innovation in the field of design. Currently a partner at Pentagram in New York, she is best known for her identity and branding systems, promotional materials, packaging and publication designs for such clients as The New York Times Magazine, Perry Ellis, Bloomberg, Citibank, Tiffany & Co, Target, the New York Botanical Garden and The Daily Show With Jon Stewart.

LloydNorthover, one of Britain's most successful consultancies, working internationally in identity, branding and communication, prides itself in providing creative solutions to strategic problems. In giving companies a competitive market advantage by making them highly visible, clear and compelling, they have created many successful campaigns for Comet, De Beers, Elizabeth Arden, HSBC, Infiniti, Lexus, Mitsubishi, Morgan Stanley, Orange and Royal Mail.

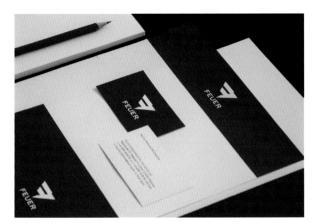

◀ ⌃ **Feuer logo** Logo design and branded stationery for an advertising design agency. The logo is instrumental in creating the company identity, so the designer will work closely with the client to convey the desired message.

CAREER OPTIONS

Junior and senior designer, creative director Specialising in brand identity. Designing logos and bringing them to life in the marketing environment (from corporate literature to shop front).

Lettering artist Creating the final letterforms of the logo, whether from a bespoke font or a hand-crafted script.

RESOURCES

• See Per Mollerup's book *Marks of Excellence*, for an excellent review of the history of logo design.

PART 2	PRACTICE
UNIT 8	COMMERCIAL APPLICATIONS
MODULE 2	**Motion graphics**

The field of motion graphics has expanded enormously from its early beginnings in film and TV opening titles and closing credits to the new media environment, interactive applications, post-production, advertising, animation and digital environments for the web and broadcast

HIGHS

• You would be working in a fast-paced cutting-edge environment.
• The better your work communicates client concepts, the more your work will be sought after.
• Motion graphics designers are multidisciplinary: they can call upon many different design skills. This enables many to keep employment and generate income from their many abilities.

LOWS

• Much of the initial concept work will be time consuming, when your clients will know exactly what they want and you will probably have to develop many versions to achieve what they require.
• Turnaround speed can be high; be realistic on what you can achieve in the time available to avoid missing your deadline.
• There are advantages and disadvantages of being a jack-of-all-(design)-trades or a specialist. It is best not to spread yourself too thinly but to be confident in what you can and cannot do.

The emphasis in the motion graphics industry is on speed of communication – how you can appeal to either a specialised demographic or a wide audience and communicate the product, proposal or information as clearly as possible. From corporations to production houses, web businesses, music videos, television and film, this industry can be divided into three specialisations.

1. Business-to-business (B2B) takes the form of idea proposals and pitches, training seminars and other info-graphics.
2. Advertising encompasses everything from web banners and TV commercials to websites.
3. Film/video specialisation covers music videos, film/TV opening and closing credits and other animated type/visuals.

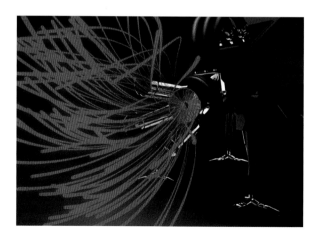

⊕ SKILLS REQUIRED

• Knowledge of communication strategies and rhetoric.
• Excellent grasp of typography, 2D and 3D composition and colour.
• Good appreciation of pace, rhythm and storyboarding.
• Good spatial awareness and geometry.
• An ability to work comfortably with complexity and layering, both literal and metaphorical.
• Advanced and up-to-date knowledge of Flash, After Effects, Illustrator and Photoshop.
• Some positions also require knowledge of Maya and 3ds Max, and experience in digital video editing software such as Final Cut is an advantage.
• Good knowledge of ActionScript.
• Diplomacy and a client-centred outlook.

◀ **Color Robot** The Color Robot campaign by Mate Steinforth shows animated pink streams of light to represent digital flows of information.

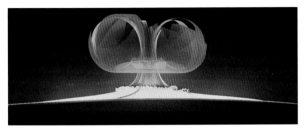

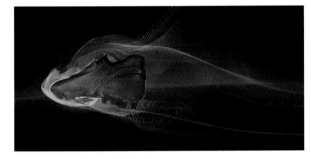

As with many specialisations, most likely you will start out in a long-established studio, under a creative director, art director or producer. Later you may go freelance or set up a small studio of your own, although the brief structure remains the same. Very occasionally clients will give you the creative freedom to push boundaries; more often they will have a specific aesthetic in mind. The most creative area is music videos and channel identity signatures such as MTV and VH-1. However, it is important to remember that these opportunities may happen only once or twice, if at all, since this industry demands a constant stream of new and fresh talent and ideas.

➕ **SEE ALSO:** ADVERTISING P178

Infiniti The Infiniti car campaign animates the road and clouds to give the illusion of speed.

Nike These two images taken from a Nike campaign give an example of visual poetics – animated flowing light trails simulating an aurora in the atmosphere of a planet.

Red Bull This Red Bull campaign shows hand-drawn fragments merged with digital imagery and photographic footage.

✱ BEST IN THE BUSINESS

Saul Bass is probably best known for his animated opening and closing credit title sequences for many Hollywood movies such as *Spartacus*, *Vertigo* and *Goodfellas*.

Kyle Cooper is another well-known producer of film titles and credits: www.prologuefilms.com/

Mate Steinforth is a good example of a freelance designer with a motion graphics portfolio: www.matesteinforth.com/

B2B studios shows the possibilities of design for businesses: www.b2bstudios.com/services/id/

Stash/Feed is a webzine dedicated to animation and motion graphics: www.feedhere.com/

Dreamshock Design Studios has a broad range of styles, clients and outputs: www.dreamshock.com/motiongraphics/

CAREER OPTIONS

Internships are a good way to start. Find a graphics studio near you; chances are they will work with all media, so you can get a grounding in the industry and see what it is like to work in a professional studio.

New media graphic designers, graphic designers or web designers, depending on specialisation.

PART 2	PRACTICE
UNIT 8	COMMERCIAL APPLICATIONS
MODULE 3	**Web design**

In the early days of the internet and the world wide web, the original professionals who took the first stabs at web development were, in fact, initially print-based graphic designers. Now, over a few short years, there are students graduating from colleges across the globe with concentrations focusing solely on web design and development, online communications and internet-based commerce. So what does a career in web-based design have in store?

Companies and organisations hire hundreds of web designers annually to help them create and perfect their online presence and identity. For the more interactive designer with a penchant for heavier coding, design studios and advertising agencies have teams of web developers, coders and information architects to handle the contemporary online needs of their clients, such as interactive interfaces, e-commerce installations, content management systems and social networking platforms. No matter where your intrinsic skills lie, the field of web design has quickly become a rich tapestry of varying disciplines and skills in which any designer can match their talents and interests.

Is it right for you?

However, regardless of whether you imagine yourself up to your elbows in deep PHP coding to create the next MySpace or face first in Photoshop creating breath-taking mock-ups of your client's new site design, your education up to that point and beyond will not be limited to the classroom. Although no higher education is truly limited to the university halls, web design for the most part is an industry for those who love to spend their time learning and exploring. Whether working freelance in a home studio or as an in-house developer at an agency, the larger population of web professionals is made up of true devotees of the modern technological age. Countless personal hours are spent learning and mastering the latest

HIGHS

• Involvement in a constantly evolving technology.
• Near-immediate edits and updates to a body of work with little fuss as compared to print design.
• More opportunities for freelance and home-based work situations for web designers.

LOWS

• The incompatibilities between browsers can be off-putting at first, and lead many people away from the field 'until they fix that'.
• The limited selection of ten fonts for content when thousands exist in print design.
• Nothing is more jarring than viewing your beautiful blue site on an older computer and seeing it rendered in an unpalatable pea-green.

⊕ SEE ALSO: MOTION GRAPHICS P170

⊕ SKILLS REQUIRED

• Firm grasp of typography, composition, layout, balance, colour theory, imagery, creation and manipulation.
• Basic understanding of XHTML and CSS.
• Growing familiarity with the usage of JavaScript, Ajax, PHP.
• Maintenance-level familiarity with older forms of web design (HTML 4.0 and tables-based designs).
• Understanding of the concepts of user interaction and client goals and their relationship to the interface.
• Desire to discover and utilise the latest web languages and innovations.
• Understanding of such principles as Web Standards, Web Accessibility and Search Engine Optimisation.
• Eye for detail, both in a visual way ('Are the images aligned?') and in a comparative way ('These two sets of codes should have identical results, what's the difference between them?').
• Familiarity with how colour and monitors work in regards to the web and how that relates to the viewer (colour blindness, cultural sensitivities, eye fatigue).

XHTML conventions or JavaScript libraries. Days are spent in a trial and error limbo as designers research and modify bits of coding to get the interface to react just as the client expects it. Months of planning are spent from initial thumbnails to final launch as developers and designers work together to create accessible sites that can be literally heard by those without vision. Millions of cups of coffee or tea are poured as these self-starters and self-educators stay up into the wee hours learning digital languages that are never uttered nor seen but experienced. Much like the frontier days of any new technology that bridges the gaps between people (the telephone, the television, the oceanic cruise-liner), all of this happens because there are always those who have the abilities and interests to see the possibilities in the enlarging world of the web, and because they can see themselves within those possibilities.

Hierarchy

Some web designers work successfully from home, conducting a large portion of their client contact by phone and email. Most of the time these solitary designers have a very good command of a wider array of web specialities, such as XHTML/CSS coding, PHP/database-driven web applications, Flash animation, as well as image correction and manipulation.

In larger work environments, a web designer may be the only professional on the team qualified to design and code while working with a team of marketers and executives. These environments may have a variety of multi-disciplinary web designers and developers, or may have specialists that focus on one aspect of each project.

> Online magazines and periodicals The popularity in people looking to the web for most – if not all – of their daily news and information has grown over the years, bringing the field of web design a variety of jobs and positions at established and independent publishers and news agencies.

⊛ BEST IN THE BUSINESS

Jeffrey Zeldman is a lecturer and author on web design. He also runs his own web design studio, Happy Cog, which has created influential web work for clients such as AIGA, Amnesty International, Mozilla, Warner Bros. Films and Stanford University. His book entitled *Designing With Web Standards* set the tone for modern-day semantic web design.

Hillman Curtis has spent a decade blending the web, Adobe Flash and film through his company Hillmancurtis, inc. to design digital media for such companies as Adobe, Hewlett-Packard, Intel, Yahoo!, Rolling Stone and MTV. Curtis and his company have been featured in many publications for their designs and have won many awards for their online work.

Molly E. Holzschlag is an award-winning lecturer and web designer, as well as author of over 35 books related to web design and markup. She has worked with the W3C and WaSP focusing on web standards, web accessibility, web sustainability and related topics.

◀ Shopping sites The fact that many sites on the internet are designed to sell means that web design positions may bring clients and projects where you will create the customers' entire virtual shopping experience.

CAREER OPTIONS

Here is a list of the basic situations an emerging web designer may find when ready to enter the working world.

Independent freelance web designer/developer

Contract freelance web designer/developer

Web designer/developer (working with an agency), design, marketing or advertising for a variety of clients.

Web designer/developer (working within a company), with a focus on the main site or sites for the company; often in charge of the office intranet, email, etc.

MODULE 4 | **Editorial design**

Modern editorial design arguably originates from the 15th-century printing press of Gutenberg, when pages of type were manually set in movable metal type. Each page was set in relation to margins, gutters and borders, and printed in multiple copies: a huge leap from handwritten manuscripts. With evolutions in print production methods and the influence of early 20th-century art and design schools such as the Bauhaus, the designer began to gain control over the page. Editorial designers now work in an unprecedented range of media and technologies. Many new forms of editorial design have been generated over time, and aesthetic considerations are wide ranging.

◀ **Early editorial design** *Aristotle*, printed by Aldus Manutius between 1495 and 1498, is an example of historical editorial design, typeset and printed in Greek.

HIGHS

• You are the designer for the layout and composition of pages/spreads of the publication.
• You see your work in the bookshop or on the internet.
• You work on a wide variety of content (especially in book design).

LOWS

• As the focal point for many different information streams, coordination of deadlines and organisation of work can become tricky.
• There is little freedom for personal expression since the style is decided beforehand.
• As with many specialisations, design school rarely prepares you for the speed or amount of work involved for each project.
• There will inevitably be many corrections/revisions to the work on the way to the final product. You will need to be open to this process and respond well to feedback.

Editorial designers are key players in the production of books, magazines, brochures and catalogues, with the task of aesthetically transforming raw text and image to maximise legibility, impact and communication in an increasingly competitive market. Depending on the publication, there may be a need for flexibility in styling. For example, in a publishing house a designer may work on a series of titles with different demographic target audiences: teen, young professional, specialist interest and mother and baby are just a few of many possibilities. Each needs a different style, emphasis and layout. Aesthetic styles are agreed by the upper production team including the art director and design editor. It is the designer's role to implement these decisions, carry out instructions and respond to changes in the market.

Editorial designers also work on larger internet-based publications, such as news websites, corporate web presence and advertising. Smaller websites usually do not have a specialised designer. There are different design issues on the internet, such as legibility of fonts, and other considerations such as type that 'moves'. Editorial designers are driven by and focused on content, and usually work within teams in medium to large organisations; they are rarely freelancers. They are often the focal point for many streams of material, such as raw text from authors, images from photographers and illustrators and overall concept

⊕ SKILLS REQUIRED

• Excellent appreciation and grasp of typography, typesetting and layout hierarchy.
• Good spatial awareness and compositional skills.
• Strong sense of design history, especially books and magazines.
• Ability to work well with complexity and layering.
• Accurate eye for content correction – grammar, colour, mood.
• Advanced and up-to-date knowledge of InDesign, Illustrator, Photoshop and, to a lesser extent, Quark.
• Team-focused attitude and diplomacy.
• Ability to negotiate extensive revisions to your designs, and to let your ego 'slide'.

Fine art books In this biography, the archival picture selection was handled with care and clarity, weaving viewers through the chronological photographic narrative of Arthur Boyd's family album and his most significant and poignant paintings.

✱ BEST IN THE BUSINESS

Alexey Brodovich, Neville Brody and Cipe Pineles, known for their innovative magazine designs.

Jost Hochuli and Jan Tschichold, known for their book designs and contributions to modern typography.

Bradbury Thompson and Piet Zwart, known for their powerful and imaginative designs in many editorial contexts.

styling from art directors and development teams. They are expected to juggle and mesh these together to create the finished publication.

There are many ways of addressing layout and design, such as minimalist problem-solving aesthetics (originating in the Bauhaus), to contemporary design approaches, including postmodern juxtaposition to concerns about sustainability and environmental impact. As an emerging editorial designer, you need to be aware of all these issues even if they are not your specialisations.

RESOURCES

• For a good overview of contemporary editorial design work: http://www.carbonmade.com/portfolios/editorial-design

• For a useful site run by industry professionals: http://www.editorialdesign.org/

• http://www.jandos.com/

• http://www.penguin.co.uk/

• http://www.markporter.com/

• *Mertz to Emigré and Beyond* by Steven Heller

CAREER OPTIONS

Design assistant, junior designer Invaluable opportunity to learn the ropes by assisting on a wide variety of projects, but with limited room for creativity.

Senior designer Greater opportunity to be creative, designing templates as well as working with them, and possibly making image choices.

Art editor Managing the design of projects, overseeing freelance designers and working closely with editorial and production staff.

Photographic imagery Powerful imagery is the centrepiece of this spread from *Televisual Magazine*. Commissioning and/or working with imagery is part of the job of an editorial designer.

Illustration/photographic imagery Editorial designers for magazines need to be flexible, imaginative and informed about the subject matter they are working with.

PART 2	PRACTICE
UNIT 8	COMMERCIAL APPLICATIONS
MODULE 5	**Game design**

**Game design has changed significantly from the
8-bit pixellated and scrolling-based arcade variants of the 1980s
to the virtual true-to-life computer-generated environments and
open-ended gameplay of contemporary games.**

HIGHS

• Innovating – you are working at the cutting edge and pushing boundaries.
• Seeing your work in the best and most popular games on the market.
• Being part of a team whose passion is their work.
• Exploring the uncharted arena of virtual reality.

LOWS

• Solutions to briefs may not come first time and may need to undergo several revisions to achieve the form and style that the art director is looking for.
• You will be one small part of a very big team even if you are a freelancer. The team and the game come first – leave your ego at the door!
• This career will rarely, if ever, be a 9-to-5 job. Be prepared for long days and possibly late nights.

● **Okami** The use of strong black lines in these character designs for the game Okami is inspired by traditional Japanese ink painting or *sumi-e*. In Okami, a magical calligraphy brush allows the player to interact with the digital world. The visual imagery reflects both the game's content, and method of interaction.

For the majority of games designers, employment will be in production studios with people who have been in the industry their whole career. These professionals are there because they know their field, work hard and are enthusiastic about what they do. As a new graduate, finding your way into the industry may seem daunting at first, but whether you excel in typography and page layout and see yourself as an interface designer, or you are skilled at producing 3D characters that cannot be distinguished from real life, there are a few principles to keep in mind.
• First, games should seamlessly entertain the audience and keep them enthralled as they escape reality, temporarily, into the game-based world. With the demographic of the game as paramount in the creation process, self-expression may be truncated at times and must be distilled into the parameters set up by the concept team. Furthermore, as the gamer should be able to totally lose themselves in the game, acute judgment

⊕ SKILLS REQUIRED

• Excellent communication skills, a 'team player' attitude and diplomacy will get you far, since you will be working hard with the same people for long hours.
• The ability to take criticism constructively.
• Speed of creativity and application; colleges rarely prepare you for the speed and workload needed for every brief.
• Creativity and artistic flair are essential, as is a polished portfolio.
• Advanced and up-to-date knowledge of the right software for your specialisation: Photoshop, Illustrator, Flash, After Effects, 3ds Max and/or Maya.
• Knowledge of mathematics and geometry for designers who specialise in 3D design, as well as those who are involved in physics programming.
• A storyline-based thought process and visualisation techniques involving 'skinning' characters, objects, and areas.

and care for detail is necessary to remove anything that jars and brings the gamer out of that experience.
• When working on briefs with other designers and art directors you will need to meet other team members in the middle and compromise on outcomes. So whether you see yourself as a freelancer or as part of a studio team, good networking and interpersonal skills are a must.

CAREER OPTIONS

There are a variety of careers in game design, from programming or coding game engines, to marketing the product.

Internships are the way in for most students. These give you a feel for the environment, and are a good indicator to a potential future employer that you are committed to your career.

Concept artists provide the initial images that shape any new game.

3D animators/artists take the initial images and translate them into three dimensions.

User interface artists create the in-game information graphics, text and buttons.

RESOURCES

• Gamasutra is a great online resource, from career and community resources and job boards to articles, advice and reviews for the full spectrum of gaming and game design: http://www.gamasutra.com

• Sloperama comes from 'seasoned professional' Tom Sloper, with advice and considered comments for those newly entering the games design industry: http://www.slorerama.com

• A Digital Dreamer has excellent information for many aspects of digital design and also has a great section on game design: http://www.adigitaldreamer.com/

Spore This screengrab from the game Spore shows how textures and patterns have been mapped onto the surfaces of the landscape, buildings and creature.

Spore for PC The PC version of Spore includes the clear, unobtrusive user interface at the bottom. The 3D buildings and skewed perspective are typical of the design of such games, produced in programs such as 3Ds Max, Maya, Blender, Lightwave, Milkshape, Sketchup Pro, Ulead and Truespace.

PART 2 | PRACTICE

UNIT 8 | COMMERCIAL APPLICATIONS

MODULE 6 | **Advertising**

RESOURCES

• The UK NHS Change for Life campaign http://www.nhs.uk/change4life/

• Barnado's excellent website gives contemporary and historical examples: http://www.barnados.org.uk/resources/

• For award-winning commercial campaigns: http://www.mcsaatchi.com

In the 1940s, Elmer Wheeler said: 'Sell the Sizzle, not the Steak.' And that, ladies and gentlemen, is advertising. When you want a snack, you don't just go for the cookie; you go for the delicious attributes the cookie wrapper so convincingly conveys: Chocolatey, Nutty, Crunchy. Advertising is not just 'selling' – it is 'influencing'. The designer whose strengths lie in developing innovative and convincing concepts can play a pivotal role in this high-energy, fast-paced industry. Advertising designers can sway the public consciousness not only through commercial advertising campaigns, but also as part of promoting social change, and raising awareness of local and global issues, such as health, sustainability and politics.

⌃ **Health campaign** The existing Heinz identity is at the centre of this 'pitch' promoting childrens' health. It shows an intelligent appropriation of an established brand identity, for the purpose of influencing the public on global, social issues.

HIGHS

• Upward momentum and building a network: exciting opportunities abound to meet with other professionals in your area. Getting out there and meeting people is the name of the game and how you could meet your next employer.
• You are involved in strategies to help clients make high-level business decisions: how to market themselves to the world with proper appeal and timing, which products to develop or how best to get the message 'out there'.
• Larger cities have local advertising clubs that hold special events, award ceremonies, educational seminars and professional workshops, and have online resource libraries and forums.

LOWS

• The larger the budget, the larger the possibility of failure. Proper management is crucial with larger accounts, which can easily overwhelm a small team.
• Advertising can create notoriously high-stress environments as a client's customer yield develops: the more people you need to reach, the more factors need to be taken into consideration. This usually necessitates more money, meaning the higher the possibility of not achieving a comparable return on a client's investment.

Advertising is a competitive field. Better advertisements reach more minds, influencing more, and attracting more attention and sales. With a team, the freelance or in-house advertising designer creates a campaign concept for a client to present themselves and their next product to the public. As the visual arm of a marketing team, the designer must call upon psychology, marketing, communication and humour to create successful market penetration through media such as: TV, radio, newspapers, magazines, email, the internet. The more innovative, the more thought-provoking, the more memorable – the advertising designer keeps ahead not only of the curve, but also of themselves.

Advertising designers

Undoubtedly, advertising employs more talent to produce creative work than any other occupation, since everything is advertised in some way.

Stress comes in part from the hours: you can expect to work long, inconvenient hours since the agency needs to meet the timing of clients, who are often in other time zones or need to use business hours to meet their own clients' needs. In a larger agency you're more likely to specialise in a certain arena than in a small agency, where you're more likely to do a little (or a lot) of everything.

There are three main positions: graphic designers, art directors and creative directors. These roles can be filled

⊕ SKILLS REQUIRED

• Artistic ability and a knack for good, clever design – being artistic and being a good designer are two different things, but both are needed. Being able to cleverly capture and communicate a client's message both within the current cultural style and while keeping it innovative and graphically sound is a skill that will take you far.

• Communication awareness – having good communication skills is one thing, but knowing your target audience and how to speak to them is such an important asset. Research and knowledge of customer psychology and cultural tastes play an important role in any successful advertising effort.

• Competitive edge – at times the advertising industry has been called 'cut-throat'. One ad can make or break your career. Most likely you will be working to deadlines and under pressure, and a competitive nature to succeed will help you to thrive in that environment.

• Experience with Photoshop, Illustrator, InDesign, Flash, QuarkXpress, PowerPoint and other programs is a must, along with a working knowledge of each step of an ad campaign, the production processes involved and how to work on schedule to meet client expectations.

by freelance and contract workers, or they may be full time as part of a creative department. Regardless of the position you may take, a good advertising piece has a way of sticking with you – whether it's a memorable jingle, a clever catchphrase or a beautiful image. If you feel you have always had the eye for the perfect way to sell something to the world, advertising design provides a rewarding and exciting career for the up-and-coming graphic designer.

⊙ **BMW campaign** The campaign for the BMW Motorrad International GS Trophy appeals to our shared desire for escapism.

CAREER OPTIONS

Working in advertising usually means at an agency, which provides great opportunities for teamwork, networking, higher budgets, broader-scoped campaigns, awards, and unmatchable experience.

Working for bigger-name clients is more common in big cities, and movement between agencies is an option for many designers as they graduate to head designers and art directors and on to opening their own agency.

Copywriter, marketer, account manager, production artist The person who enters advertising design will often wear more than one hat.

Interns and internships are in heavy rotation due to the fast-paced, low-attention-span nature of the public eye as it scans for the latest 'thing'. This is also because, in part, interns are temporary, like 'trends' and 'fads', and their work is creative, fresh, and for free. Being at an agency offers interns a lot of benefits – contacts, clients, and projects – but teaches them only one thing about working in advertising: whether they love it or hate it.

✦ BEST IN THE BUSINESS

BBDO employs 17,200 people in 287 offices in 77 countries worldwide, and is an award-winning agency network, headquartered in New York. Opening its doors in 1928, it was named Agency of the Year in 2005 by *ADWEEK*, *Advertising Age* and *Campaign Magazine* in recognition of amazing work for high-profile clients such as Pepsi, Ikea, FedEx, BBC News, General Electric, Campbells, Gillette, Motorola, Chrysler, Pfizer, Wrigley, Mitsubishi and UNICEF.

Ogilvy & Mather was founded in 1948 and is an international advertising, marketing and public relations firm that operates 497 offices in 125 countries around the world and employs approximately 16,000 professionals.

Opened by David Ogilvy, the company quickly became a leading worldwide agency by the 1960s as it helped build brands for American Express, BP, Ford, Barbie, Maxwell House, IBM, Kodak, Nestlé, Pond's and Dove.

Leo Burnett was opened in 1935, and the agency gained momentum in the 1950s when they created the Kellogg's Frosted Flakes 'Tony the Tiger' campaign. Since then the agency has undergone many changes, but has garnered many big-name accounts along the way, such as McDonald's, Coca-Cola, Walt Disney, Marlboro, Maytag, Kellogg's, Tampax, Nintendo, US Army, Philips, Samsung, Visa, Wrigley and Hallmark. Today the agency has 97 offices in 84 countries across the globe.

PART 2	PRACTICE
UNIT 8	COMMERCIAL APPLICATIONS
MODULE 7	**Information design**

Information design (sometimes called 'information architecture') is a profession not for the faint hearted, but deeply rewarding for the right kind of person. Perfectionists and innately curious people are frequently attracted to information design as a profession, along with those who want to produce useful design, which serves society rather than selling products. The best description of information design is that it's 'user-centred', and research- and analysis-heavy.

⌄ ⌄ **Symbols** Designs such as these by MetaDesign, must be easy to understand and graphically highly legible.

HIGHS

• Rewarding (meaningful and useful).
• Serves society (potential for good).
• Working with multiple content(s) and complex data.
• Combines design and scientific rigour.
• Witnessing your design functioning in society.
• Working with interdisciplinary teams.
• Many different media and contexts for design.

LOWS

• Detail-oriented (not for everyone).
• Content-driven (not style-driven).
• Involves complex problem-solving.
• Less room for unbridled creativity (emphasis on pragmatic/efficient, rather than intuitive).
• Work is often 'invisible'.

Signage, computer-generated information systems, graphs/charts, visualising scientific and technical data, digital control displays and computer interfaces, and the design of legal and technical documents are all part of information design, but the field is expanding. People whose leanings are towards mathematics and science, but who also have a creative side, are also drawn to information design, since it requires the same kind of aptitude, but with a creative aspect. It requires all the skills of a designer, including problem-solving, the ability to communicate clearly, a high degree of typographic knowledge, image generation and great research skills. However, the information designer must possess an additional level of rigour, be interested in resolving the tiniest details of a job and be able to nail the relationship between form and content.

In addition to all the design skills mentioned, it's necessary for an information designer to understand how systems work, and also how they change in different environments (print/digital/3D space). They need to have a strong grasp of how messages are perceived, and how information is processed by readers/audiences (cognitive processing), and be prepared to spend untold hours analysing and bringing order to chaos. Information design is important, meaningful, useful and functional. It is a powerful form of design that should speak to people in a clear, unambiguous language, putting the message first

❝Information design is the newest of the design disciplines. As a sign of our times, when the crafting of messages and meaning is so central to our lives, information design is not only important – it is essential… With ever more powerful technologies of communication, we have learned that the issuer of designed information is as likely as the intended recipient to be changed by it, for better or worse❞

Saul Wurman, Foreword to Information Design, *edited by Robert Jacobson*

⊕ SKILLS REQUIRED

• Ability to approach complex information logically and creatively.
• Understanding of systems and messages.
• Analytical mind.

without sacrificing any of the innovation or beauty of design. If it works, you barely notice it. It makes life easier, and it can illuminate a subject matter you previously thought nothing about. If it doesn't work, it can distort information, create confusion (for example, a badly designed map or guide can make travelling harder, or even dangerous in the case of road signs) or the information simply gets lost. How many poorly designed charts or graphs have you seen that distort the information?

There's very little that's arbitrary/subjective in this profession, and information designers frequently work with complex data, finding a way to visualise that information in the most direct and unambiguous way. They have been called 'the unsung heroes' of the design profession, because much of their work is invisible. Think of the way airport signage works. It gets you there, but you barely notice the design, which is exactly what it should do. The forms you fill in for taxes or job applications have all been designed by someone, but the design is barely noticeable.

RESOURCES

- The American Institute of Graphic Designers: http://www.aiga.org/content.cfm/guide-designersatwork
- http://www.designcouncil.org.uk/en/About-Design/Design-Disciplines/Information-Design-by-Sue-Walker-and-Mark-Barratt//
- Edward Tufte's books and work can be seen at: http://www.edwardtufte.com/tufte/
- An information design consultancy, with a user-centred approach: http://www.textmatters.com/
- International consultancy, MetaDesign, specialises in many aspects of identity, interaction and information design: http://www.metadesign.de/

CAREER OPTIONS

Designer in a company with a specialism in information design, systems design, user documentation or signage.

Web designer in a company dealing with information architecture.

Designer in government agencies that deal with delivering complex information to the public, such as health services, transport and weather.

⊙ **Supplementary brochures** MetaDesign provided branding and identity support, in repositioning Dusseldorf Airport in the marketplace. These items needed to be coordinated with the rest of the information design (see p54).

⊙ **Maps** MetaDesign developed a new wayfinding system, to aid passengers in navigating Dusseldorf Airport as part of their integrated signage project in 1996–1998. Such maps and instructional guides are a core part of an information designer's work.

Resources

The International Organisation for Standardization (ISO) 'A' series is a system for sizing paper that was first used in Germany in 1922 where it is still called 'DIN A' (Deutsche Industrie Norm). Each size is derived by halving the size immediately above it. Each size is the same as another geometrically as they are halved using the same diagonal. A0 is the first size and is 1m² (10 ¾ square feet, approximately) in area. A series sizes always refer to the trimmed sheet. The untrimmed sizes are referred to as 'RA' or 'SRA'. About 26 countries have officially adopted the A series system and it is commonly used everywhere in the world except Canada and the United States.

The 'B' series is used when a size in between any two adjacent A sizes is needed, which is relatively rare. The British and American systems, unlike the metric A system, refer to the untrimmed size of the sheet. As quoting just the A or B number can cause confusion, both the A or B size and the size in inches or millimetres should be given when specifying paper.

ISO A series

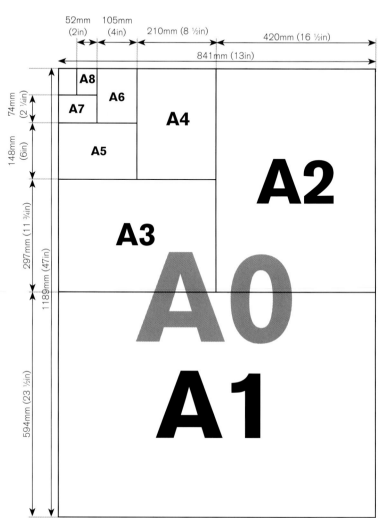

British standard book sizes

	Quarto		Octavo	
	mm	in	mm	in
Crown	246 x 189	9 ½ x 7 ½	186 x 123	7 ½ x 5
Large crown	258 x 201	10 x 8	198 x 129	8 x 5
Demy	276 x 219	11 x 8 ½	216 x 138	8 ½ x 5 ½
Royal	312 x 237	12 ¼ x 9 ½	234 x 156	9 ½ x 6

U.S. book sizes

mm	in
140 x 216	5 ½ x 8 ½
127 x 187	5 x 7 ⅜
140 x 210	5 ½ x 8 ¼
156 x 235	6 ⅛ x 9 ¼
136 x 203	5 ⅜ x 8
143 x 213	5 ⅝ x 8 ⅜

North American paper sizes

Size	mm × mm	in × in
Letter	216 × 279	8 ½ × 11
Legal	216 × 356	8 ½ × 14
Junior Legal	203 × 127	8 × 5
Ledger[2]	432 × 279	17 × 11
Tabloid	279 × 432	11 × 17

ISO B series

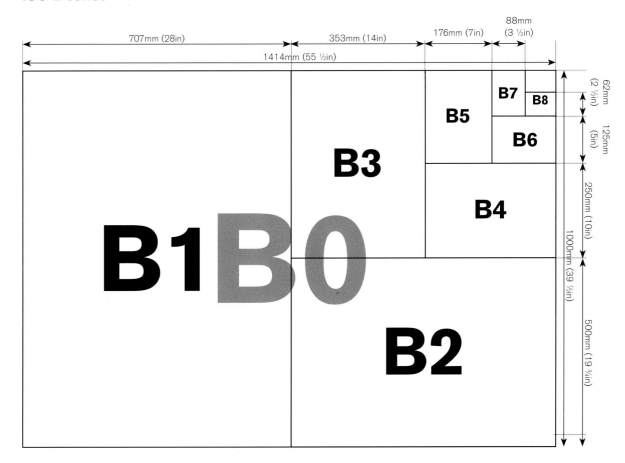

Envelopes

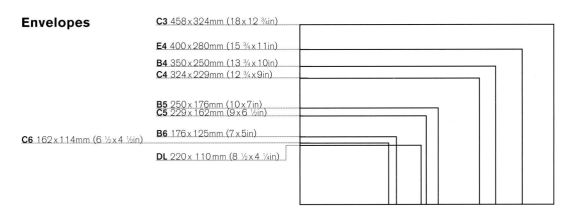

C3 458 x 324mm (18 x 12 ¾in)

E4 400 x 280mm (15 ¾ x 11in)

B4 350 x 250mm (13 ¾ x 10in)
C4 324 x 229mm (12 ¾ x 9in)

B5 250 x 176mm (10 x 7in)
C5 229 x 162mm (9 x 6 ½in)

C6 162 x 114mm (6 ½ x 4 ½in)   **B6** 176 x 125mm (7 x 5in)

DL 220 x 110 mm (8 ½ x 4 ¼in)

Glossary

AAs: 'Author's Alterations' are edits made to the content of a file by the client. They are usually handled before the job is sent to press. The client makes edits while the job is at the printer, usually in the proofing stage, and AAs can prove costly.

Abstraction: An aesthetic concept describing something that is drawn from the real, but has been 'distilled' to its barest minimum form, colour or tone, often removed from its original context.

Additive colour: System used on monitors and televisions, based on RGB (Red, Green, Blue). When combined, these form white light.

Adobe Acrobat: The family of Adobe programs that create and manage PDFs.

Alignment: The setting of text relative to a column or page.

Analogous: Similar, comparable, alike; for example, two colours that are near to each other on the colour wheel, such as green and leaf green, are analogous.

Anchor: Signified by a singular 'a' in a start and end tag, this creates a hyperlink on a web page.

Anchor point: A point on or at the end of a curve or line that can be 'grabbed' by the cursor and moved around the canvas, either to change the curve shape or to move the entire curve.

Associations: Connections between colours and emotions, culture, experience and memory.

Asymmetry: A composition of elements that are juxtaposed and do not mirror the other forms on the page.

Audience: Consumers, voyeurs and occasionally participants of design work.

Axis: *See* Stress

Banding: Series of lighter or darker bands running across an area of solid printed colour.

Baseline: The line on which the lowercase letters sit, and below which the descenders fall.

Baseline grid: Locks text onto consistent horizontal points.

Block-level: (Web coding) Starts a new line; can have width, height and position.

Blog: Web log, or a log or diary for the web; all blogs together are known as the blogosphere.

Brainstorming: A visual aid to thinking laterally and exploring a problem, usually by stating the problem in the centre of a page and radiating spokes from the centre for components of the problem. Each component can then be considered separately with its own spokes, so that each point, thought or comment is recorded.

Calibration: Colour settings that should be set to show colour on screen as it will be in print.

Canvas: The virtual 'ground' into which images are placed.

Centred: Text that is aligned neither to the left nor to the right – symmetrical, with an even gap at the end of each line.

Class: A group of elements sharing common styling rules. Can appear multiple times on a page, prefixed by a period (.).

Clip: The name for a sequence of images or length of developed film or video.

CMYK: Cyan, Magenta, Yellow, Key (Black) – the four colours that make up the full-colour printing process.

Coated-one-side paper: Coated on one side and matt on the other.

Coated paper: A hard, waxy surface, either gloss or matt, and non porous (ink sits on the surface).

Code folding: Allows a developer to condense blocks of elements by their tags, so that a long anchor tag is visually compressed to, say <a>...</a>, facilitating quick navigation through a document.

Collage: Derived from the French word for 'to glue' involving the assemblage of elements of texture, found materials and newspapers.

Colourimeter: Hardware that attaches to or hangs in front of your screen, allowing you to calibrate and profile your monitor.

Column: Vertical block of text.

Control point: A point that can be selected and moved three-dimensionally in a design program, manipulating the surface.

Complementary colours: Colours, such as red and green, that lie opposite each other on the colour wheel.

Composition: The arrangement of elements or parts of a design (text, images) on the page (or ground).

Concertina folds: Folds in alternate directions.

Connotations: A colour's broader associations, for example, green: jealousy, naivety, illness, environment and nature.

Contrast: Differentiation between two or more elements, in this context, of image colour. For example, high contrast is between black and white, or blue and orange; low contrast is between two similar shades of blue such as mid- and cornflower blue.

Crop mark: Vertical and horizontal lines at the corners of an image or page to indicate to a vendor where to trim off the bleed area.

Customer profile/Profiling: The process of creating a series of parameters or set of information that defines the desires, trends or interests of a demographic so that designs can be pitched or marketed to them.

Data: Facts or pieces of information of any kind.

Denotations: What the colour literally means, or is, for example, a red rose is a green stem with red petals.

Depth of field: Distance between the object of focus and where the focus starts to blur. For example, a photographer may want a product to be in sharp clear focus but the background to be blurred, so would choose a smaller aperture (f22), a slower film speed (ISO 100) for higher resolution, and have extra lighting and external flashes set up.

Diagram: Drawing or plan that explains the parts of something, or how something works.

Didactics: A pragmatic and unambiguous method of giving clear information.

Digital presses: Automate direct image transfer from digital file to paper without the creation of plates.

Documentation: The recording in written, visual or aural form of what is of interest.

Dot gain: A printed dot that becomes bigger than intended due to spreading, causing a darkening of screened images, mid-tones and textures. Varies with different paper stock, such as newsprint.

Downsampling: A form of compression that lowers the resolution of images by eliminating unnecessary pixel data.

DPI: Dots Per (square) Inch; the common form of resolution measurement. Designers typically use 72dpi-sized images for web images, and 300dpi-sized images for photo-realistic prints.

Earmark: Identifying or distinguishing marks or characteristics of a typeface.

Element: One small part of a composition such as a point or line, an image, a letter or a word.

Embedding: A PDF removes the need for multiple requisite files by including fonts and compressed imagery into one file.

Ephemera: Objects such as newspapers, bus and train tickets and other found textures and typography.

F stop/focal length and aperture: Size of aperture or 'iris' inside a camera, which controls the amount of light that hits the film or pixel sensor; the range on a general camera is f4 (large aperture) to f22 (small aperture). A large aperture (f2, for example) brings more light into the camera and results in a softer image; a small aperture (f16, for example) allows less light into the camera but gives a sharper image.

Filter: Plates of glass or plastic attached to the front of the lens in order to accentuate different qualities. For example, a polarizing filter cuts down light glare; a colour filter enhances different colours.

Flat plan: *See* Page plan

FLA: The uncompressed and editable file format from Flash.

Flexography: Method of printing that uses rubber relief plates.

Flush left/Flush right: *See* Ranged left/ranged right.

FLV: Flash Video, the file extension format for displaying video on the internet supported by YouTube and news-feed streaming.

Font: One size, weight and width of a typeface: Garamond Roman 12pt is a font.

FPO: For Position Only; the use of a temporary placeholder or low-resolution image in place of the high-quality counterpart during the design process.

French folds: Sheets of paper folded in half, so that they are double thickness. The two folds are at right angles to each other, and then bound on the edge.

Gamut: The complete range of colours available within one system of reproduction, for example, CMYK gamut or RGB gamut.

Gang-run printing: Printing many different jobs on one large sheet.

Gatefold: A way of folding paper so that the outer quarters of a page are folded to meet in the centre. The result works like symmetrical doors that open onto an inner page.

Gestalt psychology: A theory that suggests that mind perceives and organises holistically and finds patterns in that which appears to be unconnected.

Global village: A process where different people from different areas of the world can meet and exchange information fast via the internet. This makes the world appear smaller. Popularised by Marshall McLuhan.

Gloss paper: A shiny form of paper, used for magazines, books, etc.

Gravure: Method of printing that uses plates with recessed cells of varying depths.

Grid: Series of horizontal and vertical lines on a page, used as a visual guide for lining up words and images.

Ground: The page, surface or area in which the design will be placed.

Gsm: Grams per square metre (paper weight), or g/m^2.

Gutter: The gap between two text blocks or spreads on separate pages either side of the book fold or binding.

Handle: Anchor points in a design program connected to the main vector path by tangential lines which can be manipulated to change the shape of the curve.

Harmony: Image with a balance of two or more colours that work together, for example, leaf green and beige.

Hierarchy: The different 'weight' or layout importance given to type or images to emphasise different aspects.

Href: The hypertext reference attribute in a tag is the active participle that instructs the browser of the intended jump location.

Hyphenation: The point at which a word is broken at the end of a line in continuous text, and a hyphen is inserted.

ID: Unique identity of an element (web coding); can only be used once on a page; denoted by hash (#).

Inline: Used for visual styling; provides no structure to a document but applies effects to text.

ISO: International Organization for Standardization. This sets a standard range for virtual film speeds in digital cameras: ISO 100, for example, works best in good lighting conditions for stationary objects; ISO 1600 works best in poor lighting conditions and for mobile objects.

Justified: Lines or paragraphs of type aligned to both margins simultaneously, creating straight vertical edges and differently evened spacing in between words.

Juxtaposition: The process of putting two or more unrelated or opposite elements or objects together to create different effects.

Kelvin: A unit of colour temperature.

Keyframe: Either the frame of an animation at a key stage or a frame in a clip where a transition starts.

Kerning: Adjustments to the spaces between two letters (used extensively for capitals).

Laid paper: Has lines on its surface from its means of production. Often used for stationery.

Lateral thinking: A form of research where the emphasis is on indirect, creative, forms of inquiry.

Law of Closure The mind creates a solid object on the page from suggestions of contours and shapes.

Layout: Placement of words and images on a grid or document to organise information.

Leading: The horizontal space between lines of type. Related to the historical use of strips of lead in letterpress.

Lens: Different lenses extend the capabilities of the camera:

- A normal lens on a digital or film SLR is 35mm, considered to be near enough to human vision.
- A macro lens captures sharp, extreme close-ups of objects.
- A wide-angle lens captures a wider vision, but with perspective distortion.
- A telephoto lens captures objects at distance.

Letter spacing: (Tracking) The space between letters, which can be adjusted.

Line: A continuous form of connection between two points ('___').

Linear reasoning: A form of thinking that implies strategic thought process, one in which step-by-step logic is employed.

Linen paper: Similar to Laid paper, but finer lined.

Linguistic: Of, or relating to, language.

Lossless: A compression format for images and files that removes redundant data to shrink file size, re-creating an identical copy when reopened.

Lossy: A compression format that removes or 'loses' certain areas to achieve a smaller file size, yet reopening the file causes the program to 'guess' at the missing data, possibly creating a lower-quality version.

LPI When printing halftones, such as in one-colour newspapers and reproductions, the 'Lines Per Inch' is the number of lines that compose the resolution of a halftone screen.

LZW: The Lempel-Ziv-Welch algorithm, a popular universal lossless data compression format. Some vendors prefer this compression when dealing with such file types as TIFF.

Margin: The usually blank space to the top, bottom and sides of a page between the trim and the live printing area. Headers, footers and page numbers are traditionally placed within this area.

Market research: The process of collecting and collating data from questionnaires, interviews and comments from the public regarding a concern, a problem or a possible solution.

Matte: A dull, non-shiny quality of paper, used for newspapers, for example.

Measure: The length of a line of text on a page, based in inches, centimetres, points or picas.

Metaphor: Word or image that sets up associations; for example, a 'piece of cake' is a metaphor for easy.

Modern typefaces: Late 18th century typefaces with highly contrasted thick and thin strokes, and vertical axis/stress.

Montage: Derived from the French word for 'assemble'; a picture made from pieces of other pictures.

Mood board: A basic aid for visual stimulus that designers of various disciplines use. It can help lateral thinking and be thought of as visual brainstorming.

Negative space: The white or coloured area around an element, for example, a margin of a page.

Non-representation: The opposite of Representation.

NURBS: Non-Uniform Rational B(Bézier)-splines (NURBS) – mathematically determined and generated curves and surfaces first developed by Pierre Bézier to model freeform surfaces.

Offset lithography: The digitally produced printing plate is treated chemically so that the image will accept ink and reject water.

Old-style typefaces: Roman serif typefaces with an oblique axis/stress to the letters. Based on pen-drawn forms. Also called 'Humanist'.

Onomatopoeia: In typography, the use of type to suggest the sounds of a spoken language, such as adding a large 'o' to the word 'open'.

Optical adjustment: Making adjustments to letter spacing by eye, not mechanically.

Order: Higher orders of control points give more flexibility to manipulation of a curve or surface.

Ornaments: Typed characters that embellish the page. Also known as 'flowers'.

Page plan/Flat plan: A document with a series of numbered thumbnails set out in an ordered grid that represent each page in a book.

Panel: Device used to highlight information. Also known as a 'sidebar'.

Pantone Matching System (PMS): An international system to ensure reliable colour selection, specification, and control globally among designers, clients and vendors.

Path: A drawn line in a design program, mathematically determined; also called a vector.

Paper grain: The direction of wood fibres that make up a piece of paper.

Perfect bind: Method similar to paperback binding, where loose sheets are encased in a heavier paper cover, then glued to the book spine. Edges are trimmed to be flush with each other.

PEs: 'Printer's Errors' are mistakes and omissions found at the proofing stage by the designer or client that did not, for whatever reason, make it from the supplied file to the press. The cost of these errors is usually absorbed by the vendor as a matter of customer service.

Photomontage: The assemblage of various fragments of photographs.

Pica: *See* Point size

Pixel: The smallest element of a computer screen or printed image. The word 'pixel' is an amalgamation of picture (pix-) and element (-el).

Planographic: A printing process that does not use a raised surface.

Plates: Enable the printing of separate colours.

Poetics: A style that is unclear, artistic and open to interpretation.

Point: A dot on a page such as a period (.).

Point size/Pica: The relative size of a font. There are 72 points in an inch.

Polygon count: The higher the count, the more polygons are generated on the surface and the smoother the surface becomes.

Polygon mesh: A modelling system that divides surfaces into triangles or polygons, enabling complex surfaces to be determined with flat faces and straight lines between three or more points on an x, y, z 3D coordinate system.

Positive space: A form, image, or word printed or formed on the page.

PPI: "Pixels Per Inch" or "pixel density" is interchangeable with DPI, but usually refers to the resolution of an unprinted image displayed on screen or captured by a scanner or digital camera.

Primary colours: Red, yellow and blue.

Primary research: Gathering material that does not pre-exist, such as photographing, drawing, making prototypes and interviewing people.

Profiling: *See* Customer profiling

Quality-control strip: Usually incorporated in printed sheets outside the grid to monitor the quality of plate making, inking and registration. Checking black sections helps point out colour casting.

Quantitative: Related to quantities of things, or measurements (numerical).

Ragging: When text is aligned left, some words at the end of the lines might jut out farther than the rest and cause uneven-looking paragraphs.

Ranged left/Ranged right (Flush left/Flush right): Text that is aligned to a column, either left or right.

Raster: Assemblages of pixels on a 2D grid system that can be viewed on computer screens or print media.

Ream: Standard quantity of paper: 500 sheets.

Recto: The right-hand page in a book.

Registration mark: Hairline mark at the corner of a printed page to help ensure plates are lined up correctly and designate what will be cropped off at finishing time.

Relief: A printing process that uses a raised surface, such as letterpress.

Render: The image produced where surfaces and textures are mapped onto the wireframe.

Representation: Something that looks like, resembles, or stands in for something else. In drawing, this is also known as 'figurative', as it deliberately attempts to mimic the thing drawn.

Resolution: The clarity of a digital image. A low-resolution image (30dpi, for example) will have clearly visible pixels; a high-resolution image (300dpi, for example) will not.

Rhetoric: A style of arguing, persuading or engaging in dialogue. For a designer, it is a way of engaging the targeted audience.

Rollover folds: A way of folding a page so that successive folds turn in on themselves and the page is folded into a roll.

RSS: Really Simple Syndication (previously Rich Site Summary); allows users to subscribe to blogs, sites or other serial content in order to read specific articles without continually browsing different pages. RSS feeds usually contain a summary, published date and author details.

Saddle stitching: Book binding method where sheets of paper are folded in the centre, stitched together along the fold, then glued into the cover spine.

Sans serif (without serif): Typefaces such as Univers, Helvetica, Aksidenz Grotesque and Futura. Predominantly associated with the 19th and 20th centuries.

Satin: A form of paper between matt and gloss.

Schematic: Simplified diagram or plan related to a larger scheme or structure.

Screen-printing: Method of printing that uses stencils.

Secondary colours: A mix of any two primary colours.

Secondary research: Gathering material that already exists, such as design work, colour samples, written texts, newspaper/magazine articles, archive images (e.g. historical samples of advertising).

Semantics: The study of meaning in language and elsewhere.

Semiotics: A system that links objects, words and images to meanings through signs and signifiers.

Serif: Structural details at the ends of some strokes in old-style capital and lowercase letters.

Shift-scheduling: Allowing presses to run all day and night.

Simultaneous contrast: The human eye tends to differentiate between two neighbouring colours by emphasizing their differences rather than their similarities – background colours affect foreground colours (the image).

SLR: Single Lens Reflex. These types of camera use a viewfinder and mirrors so that the photographer's sightline goes through the main lens and results in a what-you-see-is-what-you-get image.

Small capital: A letter having the form of a capital but slightly smaller.

Snippets: Preformatted chunks of reusable code that can be collected and repurposed again and again. Many text editors will allow you to wrap tag snippets around already typed text.

Spot colour: Any flat colour, printed as a solid, and not made up of CMYK.

Statistical: Related to the collection, classification and organization of (often numerical) information.

Stock: A generic form or type of paper, such as tracing paper or 'matte coated'.

Storyboard: An organisational document similar to a flat plan, but with a sequence of thumbnails that specifically lays out the narrative for a comic strip or film.

Stress/Axis: The angle of the curved stroke weight change in a typeface. Seen clearly in letters such as 'o'.

Subtractive colour: System used in printing, based on the CMYK colours.

SWF: ShockWave Flash, the file extension format for displaying animated vector files on the web.

Symbolism: A way of representing an object or word through an image, sound or another word, for example, a crossed knife and fork on a road sign means a cafe is ahead.

Symmetry: A composition of elements that is balanced or mirrored on a page.

Syntax: The study of the rules for the formation of grammatically correct sentences.

Syntax highlighting: Allows the developer to choose how text is coloured, to help separate types of tags from content, image tags and meta information, for example.

Tertiary colour: A mix of any two secondary colours.

Thumbnail: Small, rough visual representation of the bigger picture or final outcome of a design.

Timeline: The linear timeline in both Flash and After Effects in which keyframes can be fixed in order to designate animated milestones in a production.

Tracking: *See* Letter spacing

Transitional: Originating in the early-mid 18th century, serif typefaces with more strongly contrasted thick and thin strokes, and a more vertical axis/stress.

Type anatomy: The language used to describe the various parts of letterforms.

Typeface: The set of visual attributes (design or style) of a particular group of letters; Garamond is a typeface.

Typographic rules: Printed lines that direct the reader's eye.

Url: The uniform resource locator is the basic address of any website.

Varnish: A liquid sprayed or spread onto paper to give it a hardwearing surface so that printed ink stays intact.

Vector: *See* Path

Verso: The left-hand page in a book.

Vibration: Complementary colours of equal lightness and high saturation tend to make each other appear more brilliant.

Web 1.0 and 2.0: Web 1.0 was the first boom of the internet with pages and sites to browse through. This was, however, a read-only interface. Web 2.0 was the reaction to the first dot.com crash and introduced new forms of interconnectivity, networking and community. This enabled users to comment, leave testimonials and interact with other users and content.

Weight: Colours differ in 'weight'. For example, if a man had to move two large boxes equal in size, but one pale green and the other dark brown, he would probably pick up the green one first because it appeared lighter. It is generally assumed that blue-greens look lighter whereas reds appear stronger, and therefore heavier.

Wiki: The name is taken from the Hawaiian word for 'fast' and has also come to stand for 'What I Know Is'.

Wireframe: A way to see the entire structure of the object represented in lines.

Wove or Smooth: A smooth, uncoated paper that is porous (ink sits under the surface).

WYSIWYG: 'What you see is what you get'. Used to describe a system in which the presentation of onscreen content is very similar to final output.

x-height: The height of a lowercase 'x' in any typeface.

Index

Bibliography

Eye: The International Review of Graphic Design (magazine)

J. Abbott Miller, Ellen Lupton, *Design Writing Research*, Phaidon Press Ltd

Philippe Apeloig, *Au Coeur du Mot (Inside the Word)*, Lars Müller

Phil Baines, *Type and Typography: Portfolio Series*, Laurence King

Gabriel Bauret, *Alexey Brodovitch*, Assouline

Russell Bestley, Ian Noble, Visual Research: An Introduction to Research Methodologies in Graphic Design, AVA Publishing

Michael Bierut, William Drenttel, Steven Heller, D. K. Holland *Looking Closer: Critical Writings on Graphic Design*, Allworth Press

Lewis Blackwell, *20th-Century Type: Remix*, Gingko Press

Robert Bringhurst, *The Elements of Typographic Style*, Hartley & Marks Publishers

Michael Burke, Peter Wilber, *Information Graphics: Innovative Solutions in Contemporary Design*, Thames & Hudson

Italo Calvino, *Invisible Cities*, Hyphen Press

Rob Carter, Ben Day, Philip Meggs, *Typographic Design: Form and Communication*, John Wiley & Sons

David Crow, *Visible Signs*, AVA Publishing

Department of Typography, University of Reading, *Modern typography in Britain: graphic design, politics and society*, Hyphen Press

Geoffrey Dowding, *Finer Points in the Spacing and Arrangement of Type*, Hartley and Marks

Johanna Drucker, *Alphabetic Labyrinth: The Letters in History and Imagination*, Thames & Hudson

Johanna Drucker, *Figuring the Word: Essays on Books, Writing and Visual Poetics*, Granary Books

Johanna Drucker, *The Century Of Artists' Books*, Granary Books

Johanna Drucker, Emily McVarish, *Graphic Design History: A Critical Guide*, Prentice Hall

Kimberly Elam, *Grid Systems: Principles of Organizing Type*, Princeton Architectural Press

Alan Fletcher, *The Art of Looking Sideways*, Phaidon Press Ltd

Friedrich Friedl, Nicolaus Ott, Bernard Stein, *Typography: An Encyclopedic Survey of Type Design and Techniques throughout History*, Black Dog & Leventhal Publishers Inc

E. M. Ginger, Erik Spiekermann, *Stop Stealing Sheep and Find Out How Type Works*, Adobe Press

Steven Heller, *Merz to Emigré and Beyond: Avant-Garde Magazine Design of the Twentieth Century*, Phaidon Press Ltd

Steven Heller, *Paul Rand*, Phaidon Press Ltd

Jost Hochuli, *Detail in Typography*, Hyphen Press

Jost Hochuli, Robert Kinross, *Designing Books: Practice and Theory*, Princeton

Richard Hollis, *Graphic Design: A Concise History*, Thames & Hudson

Allen Hurlburt, *The Grid: A Modular System for the Design and Production of Newpapers, Magazines, and Books*, John Wiley & Sons

David Jury, *Letterpress: The Allure of the Handmade*, Rotovision

Robin Kinross, *Modern Typography: An Essay in Critical History*, Hyphen Press

Robin Kinross, *Unjustified Texts: Perspectives on Typography*, Hyphen Press

Willi Kunz, *Typography: Macro and Microaesthetics, Fundamentals of Typographic Design*, Ram Publications

Ellen Lupton, *Thinking with Type: A Critical Guide for Designers, Writers, Editors and Students*, Princeton Architectural Press

Per Mollerup, *Marks of Excellence*, Phaidon Press Ltd

Lars Müller, *Josef Müller-Brockmann, Pioneer of Swiss Graphic Design*, Lars Müller Publishers

Joseph Müller-Brockmann, *Grid Systems in Graphic Design*, Niggli Verlag

Alan Pipes, *Production for Graphic Designers*, Laurence King

Norman Potter, *What Is a Designer: Things, Places, Messages*, Hyphen Press

Paul Rand, *A Designer's Art*, Yale University Press

Paul Rand, *Design, Form and Chaos*, Yale University Press

Paul Rand, *From Lascaux to Brooklyn*, Yale University Press

Ferdinand de Saussure, *Course in General Linguistics*, Books LLC

Adrian Shaughnessy, *How to be a Graphic Designer, Without Losing Your Soul*, Laurence King

Bradbury Thompson, *The Art of Graphic Design*, Yale University Press

Jan Tschichold, *The New Typography*, University of California Press

Jan Tschichold, *Asymmetric Typography*, Cooper & Beatty

Edward Tufte, *Envisioning Information*, Graphics Press

Edward Tufte, *The Visual Display of Quantitative Information*, Graphics Press

Edward Tufte, *Visual Explanations: Images and Quantities, Evidence and Narrative*, Graphics Press

Wolfgang Weingart, *My Way to Typography*, Lars Müller Publishers

Suggested online resources:

http://www.aiga.org/content.cfm/guide-designersatwork
http://www.artsandecology.rsablogs.org.uk/
http://www.blog.eyemagazine.com/
http://www.design21sdn.com/
http://www.designandsociety.rsablogs.org.uk/
http://www.designcanchange.org/
http://www.designcouncil.org.uk/en/About-Design/Design-Disciplines/Information-Design-by-Sue-Walker-and-Mark-Barratt//
http://www.designobserver.com/
http://www.designersaccord.org/index.php?title=Main_Page
http://www.greengaged.com/
http://www.hyphenpress.co.uk/books
http://www.kateandrews.wordpress.com/resources/
http://www.lars-mueller-publishers.com/
http://www.lovelyasatree.com/
http://www.re-nourish.com/
http://www.redjotter.wordpress.com
http://www.service-design-network.org/
http://www.socialdesignsite.com/
http://www.sustainability.aiga.org/
http://www.sustainability.aiga.org/sus_reading/sustainable_design
http://www.textmatters.com/
http://www.thersa.org/home
http://www.threetreesdontmakeaforest.org/
http://www.typotheque.com/site/index.php

Acknowledgements

Author acknowledegments

Sheena Calvert:

The Figure Versus Ground assignment in Basic of Composition, page 37, was reworked from original content created by Rob Roy Kelly. Visit www.rit.edu/library/archives/rkelly/html/04_cou/cou_per3.html

Thanks to Sîan Cook of the LCC for the content of the chart on page 15.

Thanks to Sîan Cook and Jack Blake of the LCC, along with Christine McCauley of the University of Westminster, for their help in requesting and organising student submissions.

Thanks to Kate Andrews for her contributions and suggestions to the Online resources list on page 191.

Many thanks to Rebecca Muirhead for producing the content for the following spreads, and for her extensive research, rewriting and editing throughout the book: Unit 1, p22–24, Unit 4, p92–101, Unit 5, p104–113, p119–125, Unit 6, p138–139, Unit 7, p164–165, Unit 8, p170–171 and p176–177.

Anoki Casey:

Thanks to Annette Raimondi Murray, Prepress and Colour Consultant at ANRO Inc. Print and Digital Solutions.

Thanks to John Donges, Photographer.

Thanks to Sara Hodgson, Co-Founder at Incompra Design.

Rebecca Muirhead:

Thanks to Kai Ono and Daniel Rubenstein for their expert advice on the 3d Graphics and Photography sections, respectively.

Publisher acknowledgements

Thanks to Tony Seddon at Rotovision, UK, for his helpful advice and comments on File Preparation and Sending (p132–133), File Types and Compression (p134–134) and Electronic Media Production (p146–147).

Thanks to Arvind Sond and Andy Wheater for their help with 3D Graphics (p122–123).

Thanks to Bobbie Sidhu and Jake Bickerton at *Televisual* Magazine for the magazine spreads on p86–87 and p175.

Thanks to John Grain for his help with Flash/After Effects p124–125.

Quarto would like to thank the following students, designers and agencies, for kindly supplying images for inclusion in this book:

p.6–7bl–r Vinesh Shah, Tigz Rice, Zoe Savitz, Patrick Fry, Anna Reynolds, Jonathan Duncan

p.10t, Deborah Morrison, Oregon, USA

p.16–17b Art Director Andrea Schneider, Oregon, USA

p.11t, 83t, 83m Kate Skinner

p.11b, 24t, 50br, 52ml, 75b, 112b Leena Kangaskoski

p.12–13, 89 Franziska Boemer

p.14–15, 16t, 17t, 25, 81b Lucy Brown

p.18b Victoria Weatherall

p.18, 32, 34, 43t, 64b Ian Curtis

p.19 Jo Cheung

p.20tl Lucy Halcomb, instructor: Julie Spivey/University of Georgia

p.20tr, 90t Vicky Smith www.vickysmithisnice.co.uk

p.21tr Faith Hutchinson, instructor Julie Spivey/University of Georgia

p.21b, 48b Joshua Hibbert

p.22t, 97b Damien Bertles, instructor Kent Smith/Western Washington University

p.22b Anthony Ciocca, instructor, Kent Smith/Western Washington University

p.23tm, 60t Trend Group

p.24b, 47m Simon Hessler

p.26, 29 Shaz Madani: shaz_madani@yahoo.com

p.27 Billy Woods > fantastic_bill@hotmail.com

p.28 Ben Wong

p.30, 96b James Gillen

p.35, 37, 42b, 85t Varvara Zaytseva

p.39, 154l Wikipedia

p.39 Nina Klein

p.40t Prof. Almar Mavignier www.mavignier.com

p.41b Bridgeman

p.46t, 51, 53t, 84t, 168b www.kad.com

p.46b, 50l, 54, 55mr, 58, 69mr, 88t, 91ml, 96t, 98 2FRESH www.2fresh.com

p.47, 70tl Octavo Corp/Source Library www.octavo.com

p.48t, 52b, 64t, 84b Egberto Esmerio

p.48b, 86b Elliot Hammer

p.52t Lee Yan Chak, Jack

p.53b, 56t, 61, 69tr, 78, 82, 83b, 86t&m, 89t, 95t, 97t, 138b Sägenvier Design Kommunikation www.saegenvier.at

p.55t James Allen

p.55bl, 63bl, 85b Ana Estrougo

p.55br Julie Hadjinian, instructor Kent Smith/Cristina de Almeida/Western Washington University

p.56b Design: Hannah Firmin Author: Alexander McCall Smith. ABACUS

p.57r The New York Times Co. Reprinted with permission. Copyright ©

p.59, 99bl Paone Design Associates www.paonedesign.com

p.60bl Simon Phillipson

p.61b Rashika Varsani

p.63t, 76 Ben Smithers

p.63b, 77br Strichpunkt www.strichpunkt-design.de

p.64tl, 74b Kai Matthiesen

p.65 Anna Cennamo

p.66 Corbis

p.69tl Rosa Murphy

p.69ml Jonathan Duncan

p.69b, 77b, 96m Pavel Skala

p.71 Matt Busher

p.71bl&m David Dabner, LCC

p.70tr Monotype Imaging www.monotypeimaging.com

p.73m,ml Faith Hutchinson, instructor: Julie Spivey/University of Georgia

p.73mr Randy Yeo

p.73b, 127r, 175t David Lancashire Design www.davidlancashiredesign.com.au/

p.76bl Amy Maw www.jkr.co.uk

p.76br Design Bridge www.designbridge.com

p.77bl Oksana Shmygol instructor: Simon Gray/ *dept. of* DESIGN www.dod.cz

p.80l Carol Herbert, instructor: Julie Spivey/University of Georgia

p.80tr, 96ml Pavel Skala instructor: Simon Gray/ *dept. of* DESIGN www.dod.cz

p.83b, 112t Sarah Hall

p.86–87b *InMotion* magazine (Bobbie Sidhu)

p.87t Becky Lyddon www.lardesign.co.uk

p.87m Getty Images

p.88ml All ornaments designed by Zuzana Licko, Emigré, www.emigre.com

p.89b Giordano Di Stasio

p.90b, 127tl Aarefa Tayabji

p.91t Andrew McGarity

p.91mr Sophie Lepinoy

p.91b Daniel Mather

p.97bl, 101bl London College of Communication LCC, Advertising Department

p.100t TFL

p.118 Kai Ono

p.120, 121b grand union design ltd www.grandu.co.uk

p.123m Arvind Sond

p.124 Chris Patmore

p.138tr Alexander Isley

p.139 why not associates www.whynotassociates.com

p.160tl Firefox: Firefox® is a registered trademark of the Mozilla Foundation; Safari: Copyright © 2009 Apple Inc. All rights reserved; Opera: Copyright © 2009 Opera Software ASA <http://www.opera.com/>. All rights reserved; Explorer: © 2009 Microsoft; Chrome: ©2009 Google.

p.161 Google ©2009

p.165 Jean Jullien www.jeanjullien.com

p.168t Natalya Terekhova instructor: Simon Gray/*dept. of* DESIGN www.dod.cz

p.170 Mate Steinforth www.matesteinforth.com

p.175bl and br *Televisual* magazine (Bobbie Sidhu)

p.176 Okami ©CAPCOM CO., LTD 2006, 2008 ALL RIGHTS RESERVED

p.177 Spore ©2009 Electronic Arts Inc. All Rights Reserved

p.178 Louise Matell

p.180 MetaDesign www.metadesign.de

shutterstock

istockphoto